THE BIBLE IN 10 DAYS

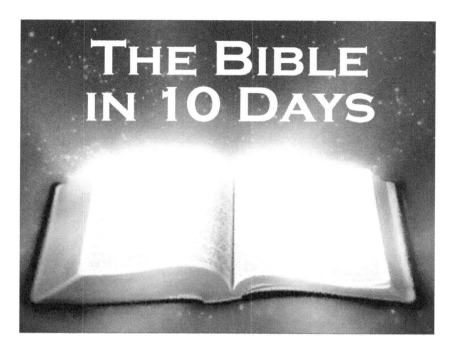

THE BIBLE IN 10 DAYS

*Connecting the
Pieces into One
AMAZING Story*

PAMELA HARRISON

The Bible in 10 Days

Copyright © 2019 by Pamela Harrison

ALL RIGHTS RESERVED

All Scripture quotations, unless otherwise indicated, are taken from the Holy Bible, New International Version®, NIV®. Copyright ©1973, 1978, 1984, 2011 by Biblica, Inc.™ Used by permission of Zondervan. All rights reserved worldwide. www.zondervan.com

The "NIV" and "New International Version" are trademarks registered in the United States Patent and Trademark Office by Biblica, Inc.™

Scripture quotations noted CEB are taken from the Common English Bible, copyright 2011. Used by permission. All rights reserved.

ISBN: 9781790919932
Imprint: Independently published

Published by High Seas Ministries, Inc., P.O. Box 1963, Georgetown, TX 78627

Printed in the United States of America

High Seas Ministries

For our children, grandchildren, and High Seas Ministries family

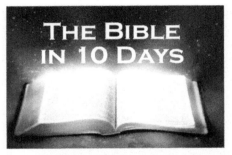

Connecting the Pieces
into One AMAZING Story

Five-DVD Set

NOW AVAILABLE

This 5-disc, 20-lesson DVD set is a presentation of the book taught by the author, Dr. Pamela Harrison. Each of the 10 segments in the book is divided into two video lessons. The format allows you to experience Pam's dynamic teaching of God's Word and then follow up with your own reading, personal study, or small group discussion. Buy now on Amazon!

CONTENTS

ACKNOWLEDGEMENTS

Most books are not conceived or written in isolation. This one certainly was not. The idea first came as a not-so-subtle hint, then a suggestion. I was nudged, encouraged, and ultimately convicted that there might be a need and an audience. After a bit of resistance and a lot of prayer, I gave in to the encouragers and the word I heard in answer to that prayer. Some of the encouragers also became readers and editors throughout the process. I would like to acknowledge their invaluable contributions.

Reverend Jim and Susan Turley, our friends of many years and spiritual mentors: It was your insistence and persistence that finally made us seriously consider this project. Without your coaxing and convincing, I'd still be thinking about it over pasta with you at Tony and Luigi's after church. Thank you for your confidence in me and for being, perhaps, God's voice in this endeavor. Your honest and passionate reviews of my work as it progressed added dimensions that I had missed or minimized. Your intelligence, theological understanding, and maturity in the faith not only supported me but challenged me and kept me on mission more than once.

Jane and Charles Shatzer: You attended our Bible study on a cruise in August 2014 and we quickly discovered in you a like-minded brother and sister in Christ. You also encouraged me to "write this down", offering to help any way you could. And what an amazing help you were! You not only read every word I sent you but researched additional resources and offered your thoughts with candor and grace. You were my unpaid but immensely appreciated editors.

Reverend David and Marilyn Downie: When you attended our ship study in the fall of 2014, I knew that if I ever did feel completely called to put the study in book form, I wanted you on my team. Thank you for finding time in your full lives to read my initial efforts and provide feedback in your typically thoughtful and affirming way.

Pat Stroh: Your gentle reviews and consistent support throughout the process assured me that I was headed in the right direction. Every time you told me how much this book was needed, I was encouraged to keep writing. You were a great blessing to me.

Laura Walker: Your experience teaching the first version of the book provided much-needed and greatly-appreciated insights for this new edition. You and Mark are treasured friends and supporters.

As with everything in my life, this project could not have been accomplished without the love and support of my partner in life and partner in ministry—the greatest blessing of this life on earth—my husband Keith. When we sat down in 2015 to consider the cost in energy, time, and emotional investment for the first edition, you never blinked. As we began this second effort, including the development of the DVDs to accompany this version, you simply asked: "What are you waiting for?"

Finally, of course, there's really only One to acknowledge. This book and the accompanying DVDs are not made up of my thoughts or words. The source of this, as of all good things, is our loving, gracious, and amazing God. Hallelujah!

SCRIPTURESCOPE QUICK REFERENCE

DAY ONE

INTRODUCTION

PROLOGUE AND GENESIS

INTRODUCTION

Why study the entire Bible in just 10 days?

There are many different approaches to studying the Bible, each with its advantages and disadvantages. Many Bible-reading plans require 1 to 3 years to complete—essentially, the marathon approach to getting from the first verse of Genesis to the last verse of Revelation. And, like a marathon, they take patience, pacing, and, sometimes, sheer will to accomplish the task.

The benefit is a methodical study of the Bible, slowly and with plenty of time to think about what you are reading. The negative is the challenge of connecting what you read two years ago with what you are reading today. In fact, many well-intentioned readers never reach the finish line. They feel guilty that they have failed to meet their goal of reading the entire Bible—failed themselves, failed God. We understand that feeling, as it has happened to us as well.

There are also shorter regimens. *The Bible in 90 Days©*, for example, requires a daily commitment of an hour of reading for three months. The benefit is a "big picture" reading of the Bible's overarching story and, often, a new desire to spend more time understanding how the events, characters, and themes connect throughout.

The negative is that reading every word of the Bible's 66 books at this pace allows little time to ponder those connections. We also understand both the pluses and minuses of this approach. In fact, it was our participation in the B90 program that inspired us to create a third option.

What if you could learn the big picture AND understand all the connections—how it all fits together into one story—in 10 hours of reading?

That's what this 10-day study is all about—learning the complete story quickly and connecting the characters, events, and themes as you do it. No, you won't be able to read every word of the Bible in just an hour a day for 10 days, but you will learn the important details—characters, places, events, teachings—from each of the 66 books that make up the Bible. You will also learn how those details are woven together into one meta-narrative, one big story. Hopefully, this study will encourage you to pursue a more detailed and intensive Bible study on your own. Or, perhaps what you learn here will inform and enlighten other studies you are currently pursuing. Most importantly, you will see God's plan of creation, covenant, and salvation for the world—for you—as told through the Bible.

Like much of God's work, this study was born out of the marriage of opportunity and calling. In this case, the opportunity was available on cruise ships, where long days at sea leave guests looking for options to occupy their time. Some find comfort in a familiar and beloved activity—a study of the Bible among fellow Christ-followers. Others are searching for answers to their deepest questions, while a few are just curious, hoping to learn something new. Often they feel safer doing this among people they never expect to see again.

The calling came unexpectedly to two long-time cruisers, recently retired from lives as professional educators, but newly recommitted to lives of serving God. As an answer to prayer, God called us to use our knowledge of the Bible, our experience as teachers, and our love of cruising to reach guests and crew members on ships. Out of this calling evolved *High Seas Ministries,* a ministry committed to Bible teaching and worship for guests and crew members of the cruise ship industry.

After hundreds of hours teaching this study on ships, God has now asked us to put a version in writing that might be of benefit to those who have sailed with us as well as those we will never meet. It is designed to be used either individually or in fellowship with others. The 10 days might be consecutive or perhaps weekly, as in a Sunday School or small group setting. How you use it is up to you. As with all of God's work in our lives, we have tried to respond to God's call as willing, available servants. We pray that this 10-day journey—however you choose to make it—will lead you to a new understanding of the amazing story of the Bible.

Pam and Keith Harrison
High Seas Ministries

PROLOGUE

As we begin the first day of our Bible journey, it's important to prepare our minds for where we are going and what we are about to see. As most of us have learned over the years, it's always good to look at the map a bit before we hit the road. In this case, it's important to know what to expect through this journey and how best to enjoy it.

This 10-day study is designed to give you *knowledge* and *understanding* about the Bible. Benjamin Bloom, an educational psychologist who lived in the mid-20th century, is credited with developing a hierarchy of thinking and learning that has become known as Bloom's Taxonomy. The bottom most basic levels on the taxonomy are *knowledge* and *understanding (comprehension)*. The top levels are synthesis and evaluation; in between, you find analysis and application.

Often we try to analyze and apply the Bible's teachings using Bloom's mid-level processes without Bloom's foundation—a solid *knowledge of what those teachings are.* We don't know who said them, why, in what setting, and for what purpose. Grasping this foundation in knowledge and understanding is what this study is about. You cannot analyze the Bible, explain its meaning or relevancy to today's world, or apply it to your life unless you know what it says.

Bloom knew this, but often that's exactly what we try to do. And we end up depending on what someone else determined to be true about the Bible rather than deciding for ourselves. This study is designed to give you the foundation of knowledge and understanding you need to be able to analyze, apply, and evaluate *for yourself* what you have read.

And, keep in mind that this study—while as complete as it can be in 10 days—is no substitute for reading the entire Bible. This 10-day journey, connecting the amazing story of the Bible, may well serve as preparation and motivation for a more comprehensive study of this all-time best-seller. Or, put another way, you might think of these 10 days as an appetizer, a taste, motivation to enjoy the full meal!

ORGANIZATIONAL NOTES. The scriptural quotes come from the New International Version (NIV) unless otherwise noted. The CEB notation refers to the Common English Bible; KJV refers to the King James Bible. And, as the title indicates, this book is a *companion* to the Bible. The entire Bible is not presented here, so to maximize your understanding keep a version nearby to reference. Placing this book and a Bible side-by-side will add to your study of this book as you can see exactly where characters, events, and teachings appear in the complete Bible. If you do not own a Bible, you can download one for free from several sites, including www.youversion.com.

Although the Bible is itself one book, it is comprised of 66 smaller books written by many different authors over a period of several centuries. The Bible is divided into two sections, or testaments, called the Old Testament (OT) and the New Testament (NT). The OT is also referred to as the Hebrew Scriptures as it contains the holy writings of the Jewish faith. The NT is sometimes called simply the Gospel or Gospels, although that term literally refers to the "good news" found in the first four books of the NT written specifically about the life, death, and resurrection of Jesus Christ. Our study will cover both the OT and

NT from a Christian perspective, meaning that what happens and is taught in the OT sets the stage for what happens and is taught in the NT.

The OT contains 39 books, and the NT contains 27 books. The first six days of our study are devoted to the OT books, the remaining four days to the NT books. In the Bible, all of the books are organized and presented in verses (sometimes in poetry but predominantly in prose) and most contain multiple chapters. When citing a scripture passage from the Bible, this format is usually followed: Book Name Numeric Chapter: Numeric Verse(s), for example Genesis 1:3-4. This format will be used throughout this study.

Both the OT and the NT contain several kinds of literature, organized into: history books (action); books of wisdom (interpreting that history for daily living); and prophecy (building on that history for the future). We will discuss which kind of literature (history, wisdom, or prophecy) each book represents as we go through the daily reading. The OT is directly connected to the NT through characters, events, places, and teachings. In fact, you cannot fully understand the teachings of the NT without understanding the OT.

One final note on the organization of the study: If you are already familiar with the Bible, you will certainly notice that not every character, place, event, and teaching is included here. The reason should be obvious—I've condensed the entire Bible into a 10-day study. Nevertheless, it's important to mention that I do realize that I have left out some familiar stories. I assure you that this was done thoughtfully, as I tried to make each day's lesson manageable time-wise while remaining faithful to the purpose of the study.

The decision of which details to omit was always a difficult one, as nothing in the Bible is insignificant or trivial. I omitted things only after deciding that leaving them out would not impact your understanding of the meta-narrative, much like what a screenwriter does when adapting a novel. And, following that metaphor to its conclusion, just as you cannot get all the details without reading the novel, you need to read the complete Bible for yourself to get all the details of its story as well.

STUDY TOOLS. Each day is divided into "chunks" to organize your reading. Sometimes these chunks divide up a long book, such as Genesis, into logical sections for study. Other times, they indicate that one book has ended, and we are moving on to the next book. In appropriate places, I've also added highlight boxes to indicate what characters, events, places, and teachings are coming up in the next chunk or chunks. These are designed to help you find specific pieces of information both as you read and later for reference purposes.

Also scattered throughout each chapter you will find *ScriptureScopes,* shaded boxes that focus on a particular scripture in more depth. They are designed to take a deeper look into a passage for its meaning, relevance, and connections to the meta-narrative. This is, of course, one of the primary goals of this 10-day study, as the sub-title suggests—to connect the amazing story of the Bible. These *ScriptureScope* sections may also seem to be written in a more personal way than the rest of the text. Indeed, in many cases they include my experience with that particular passage—how it speaks to me. I hope they will encourage you to also experience the Bible on a more personal level and allow it to touch not only your mind but your heart. For future reference, a list of *ScriptureScope* passages is included at the front of the book.

At the end of each chapter, you will find some questions under the heading *Reflecting Forward*. These are designed to help you think more deeply about the day's reading while looking ahead to what comes next. Whether you are doing this study on your own over 10 days or in a small group over 10 weeks, you will get more out of it if you think about it between sessions of reading or study. These questions will help you do this. They are also great starting points for small group discussion.

You will also find at the back of this book several helpful tools that I will reference as we move through the daily lessons. A Bible Chronology provides an understanding of how the books of wisdom and prophecy in the OT and the NT fit into the story told in the history books. It's important to keep in mind that this chronology is just one Bible scholar or group of scholars' understanding. The timeline of both the action in the Bible as well as the writing of the wisdom and prophecy books is greatly debated among Bible historians.

The Kings and Prophets table will be referenced particularly on Days Three and Four to help in understanding how these roles functioned and how the writings of the OT prophets reflect the historical writings. Again, the dates offered are one interpretation; there are other schools of thought. The table of Jesus' life as told through the gospels of Matthew, Mark, Luke, and John creates a chronology that synthesizes all four books. And, finally, the table of Paul's travels and writings offers one possible understanding of where he was when he wrote the letters as well as the order in which they were written.

FINAL THOUGHTS. If you attended church as a child, you might have gone to Sunday School or Church School. If your experience was like mine, on one Sunday you learned about Moses being put in the Nile River in a basket. The next Sunday, you studied Jonah and the whale. The next Sunday's lesson was on Joseph and his coat of many colors, and Jesus and the little tax collector Zacchaeus took center stage the following Sunday. While I loved the stories (and especially the activities we did along with them!), I had no idea how they fit together chronologically, geographically, or any other way. That's not the way we learn the history of the world or of our country in school—but it's typically the way we have studied the Bible.

In truth, the Bible is one overarching story—a meta-narrative, meaning a grand narrative that encompasses many other narratives. As such, to fully understand it you need to study it from beginning to end, in chronological order. This is the benefit of reading the entire Bible, cover to cover, and this is the opportunity you are presented in this study, in a concise 10-day synopsis.

The Bible is not just a group of unrelated stories and lessons, as many of us have learned it. Rather, it is the story of creation (and re-creation), covenant (both old and new), and salvation (individually and of the world)—OUR salvation, yours and mine. It is history, wisdom, and prophecy. Finally, it is a fascinating, edge-of-your-seat, drama of God working through history—through individuals just like you and me—to save the world.

John Newton, the 18th-century slave-trader whose conversion led to the writing of perhaps the most familiar hymn, *Amazing Grace,* wrote the following as one of the less-familiar stanzas:

> The Lord has promised good to me;
> His Word my hope secures.
> He will my shield and portion be
> As long as life endures.

God's Word is found in the Bible. The "Word" can also refer to Jesus, as we will learn in Day Seven. Newton discovered the power of the Word—both definitions—in his own life, providing good where there had been evil, hope where there was despair, strength instead of weakness, and life over death. May you, like Newton, find the power of God in the amazing story of the Bible.

GENESIS 1 – 11
IN THE BEGINNING

The first eleven chapters of Genesis are often referred to as Primeval History. They cover the time from creation up to the calling of Abraham and provide a foundation for the rest of the Bible. These chapters identify key

Creation

Adam and Eve

Sin

Noah and the Flood

Covenant

Babel

events, places, persons, and nations that set in motion the meta-narrative of the Bible, ultimately leading to the birth of Jesus in the NT. All three of the major themes guiding our study—creation, covenant, and salvation—are introduced in these chapters.

Genesis begins with God's creation of the heavens and the earth, told first in chapter 1 with God speaking the universe into being in six days, followed by a seventh day of rest. In chapter 2, a second creation story is told, focusing specifically on the creation of man and woman. These stories do not contradict each other but rather complement each other. Think of chapter 2 as an inset on a map—it's part of the big picture the map presents, but its importance is highlighted and brought to your attention by enlarging a particular section.

Note also that these stories of creation do not attempt to describe in scientific terms *how* God created the world, but rather *who* created, *what* was created, and *why* it was created. For more on this, see our first *ScriptureScope* below.

TO BE LIKE GOD

In Genesis 1:26 we read: *Let us make man [humanity] in our own image to resemble us.*

After speaking the universe into existence during the first five days, on the sixth day we now find God referring to himself as "us". Is this just some archaic Biblical language, God referring to himself in the plural? Absolutely not.

Two points are important to understand. First of all, God is letting us know right up front that he is a triune God, or put another way, the Trinity. This triune nature of God is a complicated thing to understand—theologians have been trying to explain it for millennia. So, we won't get it completely here, but the important understanding is this: The three God-Persons are God the Father, Jesus the Son, and the Holy Spirit.

As we go through our daily reading, we will meet these different Persons at different times in the story, but God is saying in Genesis 1:26: *We were all three here in the beginning. We are the Trinity, and we created the universe and everything in it.* This triune nature of God is one of the aspects of Christianity that distinguishes it from every other religion.

The second important point is this: God indicates that humanity was created in "our image." Does this mean that we look like God and God looks like us? Two eyes, two ears, hair on our heads (okay, some of us have hair), two arms and legs? Again, no.

God created man and woman to be in perfect relationship with each other and with him. God's triune nature means that he is relational within the three God-Persons. By creating humanity in "our image" we are created to be relational in that way as well—with ourselves, with God, and with each other.

And finally, God, as we will learn throughout our reading, is not interested in outward appearances, but what is in the heart—who and what we are on the inside and have the potential to be. This means that being created in his image should give us hope.

We have the potential—despite all of our human weaknesses and frailties—to be like our gracious, loving, and relational God. Not to *be* God, but to be *like* God. And that is *very* good news!

In chapter 3, Eve is tempted by the serpent to eat the fruit of the forbidden tree of knowledge of good and evil (traditionally, an apple). She gives into temptation, then offers it to Adam, and they are both sent out of the Garden of Eden, separated from God.

This action is traditionally referred to as "the Fall", meaning that Adam and Eve fall out of perfect relationship with God—they fall from a life of obedience to disobedience. Without that perfect relationship, they also are out of perfect relationship with themselves, each other, and with creation—the relationships we discussed in the *ScriptureScope* above. They no longer share in the eternal, divine life with God for which they were created. Here, eternal life means not just life that lasts forever but life like God's life—divine, perfect, holy.

It is this "Fall" which fuels God's plan for redemption throughout the Bible—to reclaim and redeem humanity back into perfect relationship with each other, with creation, and with God. Beginning in Genesis 3, God starts working to save the world—work that culminates with the crucifixion and resurrection of Jesus.

Later, in chapter 4, Adam and Eve's son Cain kills his brother Abel and for the first time this lack of relationship and separation from God is given a name —"sin" (4:7). Adam and Eve have another son, Seth, and it is from Seth's descendants that we will find Noah, Abram (Abraham), David, and, ultimately, Jesus. The problem of sin that begins in the garden continues to grow so much that God decides to reclaim his entire creation by starting over—wiping the slate clean, beginning again with one righteous family and a pair of animals from each species to repopulate the earth.

In chapters 6 through 9, God floods the earth and calls upon Noah to build an ark to save his family and the animals. The ark survives the flood and God makes a covenant with Noah (see *ScriptureScope* on the next page), promising never to destroy the world with water again. This introduces the theme of covenant, an agreement between two parties that is typically identified by a sign. The importance of covenant in the Bible cannot be overstated. The word is first used here with Noah, but God's covenants with Abraham and his family, the Israelite people, and King David form the foundation of the OT and lay the groundwork for the new covenant that Jesus brings in the NT.

A covenant is more than a contract. A contract allows for the agreement to end if one of the parties fails to do what was promised. A covenant, however, says that the agreement is forever in place even if one of the parties is not faithful to its terms. This is the critical aspect of Biblical covenants, which are made between God and people. While God's creation, humanity, repeatedly fails to do what was promised, God continues to honor the covenant. We will see this throughout our study, both in the OT and the NT.

GOD'S REMINDER

In Genesis 9:16 we read: *Whenever the rainbow appears in the clouds, I will see it and remember the everlasting covenant between God and living creatures of every kind on the earth.*

These are God's words to Noah after he destroyed the world with the flood. They are spoken by the God who became so disappointed in his creation that he determined there was no other path but to begin again, with one righteous man and his family. They are also the words of a God who vows never to destroy his creation in that way again, even though he seems pretty sure that men and women will continue to disappoint him.

God creates the sign of the rainbow to remind himself—not us—of this new covenant he has made. When we look at the rainbow, we can remember that this is a sign of a God who created, who is creating, who loved, who still loves, and who ultimately loved us enough to send his own Son to save us once and forever from our sinful natures.

Despite God's plan to save the world through Noah, the problem of sin reappears in Noah's descendants, to the point that the nations try to build a tower in the city of Babel to reach and be equal with God in heaven (chapter 11). The city of Babel is known later in the OT and the NT as Babylon. This act of rebellion leads God to develop a new plan to save the world, this time through Abram and Sarai, whose story begins now.

Abram and Sarai

Covenant Promises

Hagar and Ishmael

Name-changing

Circumcision

Isaac

Esau and Jacob

GENESIS 12 – 27
ABRAHAM AND ISAAC

As we meet Abram, son of Terah, in chapter 12 we learn that he is married to Sarai;

they have no children. God calls him to move his family to inhabit the land of Canaan to the south and promises to make his family into a great nation. Abram obeys God. In chapter 15, God makes a covenant with 75-year-old Abram. He promises that he will make Abram's descendants as numerous as the stars and that they, as a great nation, will possess the land of Canaan (which currently is inhabited by several other tribes and peoples). God also promises to give him his blessing and tells him that Abram's family will be a blessing to the rest of the world. These three things—descendants (or family), land (or inheritance), and blessing—are important, as they are the foundation of both the OT covenant and the NT covenant to come through Jesus.

Abram obeys and shows great faith in a very unlikely scenario. Abram is seventy-five; Sarai is sixty-five. They have never had children, and the possibility seems so remote to Sarai that, after waiting ten years for God's promise to come true, she gives Abram her maid Hagar to bear him a son. In chapter 16, Ishmael is born, whom Abram loves. Although trying on occasion to "help God keep his promise" (*Anyone ever done that??*) Abram and Sarai continue to wait for God's promise of a son born to them.

In chapter 17, because of Abram's great faith, God changes his name to Abraham and Sarai's name to Sarah. This is the first example of name-changing in the Bible, but there will be others. Name-changing is an outward sign of an inward transformation, a renewed dedication to God and God's purpose.

God also establishes circumcision as the sign of Abraham's renewed covenant with God. Circumcision was not unheard of at this time. During the golden age of Egypt's 12th dynasty and the Sumerian civilization, it was common among Ethiopians, Syrians, and some Egyptians as a rite of passage to manhood. God's use of it as a physical symbol of purity and contrition would later, under the new covenant, become a spiritual "circumcision of the heart".

In chapter 21, when Abraham is one hundred years old and Sarah is ninety, their son Isaac is finally born. God assures Abraham that he will make a great nation out of Ishmael's descendants (the nation of Islam), but that Isaac is the one who will fulfill the covenant. Despite this reassurance, God commands Abraham to sacrifice Isaac. Talk about hard to understand! See the *ScriptureScope* below for what happens as Abraham follows God's command.

AMAZING LOVE

In Genesis 22:10-12 CEB we read: *Then Abraham stretched out his hand and took the knife to kill his son as a sacrifice. But the Lord's messenger called out to Abraham from heaven, "Abraham? Abraham?" Abraham said, "I'm here." The messenger said, "Don't stretch out your hand against the young man, and don't do anything to him. I now know that you revere God and didn't hold back your son, your only son, from me."*

Many scholars have debated the inclusion and meaning of the story of God testing Abraham through the sacrifice of Isaac. The rest of us have trouble understanding how a loving God could ask a father to do this. In the big picture, however, this is exactly what God did for us through Jesus.

This passage, like so many in the Old Testament, points directly to the life, death, and resurrection of Jesus Christ in the New Testament. Verse 12 makes the meaning clear: Only a man who loved God as Abraham did would sacrifice his son because God commanded him to do so. Only our God, who so loved the world, could send his Son, his only Son, to die for us.

In chapters 23 and 24 Sarah dies, and Abraham finds a wife for Isaac—Rebekah, the granddaughter of his brother. Isaac and Rebekah have twin sons, Esau and Jacob. We read in chapter 27 that, with Rebekah's help, Jacob deceives his brother and his father to gain first-born Esau's blessing and birthright.

When Isaac discovers that he has been duped, he gives this blessing to Esau: *You will live by your sword and you will serve your brother. But when you grow restless, you will throw his yoke from off your neck.* (Genesis 27:40) What image does this bring to mind? How might Esau "throw off his yoke"? Revenge? Murder? We will see how this prophecy comes true. Needless to say, Jacob is a little nervous that his brother might kill him, so he flees to live with his uncle Laban, Rebekah's brother.

Jacob's Ladder

Laban

Leah and Rachel

Twelve Sons (Tribes)

Jacob becomes Israel

Esau's Forgiveness

Joseph into Slavery

Tamar and Judah

GENESIS 28 – 38
JACOB

These chapters focus on Jacob (which means "heel-grabber" or "scoundrel") and his family. Here we gain even more insight into Jacob's character—and most of the time, it's not a pretty picture. Jacob is, perhaps, the most unlikely of Biblical heroes. He has already demonstrated his underhanded approach to getting what he wants by stealing his older brother's birthright and blessing. Now we see that, unlike his grandfather Abraham--a man of great faith in God's promises--Jacob's approach to God is what we might call in 21st century language *transactional*, based on a "what's in it for me" mindset. For example, on the way to see his uncle Laban, we read in chapter 28 that Jacob has the first of several encounters with God. This one is typically referred to as "Jacob's ladder" and results in Jacob bargaining with God that if God will take him safely to Laban, then he will worship him as his forefathers before him did.

When Jacob arrives at Laban's home in chapter 29, Jacob falls in love with Laban's younger daughter Rachel and agrees to work seven years to marry her. The deceiver Jacob has met his match, however, in Laban. At their wedding, Laban substitutes the older daughter, Leah, for Rachel. We don't know if the veil was extra thick or if Jacob had too much wine or both, but he does not know he has been the victim of "bait and switch" until it's too late. So, he agrees to keep Leah and work another seven years for Rachel also.

Jacob eventually works an additional six years to earn his own flocks, so after twenty years of working for Laban, Jacob takes his family and his flocks and leaves (chapter 31). During those twenty years, Leah and Rachel and their two maidservants have produced eleven sons and at least one daughter for Jacob. As she dies, Rachel gives birth to one more son, Benjamin.

As Jacob flees Laban, he must cross through Edom, the land of Esau's family. He is, understandably, afraid to meet his brother. We read in chapter 33 that the night before they meet, Jacob has a dream in which he wrestles through the night with God. (*Have you ever wrestled with God through the night? I know I have.*) As day breaks, God releases him, blesses him, and changes his name to Israel. Remember the name-changing of Abram and Sarai? Similarly, here the changing of

Jacob's name symbolizes his transformation from someone who bargains with God to someone who serves God. And what about the meeting with Esau? See the *ScriptureScope* below.

JUSTICE—MERCY—GRACE

In Genesis 33:4 we read: *But Esau ran to meet Jacob and embraced him; he threw his arms around his neck and kissed him. And they wept.*

Once Jacob finally got away from Laban, he faced another challenge— his twin brother Esau, the same one he had deceived out of his first-born child status and blessing. He certainly had no reason to expect Esau to be anything but angry and bent on revenge, even after twenty years had passed, so he sent gifts ahead with his servants to 'soften him up'. Jacob soon discovered, however, that it was not Esau who would be given gifts in this situation, but Jacob himself, for Esau had forgiven him and greeted his younger brother with affection.

Remember Isaac's blessing to Esau in Genesis 27:40? He told Esau that he would serve his younger brother "but when you grow restless, you will throw his yoke from off your neck." Most of us would think that means Esau would get revenge, perhaps even killing Jacob. But, we read here that Esau removed the yoke not by harming Jacob or taking back what was rightfully his but by *forgiving* his brother. We aren't told why or how Esau forgave Jacob, but we are shown the result of this forgiveness—peace for both the offender (Jacob) and, most importantly, for the one who forgives (Esau). Jacob, who deserved justice, received not just mercy, but grace.

In the 21st century—as in Jacob's time—most people want to see justice done, especially justice for everyone else. When a wrong is done, we want to see that wrong avenged—someone must pay! We see justice as "getting what you deserve."

Mercy, on the other hand, comes by throwing ourselves at the feet of judgment and pleading for the opposite of justice —"not getting what we deserve." What, then, is grace? Is grace just another word for mercy? Not exactly.

Grace, as dispensed in the Bible both here by Esau and later by Jesus from the cross, can be defined as "getting something you do not deserve and have not earned." As a brother in Christ once shared with me, "grace always comes as a surprise." It is more than mercy—more than "not getting justice"—as grace is a gift of new opportunity, new life. In Jacob's case, he deserved anger and conflict from his brother because of his actions toward him twenty years earlier. If Esau had stood aside and let him pass through his land without harming him, he would have demonstrated mercy toward his brother. But Esau did much more than that—he hugged his brother, kissed him, and offered him hospitality and love.

Jacob, who deserved death, received forgiveness and a new chance at life…just as those who believe in Jesus Christ receive forgiveness and abundant new life, despite their brokenness and sin-filled lives. This is grace.

In chapter 37, Jacob's favorite son Joseph (whose mother was Rachel) is sold into slavery by his jealous brothers. They resent Joseph because of his favored status and his dreams of greatness. Rather than tell their father Jacob the truth, they convince him that Joseph died from an attack by a wild animal.

This seems to be the end of Joseph, as the story shifts in chapter 38 to the household of one of Jacob's other sons, Judah. Here we learn that Judah's sons have both died, leaving his daughter-in-law Tamar with no husband and no one to carry on the family line. Tamar decides to pose as a prostitute to get Judah to sleep with her. She becomes pregnant and produces twin sons, Perez and Zerah. Thus, the line of Judah continues—which seems fairly insignificant until you read the lineage of Jesus in the gospel of Matthew.

There, among all the fathers, sons, and grandsons throughout history, we find only five women mentioned. The first one is Tamar, for from her son Perez descended King David. From the line of King David descended Joseph, who was engaged to Mary when she was told by the angel Gabriel that she would be the mother of Jesus, the Christ. Because the husband's line determines the lineage, Joseph fulfilled the prophecy that the Messiah, Jesus, would come from the line of King David from the house of Judah— thanks in part to Tamar.

Potiphar's Wife

Pharaoh's Dreams

Joseph in Charge

Famine in Canaan

Reunited in Egypt

GENESIS 39 – 50
JOSEPH IN EGYPT

In chapter 39, we find out Joseph made it to Egypt as a slave and served in the house of high-ranking Potiphar before landing in prison. (It seems he rejected Potiphar's wife's advances, which did not please Potiphar's wife.) As a prisoner he interprets the dreams of his fellow prisoners while clinging to faith that God will deliver him. Joseph is consistently promoted to positions of responsibility and respect, both when in Potiphar's house and now in the prison.

In time he is released from prison to interpret Pharaoh's dreams, predicting seven years of abundance followed by seven years of famine. Pharaoh puts Joseph in charge of all of Egypt, and Joseph puts a plan in place to ensure Egypt has food when the rest of the world does not.

Meanwhile, back in Canaan, Jacob reluctantly sends all of his remaining sons except Benjamin (Rachel's other son) to Egypt for food. And before whom do they appear to ask for food? Joseph, of course, but they do not recognize him. He recognizes them, however, and requires that they bring Benjamin, his brother, before he will grant their request for food. There is much more to the story, which you can read for yourself in Genesis 42 – 45.

Ultimately, Joseph reveals his identity to his brothers, and Jacob and the remaining family in Canaan come to Egypt to join them. In chapter 47 we read that Pharaoh gives them the land of Goshen for their flocks, and they live there until Jacob dies. Joseph's brothers fear that Joseph will now enslave them once Jacob is gone, but Joseph assures them that he has forgiven them (see *ScriptureScope* below).

In the last chapter of Genesis, Joseph dies and is buried in Egypt. These events, beginning with Joseph's enslavement in Egypt, explain how the Israelites came to be in Egypt rather than Canaan, where God led their forefather Abraham. In Day Two, we will continue their saga as we study the great salvation story of the Old Testament.

DIFFICULT TO SEE

In Genesis 50:20 CEB we read: *You planned something bad for me, but God produced something good from it, in order to save the lives of many people, just as he's doing today.*

These are the words of Joseph to his brothers, who fear his retaliation now that their father Jacob has died. The "something bad" they planned for him, of course, was selling him into slavery. The saving of many lives was the feeding of the Egyptian people and the reuniting of Joseph's family because of his leadership in the years of famine.

Not only do Joseph's words demonstrate, once again, the power of forgiveness and grace, but this passage also reminds us that God does work in 'mysterious ways.' It's often difficult to see it at the time—as I'm sure Joseph wondered as he was enslaved in Egypt—but ultimately, God is in charge.

Later, in the New Testament, we will read that Jesus was crucified, an apparent defeat of God's plan to save his creation. Indeed, we might suspect that the forces of evil rejoiced, thinking that God's great experiment was finished, with disastrous results. Instead, Jesus' death was part of God's plan to accomplish the salvation of his creation—the saving of many lives.

Despite how things appeared to others, God had a plan and purpose for Jesus and for Joseph, and he has a plan and purpose for each of us. Joseph teaches us to look for God's plan and God's purpose, even when they are difficult to see. And Joseph's story always reminds me of a song I learned many years ago at church camp as a youth. It remains one of my favorites:

> It is no secret what God can do.
> What he's done for others, he'll do for you.
> With arms wide open, he'll pardon you.
> It is no secret what God can do!

REFLECTING FORWARD

Use these questions to guide your discussion of Day One and lead you into Day Two.

1. Have you read or studied the Bible before? If you have, how is this study different for you?

2. On page 24, we talked about Genesis 1:26 teaching us that the Trinity was there at Creation—God, Jesus, the Holy Spirit, all three, right from the beginning. What does that mean to you? How does remembering this change the way you read and understand the Old Testament?

3. Genesis is full of "colorful" characters—many of them clearly flawed, but nevertheless key parts of God's story. Tamar, for example, did what some might call "the wrong thing for the right reason." What's the message for us here? How has God used your "wrong moves" for good purposes?

4. Read Genesis 42-45 for the complete story of Joseph's reunion with his brothers. Can you imagine Joseph's inner struggle when they first appeared? Talk about conflicted—family, after all these years, but did it have to be these guys? Have you ever experienced a similar struggle or conflict? What can we learn from Joseph?

5. Considering God's big story of salvation, what seems the most important thing to take with you from Day One to Day Two?

DAY TWO

EXODUS, LEVITICUS, NUMBERS, DEUTERONOMY, JOSHUA

Before we move forward, let's take just a moment to review our Day One reading. In the action-packed book of Genesis (literally "beginnings") we indeed found the beginning of God's story. Our three themes—creation, covenant, and salvation—were introduced in dramatic fashion. God created the universe and humanity "in our [God's] image" to be in perfect relationship with God. Sin entered the world, separating humanity from this perfect relationship. God then began working to save his creation, reclaiming and redeeming humanity back to himself out of sin and death to relationship and life. First through Noah, then Abraham, God established covenants with righteous people, promising blessing and his protective presence forever.

We saw some sub-themes emerge, for example, transformation accompanied by a name change: Abram to Abraham, Sarai to Sarah, Jacob to Israel. We also read stories of reconciliation, accompanied by grace and forgiveness. Remember Esau's forgiveness of Jacob? Joseph's forgiveness of his brothers? We certainly saw faith demonstrated—faith in a most unlikely scenario—by Abraham and Sarah. They left their home for Canaan based on a promise of descendants and land, and they waited 25 years for the birth of Isaac. Finally, we met Tamar, one of the five women mentioned in Jesus' lineage and the first hint that the One ultimately to redeem the world will be a different kind of king who brings a very different kind of kingdom.

Today, we begin with the book of Exodus, complete the remaining three books of the Pentateuch (i.e., Torah, Books of Moses, or Books of the Law), and continue through Joshua. We will see another covenant from God, but first…the theme of salvation is elevated from individuals

(Noah, Abraham and families) to the salvation of a people and ultimately a nation. There are several schools of scholarly thought on when these events happened, but you can refer to the Bible Chronology on page 264 for one interpretation.

And now, the great salvation epic of the Old Testament!

EXODUS 1 – 15
DELIVERANCE FROM EGYPT

Moses

The Burning Bush

I AM

Ten Plagues

Passover

Out of Egypt

The Red Sea

As the book begins, we learn that it has been four hundred years since Joseph's death is recorded in the last chapter of Genesis. Jacob's descendants, the Israelites, have become so numerous that respect for the family of Joseph has given way to enslavement, due to fear of their vast numbers and potential power. After enslaving them, Pharaoh then fears that they will revolt, and he gives the order to kill every newborn Hebrew (Israelite) boy.

We quickly see that women are the true heroines of these early chapters of Exodus. In chapter 1, the Egyptian mid-wives refuse to follow Pharaoh's edict that they kill any male Israelite newborn. In chapter 2, then, we meet the mother of one surviving Hebrew baby boy, Moses, who is a member of the tribe of Levi (one of the twelve sons of Jacob or Israel). She courageously hides Moses in the Nile in a basket, where he is discovered by Pharaoh's daughter. Moses' sister Miriam has seen the whole episode. She cleverly arranges for her mother to serve as wet nurse for the baby when the princess decides to take him to the palace to raise as her own. He grows up to have a striking resemblance to Hollywood legend Charleton Heston (*smile*) and also a heart for the

Hebrew slaves. He kills an Egyptian slave master and then flees to Midian where he marries, has children, and lives as a shepherd for over forty years.

In chapter 3, when Moses is eighty years old, God speaks to him from a desert plant that's on fire but does not burn up (i.e., the burning bush), directing him to return to Egypt to tell the new Pharaoh to set the Israelites free from slavery. Moses resists, coming up with a myriad of excuses (*sound familiar, anyone?*), but ultimately agrees to go, accompanied by his older brother Aaron.

A scripture which will be an important connection throughout our study appears in Exodus 3:14. Moses has asked God for God's name should the people (or Pharaoh) want to know who has sent him. God replies simply: *I AM WHO I AM. Tell them I AM has sent you.* Armed with this knowledge, Moses and Aaron return to Egypt and make their first appearance before Pharaoh in chapter 5, telling him that the God of Israel says, "Let my people go."

God tells Moses that he will harden Pharaoh's heart in order to demonstrate his glory and power over the Egyptian gods and, indeed, over all of creation. As a result, Pharaoh rejects Moses' plea for the Israelites' freedom and refuses to let them go, despite ten plagues God sends upon Egypt (see chapters 7 – 12). The Nile turns red with blood, followed by an invasion of frogs, lice, and flies. The livestock die as a result; the people become covered in skin sores from malnutrition and unclean water. Hail rains from the sky, followed by swarms of locusts and days of darkness.

In chapter 12, Moses warns the Israelites to prepare for the tenth and final plague. Death will come to all firstborn Egyptian children, but the Hebrews will be "passed over" by putting lamb's blood on their doorframes. This institutes the lasting ordinance of Passover, celebrated by the Jewish people as the great salvation story of their faith and by Christians as the great salvation story of the old covenant.

Two OT/NT connections here: First, the shedding of the lamb's blood as a covering, a protection, from death connects to the rules of sacrifice for forgiveness given to the Hebrews and covered later in today's reading. It also connects to John the Baptist's reference to Jesus as "the Lamb of God" in the NT (John 1:36—Day Eight). Second, but equally important, is the understanding that this OT salvation story contains the same essential elements as the NT salvation story—Jesus's resurrection after his death on the cross. In each case: (1) God is glorified as almighty and all powerful and (2) death is defeated. There are major differences in the stories as well, which we will see later. For now, however, the important connections are the similarities.

After the death of his own child, Pharaoh briefly relents, and the Hebrews leave Egypt. Pharaoh quickly changes his mind, however, and they are chased by Pharaoh's army to the edge of the Red Sea. God parts the waters, allowing the Hebrews to cross, but releases the waters to engulf Pharaoh's army as they follow. Safe on the other side, the Israelites sing songs of victory and trust God to provide for them, if only temporarily.

EXODUS 16 – 40
INSTRUCTION AND COVENANT

Mount Sinai

Covenant with Israel

Ten Commandments

Instruction and Law

The Golden Calf

God's Character

God's Presence

The Israelites' journey began in March-April in the Hebrew first month of Nisan. The final plague, celebrated as Passover, occurred on Day 14 of Nisan, and on Day 15 they left Egypt. We learn quickly as the former slaves begin their journey back to Canaan—the land once occupied by their ancestors Abraham, Isaac, and Jacob and the land promised to them by God—that they are "grumblers", constantly complaining about their conditions. They frequently lament that they were better off in Egypt as slaves. Responding to their needs, the Lord (God, Yahweh, I AM) provides water for them from rocks, quail in the evenings, and manna (bread) in the mornings. In chapter 17 we meet Joshua, Moses' assistant and a military commander who leads the Israelites in defeating the attacking Amalekites. Later, Joshua will become the leading character in the taking of the land of Canaan.

After three months, the Hebrews arrive at Mount Sinai (later referred to as Mount Horeb, generally thought to be the same place). There God establishes his covenant with the Israelite people, following in the tradition of the covenants established with Noah and Abraham. After promising his faithfulness to all the people, we read that God calls Moses to the mountain and gives him ten laws for the people to follow in order to live in relationship with God and with each other. These have become known as the Ten Commandments (Exodus 20:3-17).

In chapters 20 through 31, God gives Moses additional instruction on Mt. Sinai, so much in fact that it takes forty days and forty nights to accomplish. These include specific laws for creating a traveling place of worship for the journey (the tabernacle), the Ark of the Testimony (or Ark of the Covenant), and the Tent of Meeting. God also designates Moses' brother Aaron and his descendants in the tribe of Levi as priests.

Meanwhile, back at the foot of the mountain, the people have given up on Moses ever returning from the mountain top. After all, it's been over a month and the whole experience with God speaking to them from the mountain was frightening enough—how could one man survive being in God's presence for forty days and nights? They convince Aaron to create a golden calf for them to worship. He does, using the gold they've brought with them as gifts from the Egyptians who were glad to see them go after all the trouble their God had caused.

In chapter 32, they are reveling in worshipping their new "god", when Moses descends from the mountain with the two stone tablets of laws written by the finger of God. He sees what's happening and breaks the tablets in anger. He calls upon his tribe of Levi to kill three thousand people as punishment. God is so angry that he tells Moses he cannot go with them any further for fear of destroying them. See the *ScriptureScope* below.

OLD TESTAMENT GRACE

In Exodus 33:1, 3 we read: *Then the Lord said to Moses, "Leave this place, you and the people you brought up out of Egypt and go up to the land I promised on oath to Abraham, Isaac and Jacob, saying, 'I will give it to your descendants.' Go up to the land flowing with milk and honey. But I will not go with you, because you are a stiff-necked people and I might destroy you on the way."*

Yes, this sounds a bit extreme, but...any parents out there? Has your child ever done something that required you to separate yourself from him or her before you say or do something you might regret? *("Go to your room, I can't talk to you about this right now" comes to mind.)* Actually, I am certain I've played both roles in this scenario at different points in my life.

I'm also pretty sure this might be something akin to God's reaction in this situation. He has saved the Israelites from slavery in Egypt, only to have them turn on him the minute he has a closed-door session with their leader for a few days. How could their faith be so short-lived?

Moses pleads for God to relent from his decision to abandon them (verses 15-16), and, amazingly, God does. We see here again that God is relational—he desires a relationship with the nation of Israel (indeed, all of humanity). God values the relationship he has with Moses enough to allow Moses to remind him of his covenant and dissuade him from his decision.

In this interaction we also get an important—and often-referenced—description of God. Moses asks to see God, God invites him to return to the mountain, and there God allows Moses to see just his back.

In Exodus 34:6-7, we read: *And he passed in front of Moses, proclaiming, "The LORD, the LORD, the compassionate and gracious God, slow to anger, abounding in love and faithfulness, maintaining love to thousands, and forgiving wickedness, rebellion and sin."*

This passage will be quoted throughout the OT and the NT as a description of God's character. And, more importantly, we will *see* the compassionate and gracious nature of God. That's right—God did not "invent" grace with Jesus. We see it right here, in the middle of the Old Testament.

God recreates the stone tablets and, after another forty days, Moses returns to the people with a radiant face, indicating his encounter with the God of the Universe, the Great I AM, the Lord. In chapters 36 through 38, God's directives for building the tabernacle (traveling place of worship) and the ark are carried out. In chapter 40 we read that the tabernacle is set up on the first day of the Israelites' second year in the wilderness. The Lord enters the tabernacle as a cloud and will continue with the Israelites throughout their travels, guiding them as a cloud by day and a pillar of fire by night.

It has been one year since the Israelites left Egypt.

LEVITICUS 1 – 15
INSTRUCTION FOR HOLINESS

Offerings

Sacrifices

Holiness

Warning: We are about to enter one of the notoriously difficult books to endure in the Bible, responsible for the failure of many a reader intent upon reading the Bible cover-to-cover. Try to contain your excitement! *(smile)* Reading and rereading the instruction (or laws) given to the Israelites can be excruciating at times, but there are some nuggets hidden here that are critical to understanding the Bible's amazing story. Let's find them!

The primary purpose of the book of Leviticus and all the instruction contained therein is to teach the Israelites how to live in relationship to God and to each other. Remember the Ten Commandments? The first four address our relationship with God; the last six are about how to live in a holy way with each other. The rest of the instruction found in Leviticus and elsewhere expand upon these ten basic laws.

The first seven chapters focus on the various altar offerings the Israelites are to present in the tabernacle. In chapters 4 through 6, we read specifically about the offerings and sacrifices to be given for guilt and sin. These include bulls, goats, and lambs—making a clear connection back to the lamb's blood used in Passover and forward to

John the Baptist's claim of Jesus as "the Lamb of God", the ultimate sacrifice for sin.

In the remainder of this section (chapters 8 – 15) other laws focus on living in a community, including what to eat, personal hygiene, how to deal with infectious diseases, and childbirth. Most scholars agree that these were designed, at least in part, to keep the Hebrews alive and healthy in an ancient world where there were no water treatment plants and no antibiotics to fight infections. The problem is that in the 21st century, many of these regulations seem archaic at best and, in some cases, barbaric. For some help with this, see the *ScriptureScope* below for another thought on God's reasoning.

HOLY APART

In Leviticus 10:10-11 we read: *You must distinguish between the holy and the common, between the unclean and the clean, and you must teach the Israelites all the decrees the LORD has given them through Moses.*

What might we, as 21st-century Christ-followers, get out of Leviticus? Why study these laws given to an ancient people in a world so different from ours? This verse helps, I think.

Yahweh (God) has introduced a new concept to the Israelites—holiness. It's an abstract thing, and even when he tells them that he is holy, and they should be holy also, they don't really know what he means. We can understand that—it's hard for us, millennia later, to know how to be holy.

So, always the master teacher, God begins where the Israelites are—with food and basic human necessities. He uses these things to teach the concept of 'apartness'—separating them as 'holy' from the rest of the world as 'common'. They may not be ready to understand that holiness is thinking, feeling, and acting in a godly way, but they can understand eating and cleansing. They can see that these practices are different from the other nations around them and that they set them apart from others who do not worship the Lord.

Later, these early lessons on outward, physical attributes of holiness will evolve into Jesus' teachings on what it means to be inwardly holy, teachings we commonly call the Beatitudes (see Matthew 5).

In chapter 11, God further explains why the Israelites should be holy: *I am the Lord your God; consecrate yourselves and be holy, because I am holy. I am the Lord who brought you up out of Egypt to be your God; therefore be holy, because I am holy.* (Leviticus 11:44a, 45) Remember in Genesis 1:26 when God created humanity "in our image to resemble us"? Now we understand that the resemblance is not an outward, physical resemblance, but a resemblance in character and attributes. God created us to be like him in his holiness, and—thank goodness—we have the Bible to teach us how to do it!

LEVITICUS 16 – 27
REWARDS AND CONSEQUENCES

Day of Atonement

Gleaning the Fields

Love Your Neighbor

Tithing Introduced

In chapter 16, we read God's direction to Aaron, as chief priest, on how to atone for the people's sins on the annual Day of Atonement (Yom Kippur). In Leviticus 16:8, 10, 21-22 we read: *He is to cast lots for the two goats—one lot for the LORD and the other for the scapegoat. He is to lay both hands on the head of the scapegoat and confess over it all the wickedness and rebellion of the Israelites—all their sins—and put them on the goat's head. He shall send the goat away in the desert. The goat will carry on itself all their sins.* Note that this is where the secular term "scapegoat" originates—or as a student of mine once claimed that she had been designated, the "escape goat". *(smile)* Later we will compare this description of the once-a-year atonement for sin in the old covenant with the once-and-forever atonement for sin in the new covenant, accomplished through Jesus' death and resurrection.

In chapter 19, we find a law that impacts not only the future of Israel but of the world. See the *ScriptureScope* below.

GOD'S WAY OF THINKING

In Leviticus 19:9-10 CEB we read: *When you harvest your land's produce, you must not harvest all the way to the edge of your field; and don't gather up every remaining bit of your harvest. Also do not pick your vineyard clean or gather up all the grapes that have fallen there. Leave these items for the poor and the immigrant; I am the Lord your God.*

This passage is one of many in Leviticus that show God's compassion for the poor, the widow, and the outsider as well as his expectation that we will demonstrate that compassion also. He even gives us some 'tips' on how to do that —"Don't be so focused on keeping every last grape and every last kernel of wheat for yourselves; leave them for those who need them more than you do."

This gleaning of the fields was, as we'll soon read, how Ruth caught the eye of Boaz. They married and had a son, Obed, whose grandson was David, the Shepherd-King of Israel.

Closer to home, I think about this "leaving of the excess" every time I look at my closet—someone surely needs my stuff more than I do. Or when I'm eating—plates of abundance when so many are hungry. The bottom line: This little passage in Leviticus reminds me of how much I have and how little others have. In God's way of thinking, I believe that means I need to offer some up to the gleaners.

Later in this chapter we find one of the nuggets I mentioned earlier, what Jesus refers to in the New Testament as the second half of the "Great Commandment" (see Day Seven). In Leviticus 19:18b we read: *Love your neighbor as yourself.*

In the last chapters of Leviticus, we find repetition of many of the laws presented earlier in the book, but the focus changes from law-giving to consequences. Rewards and punishments for following or not following the laws are given. Ultimately, God provides a way for forgiveness and reminds the Israelites that he will remember his covenant with their ancestors Abraham, Isaac, and Jacob. In the final verses, God introduces the concept of tithing (giving one-tenth of one's earnings back to God) as a way of demonstrating our understanding that everything is a gift from God and belongs to him.

We are now at the end of Leviticus. There... that wasn't so painful, was it?

NUMBERS 1 – 19
PART ONE: THE JOURNEY CONTINUES

First Census

Nazirite Vow

Twelve Spies

Joshua and Caleb

Wandering 40 Years

After a break in the action to discuss the instruction given to Moses and the Israelites in Leviticus, we pick up again with the Hebrews' journey to the Promised Land. We are now in year two, month two. In chapters 1 through 5, as preparation to take the land of Canaan from its current inhabitants, God directs Moses to count the number of men available to serve in the army. Some additional instruction—some repetition, some new—is given. We also read some repeated events from Genesis and Leviticus.

Note: This repetition is not unusual in the Bible's historical narratives, both in the OT and somewhat in the NT. Often events or a series of events are retold from differing perspectives and sometimes there are "flashbacks". If you are expecting to always read a chronological telling of the big story, you can get confused. If this happens, refer to the Bible Chronology on page 264 to see which books cover the same periods of time.

In chapter 6, we read about the vow of the Nazirite, a person especially dedicated to God's service and a designation given to several key characters coming up in our reading. The traveling tabernacle is dedicated with each of the twelve tribes bringing the same offering of silver, gold, incense, and animals to be sacrificed. In Numbers 6:23-26 we read a familiar blessing: *This is how you are to bless the Israelites. Say to them: "The Lord bless you and keep you; the Lord make his face to shine upon you and be gracious to you; the Lord turn his face toward you and give you peace."*

Chapters 7 through 12 detail the dedication of the tabernacle as well as more grumbling and complaining from the "stiff-necked" Israelites. In chapter 13, the action picks up at the beginning of year two, month three. With the census completed, Moses sends twelve spies into Canaan to see what the land is like and what the Israelites will be up against when they enter. A little over a month later, the spies return. All but two—Joshua (the military leader) and Caleb—report that while the land is all God said it would be, the Israelites should not enter due to the size and strength of the native people. Despite protests from Joshua and Caleb, the people side with the other ten spies.

In chapter 14 we read of God's anger as he threatens to destroy the people for their lack of faith—much as he did after the golden calf incident—but, again, Moses convinces him otherwise. So, God decrees that none of this generation (everyone over twenty years old) will enter the Promised Land except for Joshua and Caleb. Instead, they will wander in the land for forty years, one year for each day the spies were in Canaan, until this generation passes away. The remainder of this section includes more laws on offerings and cleansing.

NUMBERS 20 – 36

PART TWO: FORTY YEARS LATER

Balaam's Donkey

Second Census

Division of Land

Joshua as Successor

Eastern Tribes

Total Destruction

As chapter 20 begins we realize that, without any clear indication in the scriptures, the story has jumped ahead 38 or 39 years. Miriam dies, indicating the passing of time, and the focus turns to the Israelites' destruction of nations they encounter while wandering in the desert. The Israelites (descendants of Jacob) are denied passage through Edom (the land of Esau's descendants). They decide to camp east of the Jordan River across from Jericho on the plains of Moab (land of the descendants of Lot, Abraham's nephew).

In chapter 22 we read perhaps the most familiar story from the book of Numbers, the strange but powerful story of Balaam and his donkey. Balak, the king of Moab, has summoned Balaam, a sorcerer/soothsayer who is known for 'divination' (serving as an intermediary between the pagan gods and the people). He asks him to communicate with Yahweh, the god of the Israelites. Balaam encounters Yahweh in a way that creates one of the most memorable stories of the OT.

GOD'S INTERVENTION STRATEGY

In Numbers 22:23a, 24, 26-30 CEB we read: *The donkey saw the Lord's messenger standing in the road with his sword drawn in his hand, so the donkey turned from the road and went into the field. Then the Lord's messenger stood in the narrow path between vineyards with a stone wall on each side. The Lord's messenger persisted and crossed over and stood in a narrow place, where it wasn't possible to turn either right or left. The donkey saw the Lord's messenger and lay down underneath Balaam. Balaam became angry and beat the donkey with the rod. Then the Lord opened the donkey's mouth and it said to Balaam, "What have I done to you that you've beaten me these three times?" Balaam said to the donkey, "Because you've tormented me. If I had a sword in my hand, I'd kill you now." The donkey said to Balaam, "Am I not your donkey, on whom you've often ridden to this day? Have I been in the habit of doing this to you?" Balaam said, "No."*

Note God's intervention strategy. Balaam was on a path that was reckless in God's eyes. So, what does God do to get Balaam's attention? He works through Balaam's donkey, who can see God's messenger long before Balaam can. The messenger positions himself in Balaam's path in increasingly tight places, so that ultimately the donkey has no choice but to submit. Balaam beats the donkey repeatedly, failing to see that God is speaking to him.

And don't we do the same? We are sometimes so intent on our own reckless path that God has to work through others to get our attention—sometimes by talking and sometimes by actions. And, even though they may be trusted sources, we still don't hear until finally we are halted in our path. Like Balaam, we resent their interference in our lives.

Sooner or later, however, God will get our attention. He will position himself and his message to us in such a way that we cannot avoid dealing with it and him. Sometimes we call that "hitting bottom". Often, in hindsight, we see that such extreme circumstances would not have been necessary if we had just heeded God's messengers around us. Of course, they don't always come in such obvious ways as a donkey who speaks. And some people think Walt Disney came up with talking animals!

The narrative around Moab continues through chapter 25. In chapter 26, God calls for a second census to be taken in anticipation of going into Canaan. God directs how the land should be allotted to the tribes, and in chapter 27 Joshua is appointed to succeed Moses. There is much repetition here, including the retelling of the delivery from Egypt.

One new—and significant—event occurs in chapter 32. The tribes of Reuben and Gad, and the half-tribe of Manasseh (one of Joseph's sons), ask to take their portion of the land east of Jordan rather than in Canaan. Moses agrees, provided they will fight with the other tribes to conquer Canaan. The tribal leaders accept Moses' terms. Their agreement is significant in showing the new generation's respect of Moses as their leader and God as their God.

Finally, but of extreme significance for the rest of the story, in chapter 33 God gives direction to destroy all the inhabitants of the lands they conquer as well as their gods, idols, and altars. We read God's direction in Numbers 33:55: *"But if you do not drive out the inhabitants of the land, those you allow to remain will become barbs in your eyes and thorns in your sides. They will give you trouble in the land where you will live."* We will see in Day Three just exactly what this means.

DEUTERONOMY 1 – 34
MOSES' FINAL INSTRUCTION

Greatest Commandment

History Lesson

Deuteronomy contains Moses' parting words to Israel. He is preparing to die, knowing that he will not cross over into Canaan with Joshua and Caleb. Moses teaches this new generation of Israelites about their history with Yahweh and then directs them to keep God's

Law Review

Future King

Covenant Renewal

Song of Moses

Moses Dies

Joshua Becomes Leader

decrees and commandments. The *ScriptureScope* on the next page contains a familiar and important verse followed by some that may not be so familiar.

LASTING IMPRESSIONS

In Deuteronomy 6:4-9 we read: *Hear, O Israel: The Lord our God, the Lord is one. Love the Lord your God with all your heart and with all your soul and with all your strength. These commandments that I give you today are to be upon your hearts. Impress them on your children. Talk about them when you sit at home and when you walk along the road, when you lie down and when you get up. Tie them as symbols on your hands and bind them on your foreheads. Write them on the doorframes of your houses and on your gates.*

Here, in verses 4 and 5, we find The Shema, recited as the centerpiece of Jewish prayer services. These are also the scriptures taught to Jewish children—Christ-followers might think of them as the "Jewish John 3:16". As such, we should acknowledge the significance of verse 5: "Love the Lord your God with all your heart and with all your soul and with all your strength." It is quoted by Jesus in Matthew 22:36-38 when he is asked "What is the greatest commandment?" It essentially sums up the first four commandments of the original ten and reminds us that God's love for us merits not just a weekly or occasional response of devotion, but *all* of us, *all* the time. The second half of the Great Commandment—Leviticus 18:18 *Love your neighbor as yourself*—sums up the last six of the ten commandments.

Beyond that, I'd like to focus on the examples Moses gives the Israelites of how to 'impress' God's decrees upon their children–talking, walking, evening, morning, as jewelry and adornment, in front of their homes. I don't know of many people who meet these criteria in terms of teaching God's word to their children–I know I certainly have not. But, if not God, what do we as parents and grandparents 'impress upon our children'? Our morals and priorities?

Maybe things about the university we attended? Perhaps our career? Possibly a professional sports team we follow? A particular style of music, composer, or artist? A favorite hobby that brings us joy? Our love of shopping, dining, or movies? Who are we to our children and grandchildren? If we asked them what they know about us, what would they say?

We certainly talk to our children and grandchildren about *something*. We adorn ourselves and our homes with *something*. *Something* occupies our thoughts, drives our actions, and absorbs our time and money. Why not the God of our salvation–our creator, redeemer, comforter, and friend? What could possibly be more important to 'impress upon our children' than a love of God?

Because none of the generation going into Canaan (except Joshua and Caleb) experienced God's delivery from slavery in Egypt, Moses reviews their history and God's instruction found in Exodus, Leviticus, and Numbers. In chapter 17 expectations are set for any future king of Israel, although Moses reminds the people that they don't need any other king than Yahweh. In chapter 18 Moses tells them that in the future many prophets will be sent to speak God's word to the people in place of him.

Moses makes it clear that the Israelites are not to worship Yahweh in the ways of the people they conquer in Canaan as these things are "detestable" to God. In chapter 24, they are told to "purge the evil" from Israel, both what comes from without and what originates from within. In chapter 29, Moses calls all the people to renew their covenant with God. Moses concludes the ceremony, saying in Deuteronomy 30:19-20: *This day I call heaven and earth as witnesses against you that I have set before you life and death, blessings and curses. Now choose life, so that you and your children may live and that you may love the Lord your God, listen to his voice, and hold fast to him. For the Lord is your life.* Deuteronomy concludes with Moses' song that praises God for his care of the Israelites, a song the Israelites are to sing through the generations (chapter 32). In the final chapter, Moses dies, and leadership of Israel is passed on to Joshua.

Thus ends Deuteronomy, the last of the five Books of Moses. Before going on, let's reflect. In Genesis we met Abraham, a man who taught a family about *faith*. In Exodus we met Moses, who taught a nation about *law*. In the New Testament, we will meet Jesus, who will teach the world about *love* and *grace*.

In Exodus, Leviticus, Numbers, and Deuteronomy, we read stories of deliverance and salvation; the formation of a nation from a family; disobedience and consequences; faithfulness and rewards; and, living in relationship with God and with others. Deuteronomy, which means literally in Greek "second law", serves as the gateway from the Pentateuch (the five books of Moses) to the rest of the OT as it reminds us of the past, exhorts the Israelites regarding the present, and lays down expectations for the future.

At the end of Deuteronomy, Joshua is the right hand of Moses and commander of the military. At the beginning of the book of Joshua, he will be the leader of a nation.

JOSHUA 1 – 12
TAKING THE LAND

Jericho Spies

Rahab

Fall of Jericho

Covenant Renewal

It has been over six hundred years since God made his original covenant with Abraham, promising him descendants and blessing and land. It will take at least another six years to conquer the land enough that it can be occupied. The taking of the land begins with the conquest of Jericho, followed by a northern campaign and a southern campaign.

At the beginning of the book of Joshua, the Israelites are camped on the east bank of the Jordan River, directly across from Jericho. God commands Joshua to prepare for battle. Joshua sends two young spies into Jericho to assess the enemy's strength, a reflection of Moses' sending of the twelve spies into Canaan over forty years earlier.

In chapter 2, we meet Rahab, a prostitute who lives in the city wall, giving her the opportunity to witness first-hand the activities of Jericho's city guard and army. She has noticed the Israelites camped across the Jordan and fears the coming invasion. Rahab hides the two spies and helps them escape back to the Israelite camp— in return for her family being spared by the Israelites when they attack the city.

In chapter 3, the time comes for the Israelites to cross the Jordan. God holds the waters back (as he did at the Red Sea), so they can cross. Word of this gets to the kings on both sides of the Jordan, and they begin to fear the Israelites and their God. Once on the other side of the river, God decrees that all the men must be circumcised before the battle (chapter 5). Apparently, no one had been circumcised during the forty-year trek through the wilderness and, except for Joshua and Caleb, all those who had been circumcised in Egypt had died.

It is the month of Nisan, so once the men have recovered from circumcision, the first Passover is celebrated in the Promised Land. In chapter 6, Joshua and the Israelites follow God's explicit instructions and take the city of Jericho. The battle plan is far from conventional, with God directing the Israelites to march around the city every day for seven days. On the seventh day, they march around the city seven times, blow the shofar (trumpet), shout, and….as the great African-American spiritual says, "the walls come tumblin' down!" Needless to say, the Israelites probably suffered some jeering and humiliation from the

Jericho army as they watched the daily marching, but the Israelites remained faithful to God.

In chapter 8 Joshua leads the Israelites in the renewal of their covenant with God. The remainder of this section details the battles for the land as well as some deception by a local tribe. This leads to the Israelites disobeying God's command to destroy all the inhabitants. See chapter 9 for details.

Ultimately, we learn that the two spies were faithful to their commitment to Rahab to save her and her family. As a result, she joins the Israelites and worships Yahweh. Later, in Matthew 1:5, we will learn that Rahab, the prostitute from Jericho, married Salmon of the tribe of Judah, descended from Perez, one of the sons of Tamar. They have a son, Boaz, who becomes the great-grandfather of King David. We will learn more about Boaz in Day Three.

So, out of all the action in the book of Joshua, perhaps the most significant event is that a prostitute shows compassion on two Jewish spies and believes them when they say they'll come back for her. As we noted with Joseph, God truly does work in mysterious ways. Nothing, and no one, is insignificant!

JOSHUA 13 – 24
INHABITING THE LAND

Covenant Fulfilled

Allotment of Land

Joshua's Speeches

Covenant Renewal

Joshua's Death

In these chapters we find the final fulfillment of God's covenant made with Abraham centuries earlier. Abraham's descendants have, indeed, become as numerous as the stars. They have been blessed with children and grandchildren, goods and livestock, community and fellowship. They have been a blessing to others, like Rahab and her family. Now, finally, they will live in the Promised Land of Canaan. God has kept his part of the covenant.

These chapters begin with the allotment of the land to the twelve tribes as God commanded (chapters 13 – 21). Boundaries and cities are established as God directed. At the same time, one of God's directives is repeatedly not followed. Although they were told to destroy all the native people—their gods, idols, and altars—in many cases the Israelites allow them to remain, essentially creating treaties with them. Why? Scholars have suggested a weakness of resolve, fascination with the pagan culture, or both. Whatever the reason, the results prove to be disastrous for the Israelites, as we will see in Day Three.

The remainder of the book of Joshua contains Joshua's three parting speeches. The first occurs in chapter 22 and is delivered to the tribes of Reuben and Gad and the half-tribe of Manasseh who fought to take the land but now are returning to their homes east of the Jordan. The second speech, in chapter 23, is delivered to the elders and leaders of the tribes. The third, found in chapter 24, is to all the Israelites and includes a renewal of their covenant with God. Joshua warns them to remain apart from the native people and their gods and challenges them to decide whom they will serve.

Joshua confronts the people with the following testimony from 24:14-15: *Now fear the Lord and serve him with all faithfulness. Throw away the gods your forefathers worshipped beyond the River and in Egypt, and serve the Lord. But if serving the Lord seems undesirable to you, then choose for yourselves this day whom you will serve, whether the gods your forefathers served beyond the River, or the gods of the Amorites, in whose land you are living. But as for me and my household, we will serve the Lord.* The book of Joshua closes with Joshua's death.

REFLECTING FORWARD

Use these questions to guide your discussion of Day Two and lead you into Day Three.

1. As the Israelites' story unfolded, we saw Moses interacting with God—and, more than once, trying to change God's mind. More importantly, God listened. What does this tell you about God? How have you experienced this aspect of God in your life?

2. We can't be like God if we don't know what God is like. The books we studied in Day Two give us many opportunities to learn about God's character. How would you describe God—the God you know—to someone else?

3. In Day Two, God introduced the concept of holiness to the Israelites. For them, "being holy" meant following specific rules to the letter. What does "being holy" mean to you today? Think of someone you consider "godly" or "holy". Why do you see him or her this way?

4. Revisit the discussion of Deut. 6:4-9 on page 54. If you have children or grandchildren, how do you 'impress' God's commandments upon them?

5. God commanded the Israelites to destroy all the native people and their idols when they entered Canaan, so that his people would not be tempted to reject him for these other attractions. Have you ever found yourself surrounded by people and idols that challenged your faith in God? Were you strong enough to reject them?

6. As Day Two concludes, the Israelites are in Canaan, and it seems like the story ends here. But, it's really just the beginning. Israel has not followed God's command to destroy all the pagan people and idols, and we will see the consequences of this in Day Three. Before we move on, consider a time when *you* did not rid yourself of all the idols God told you to reject. Did they later become "thorns" and "barbs" in your life? (Numbers 33:55)

DAY THREE

JUDGES, RUTH,

1 AND 2 SAMUEL,

1 AND 2 KINGS,

1 AND 2 CHRONICLES

As we move forward with the story of Israel, let's remember that it began with Abraham and Sarah, a couple who longed for a child and ended up with descendants as numerous as the grains of sand in the desert. Those descendants became slaves, then victors, and, finally, a nation under the law-giver Moses. Despite the Israelites' unfaithfulness, God remained faithful to the covenant he made with their ancestors. As a result, they entered the Promised Land and are ready to grow into the people God has chosen them to be—people who will share with the world the blessing of a perfect relationship with him. They are also about to experience the rewards of obedience and consequences of disobedience on their way to becoming the Kingdom of Israel.

JUDGES 1 – 12
DECAY AND DELIVERANCE

The book of Judges is a record of over three hundred years of moral and spiritual decline in the nation of Israel. This decay directly reflects the warnings Moses gave the

Othniel and Ehud

Deborah and Jael

Gideon

Samson and Delilah

Israelites in his final words to them in Deuteronomy. If you review the Bible Chronology on page 264, you will see that this period follows closely the taking of the land in the book of Joshua. In fact, the first chapter of Judges records Joshua's death again and the battles that follow in Canaan, emphasizing that the Israelites continue to disobey God's command to drive out or destroy the native peoples.

In chapter 2, the Lord's messenger tells the Israelites that they have broken their covenant with him by not destroying all the people in Canaan as well as their gods and their altars, resulting in the "trouble in the land where you live" predicted in Numbers (Day Two). This is followed with an overview of the book of Judges as a description of a cycle of decay and deliverance: The Israelites choose to serve other gods, such as Baal. In their weakness, they are conquered by neighboring tribes. God delivers them by calling a judge (leader) from one of the tribes of Israel. The Israelites then honor and serve God for a few years before falling back into pagan worship—and the cycle repeats.

Chapters 3 through 12 detail this cycle by describing several of the judges and their efforts to deliver Israel and revive worship of Yahweh. These include the first judge, Othniel, who is Caleb's nephew and son-in-law. (Reminder: Caleb was the other spy along with Joshua who was allowed to enter Canaan.) Any southpaws out there? The next judge is a left-handed Benjamite named Ehud. According to several ancient sources, left-handed warriors were highly prized for their ability to fight and, in particular, be extremely effective with the sling-shot.

The early chapters of Judges include the story of Deborah, the woman judge who conquers an army with the help of her general Jael, another woman. We also find the story of Gideon, who delivers the Israelites from oppression by the Midianites with only 300 of his original 32,000 men—God's way of demonstrating to Israel that it was God's power, not theirs, that defeated the foe. You can read this amazing story in Judges 6 and 7. See the *ScriptureScope* on the next page for more thoughts on Gideon's lesson for us.

OVER-PREPARED

In Judges 7:2-3b CEB we read: *The Lord said to Gideon: "You have too many people on your side. If I were to hand Midian over to them, the Israelites might claim credit for themselves rather than for me, thinking, 'We saved ourselves.'"*

One of the challenges of serving God is giving him room to do his part. When God called Gideon, immediately Gideon went into action, pulling together forces from four tribes for the fight. That's when God said, "Whoa! You have over-prepared here. You don't need this many men. Remember...you've got me."

I still need to hear that message sometimes, although my faith is getting stronger. In my zeal to answer God's call and to serve him, I forget sometimes that he is also on the team! And, like any team, I have my part to do (mostly just show up) and he has his part (mostly everything else.)

We are reminded of this every time we prepare for another *High Seas Ministries* cruise. About six weeks before we sail, I email the cruise director, requesting a location for the Bible study and notification of the study placed in the Daily Program. If we encounter a cruise director we've not worked with before, I send names of other cruise directors as references and include links to our website. I do everything that I can do—but the rest is in God's hands. I send the email and wait—not too patiently—for the cruise director's response. When the email comes, welcoming us on board, I am reminded whose ministry this really is and who is in charge!

God does not call without equipping, and he does not abandon those he calls. But, in order for God to be glorified, we may need to go into the battle a little less prepared than we want to be, trusting that God will uplift us, empower us, and be glorified through us—as long as we give him the chance.

Chapters 8 through 12 continue the cycle of decay and deliverance. In chapter 13 we meet Samson, perhaps the most familiar judge. Samson's story takes him from the strongest man alive to a broken man, blinded by his enemies and reduced to a source of entertainment for the conquering Philistines. Samson is born to a Danite woman who is childless (like Abraham and Sarah) and has been given specific directions from God to raise her son as a Nazirite, with a focused and pure commitment to serving God. (Reminder: Back on Day Two we learned about the vow of the Nazirite in Numbers.)

Samson leads Israel for twenty years and then falls in love with Delilah (chapter 16). The rulers of the Philistines promise to each pay Delilah eleven hundred shekels to find out Samson's source of strength. Ultimately, Samson confides to her that it is his hair; she cuts it off and he is captured by the Philistines. In his final hours, Samson calls upon the Lord's strength one last time and brings down the Philistine temple on all of the Philistines, thus killing more men as he died than when he lived.

The final three chapters of Judges put an exclamation point on Israel's moral and spiritual decay that have been the theme of this book. The horrific story of the Levite's concubine and attacks on the Benjamites is not only difficult to read but a graphic reminder of the depths to which Israel has fallen since the leadership of Moses and Joshua.

RUTH 1 – 4
FAITHFULNESS

The small but powerful book of Ruth occurs during the same time period as the book of Judges but provides a dramatic contrast to its dark tales of decay and disobedience. In fact, it demonstrates that

Ruth and Naomi

Bethlehem

Gleaning (Lev. 19)

Boaz

Obed--Jesse--David

even in periods of moral decay, goodness and faithfulness can be found.

(We know that, right? Our world seems to be in a mess most of the time, but examples of love and grace can be found—even here, even now.)

Naomi, an Israelite woman, has been living in the country of Moab with her husband, two sons, and two daughters-in-law, Orpah and Ruth. Her husband and sons die, and she decides to return to her home of Bethlehem in Judah (yes, the same Bethlehem that will be the birthplace of Jesus). Naomi urges her daughters-in-law, who are both from Moab, to stay in their home country. Orpah stays, but Ruth refuses to leave her mother-in-law. In Ruth 1:16-17 we read Ruth's words: *But Ruth replied, "Don't urge me to leave you or to turn back from you. Where you go I will go, and where you stay I will stay. Your people will be my people and your God, my God. Where you die I will die, and there I will be buried. May the Lord deal with me, be it ever so severely, if anything but death separates you and me."*

Ruth and Naomi return to Bethlehem, and in chapter 3 we read that Ruth works as a gleaner in the fields of Naomi's relative, Boaz. A couple of connections here: Boaz is the son of Rahab (the prostitute from Jericho) and Salmon of the tribe of Judah. And, because of the law given in Leviticus 19, Boaz allows the poor, widows, and foreigners (and Ruth falls in all three categories) to glean in his fields, picking up the stalks of barley left by the harvesters. This is what Naomi and Ruth live on until Boaz notices Ruth, sees her as a woman of noble character, and marries her in chapter 4.

Ruth then becomes the third woman mentioned in the lineage of Jesus, as she and Boaz have a son, Obed, who will become the father of Jesse and thus the grandfather of King David. The "upside-down" kingdom of Jesus begins to take form—over 1,000 years before he is born—as his lineage includes not just "saints" and pure-bred Israelites, but a prostitute (Rahab), a pretend prostitute (Tamar), and a foreigner (Ruth).

1 SAMUEL 1 – 15
THE KINGDOM OF ISRAEL

Samuel—a leader, prophet, judge, and instrument of the Lord—serves as a bridge between the period of the judges and the period of the kings in Israel's story. To understand the importance of the prophet role

Samuel, a Bridge

Hannah

Eli the Priest

Saul Anointed King

Saul Loses Kingdom

in Israel, refer to the Kings and Prophets table on page 266. This study aid will be very helpful as we continue through Day Three.

Thinking back on the judges, you may remember that they typically served as both spiritual and military leaders. They 'judged' Israel by helping Israel conquer the people oppressing them, but they also provided moral and spiritual guidance. Gideon is a good example of this style of leadership.

Samuel is arguably the last of these military/spiritual leaders, with young King David possibly in this category as well. Following Samuel, Israel will primarily be led by a series of kings who are political/military leaders. Working with them are prophets who provide spiritual guidance, both to the king and to the people. And, Samuel also serves in this role, as we will see. This period in Israel's history fulfills Moses' words to the Israelites that God would send many men to speak for him (God) rather than just one, as he did with Moses.

First Samuel begins with the birth of Samuel to Hannah who, like Sarah and the mother of Samson, was barren. She promises God that she will give her son to the Lord and raise him as a Nazirite if she is blessed with a child. True to her word, after Samuel is born, she takes him to Eli the priest to raise. In these early chapters we read that Eli also has sons of his own who do evil, but Samuel is said to *"grow in stature and in favor with the Lord and with men."* (1 Samuel 2:26). Note that this same description is given to Jesus in Luke 2:52.

In chapter 3, the Lord calls Samuel to lead Israel, which Samuel does through a period of chaos. The Ark of the Covenant is captured by the Philistines and returned only after God sends rats and tumors upon the Philistines. Samuel continues to lead Israel until the people demand a military king like the nations around them (chapter 8).

Although they have a divine king—Yahweh—God agrees to let them have a human king as well. In chapter 9 God leads Samuel to anoint Saul, a 30-year-old Benjamite, as king. Saul is tall, strong, and a great warrior—exactly what the people want in their king—and he serves Israel as king for 42 years. Saul initially listens to God and is victorious in battles against the Ammonites (chapter 11).

As time goes by, however, Saul fails to follow God's commands. God directs him to destroy the Amalekites, the Amalekite king, and all their livestock, but Saul does not. In chapter 15 the Lord, speaking through Samuel, tells Saul that he is taking the kingdom of Israel away from him because of his rebellion and arrogance and promising it to another. Samuel never visits Saul again.

1 SAMUEL 16 – 31
SAUL AND DAVID

David Anointed King

David and Goliath

Jonathan

Saul Pursues David

Samuel Dies

Saul and Jonathan Die

As God promised Saul, he has another man in mind to be Israel's king, and his story begins here. Unknown to Saul, God leads Samuel to Bethlehem of Judah to a shepherd boy who is the youngest son of Jesse (who is the son of Obed and the grandson of Ruth and Boaz). There Samuel anoints David to be the next king of Israel.

Meanwhile, back at the palace, Saul is becoming more and more depressed and tormented, as he contemplates God's promise to take the kingdom away from him. To soothe his spirit, his servants bring him a young shepherd boy who plays the harp and sings—none other than David. In chapter 16 Saul befriends David although he has no idea that this is his future successor.

The Israelites are at war with the Philistines (as usual). They are encamped across the Valley of Elah from each other, where each day the Philistines send out their giant warrior, Goliath, to challenge an Israelite to a one-on-one fight to determine the outcome of the battle. In chapter 17 David, who is too young to fight, comes to the battlefield to bring food for his older brothers and discovers the stalemate. He has faith that Israel's God will prevail, volunteers to fight Goliath, and kills the giant with a single stone from his sling. (*Perhaps David was left-handed??*)

A battle ensues, and the Israelites are victorious. In chapter 18, we learn that David wins a true and lasting friend in Saul's son Jonathan. But when the people chant "Saul has killed his thousands, David his ten thousands!" paranoid Saul begins to see David as his enemy and looks for an opportunity to kill him.

Jonathan defends David to his father and sends David away to safety, but not before David promises to always care for Jonathan's descendants no matter what happens between their families. Indeed, Saul continues to pursue David and the men who have joined him. Twice David has the opportunity to kill Saul, but does not because of his loyalty to the king, "the Lord's anointed." For a particularly entertaining incident, read chapter 24 in 1 Samuel. The *ScriptureScope* below records David's response to Saul.

RARE GRACE

In 1 Samuel 24:12 CEB we read: *May the Lord judge between me and you! May the Lord take vengeance on you for me, but I won't lift a hand against you.*

These words of David to Saul are a breath of fresh air—not only in the Old Testament but in the 21st century as well. As we read repeatedly in these chapters of death, destruction, vengeance, and justice, seemingly out of nowhere comes this picture of grace. David has multiple opportunities to kill the man who has attempted to kill him and has made his life one of hiding in caves and constant running—a man who would not consider offering the same grace to him.

Yet, David does not touch Saul. Instead, he honors his role as King of Israel and turns the final judgement over to God. My, how different this would seem in our world! The norm in our society is 'getting even', whether it's on the playground, in the courtroom, or among gangs and mobsters. A story of grace and forgiveness seems as rare today as it did three thousand years ago.

Occasionally in the media we will hear of people who forgive the killer who murdered their loved ones (think of the Charleston, SC, church killing in 2015) or the arsonist who burned down their home or the rapist who destroyed a life. And, like David's men, the world is always surprised, for most people cannot understand how someone could forgive such an offense.

As Christ-followers, we should not be surprised. After all, grace is the essence of our faith and we find examples of what we typically think of as "New Testament grace" sprinkled throughout the Old Testament as well (remember Esau and Joseph?). No, we should not be surprised; in fact, we should look for opportunities to extend Christ's grace to others in our own lives.

Chapters 25 through 30 detail more of Saul and David's encounters. In chapter 27 David ironically joins the Philistines to get away from Saul. And, in chapter 28 we see that Saul is so desperate to defeat the Philistines that he asks a medium to contact Samuel's spirit to help him. In the final chapter, Saul dies along with three of his sons, including Jonathan.

2 SAMUEL 1 – 22
DAVID AS KING

| *City of David* |
| *Davidic Covenant* |
| *Mephibosheth* |
| *Bathsheba* |
| *Nathan the Prophet* |
| *Solomon* |
| *Absalom* |

David learns of the death of Saul and Jonathan and becomes king of his tribe (Judah), a position he holds for seven years. In the meantime, Ish-Bosheth (Saul's remaining son) succeeds his father as king over the rest of the tribes. War ensues and by chapter 5, David becomes king over all Israel and reigns for an additional thirty-three years.

King David takes Jerusalem from the Jebusites and renames it the City of David. He brings the Ark of the Covenant to Jerusalem and in chapter 7 seeks counsel from the prophet Nathan regarding building a temple for the ark. Through Nathan, God tells David that David will not be the one to build him a temple. Note the wordplay in the passage below, as God declines to allow David to build a temple (a house) for him. Instead, God promises to build up David's house (his lineage).

We find the Davidic Covenant—a continuation of the covenants established with Noah, Abraham, and Israel—in 2 Samuel 7:11b-12, 16: *The Lord declares to you that the Lord himself will establish a house for you. When your days are over and you rest with your fathers, I will raise up your offspring to succeed you, who will come from your own body, and I will establish his kingdom. Your house and your kingdom will endure forever before me; your throne will be established forever.* The one *"who will come from your own body"* and whose *"throne will be established forever"* is the prophesied Messiah, Jesus.

David is true to his promise to Jonathan to care for his household when he seeks out Jonathan's only remaining son, the crippled Mephibosheth. In chapter 9 he brings him to Jerusalem, shares his table with him, and gives him all of Saul's land. Shortly after that, we read that David no longer goes into battle himself but sends his generals. He has become comfortable in Jerusalem and, one afternoon as he is relaxing at the palace, he notices a beautiful woman bathing on the next rooftop over. Her name is Bathsheba.

In chapter 11 David has Bathsheba brought to him and soon we learn that Bathsheba is pregnant with David's child. Rather than admit his mistake, David first tries to cover it up by having Bathsheba's husband Uriah the Hittite sleep with her. Uriah refuses to take this privilege because his company of soldiers does not have the same option with their own wives. So, David sends him to the front lines of the battle, and he is killed.

David marries Bathsheba and they have a son. Speaking through the prophet Nathan, the Lord expresses his "displeasure" and tells David that his taking of Bathsheba will bring calamity upon his house. In 2 Samuel 12:4 we read the parable Nathan uses to convict David of his sin: *Now a traveler came to the rich man, but the rich man refrained from taking one of his own sheep or cattle to prepare a meal for the traveler who had come to him. Instead, he took the ewe lamb that belonged to the poor man and prepared it for the one who had come to him.*

David sees that he is like the rich man, taking from the poor man to satisfy his desires. David immediately repents and, in response, writes a beautiful psalm of contrition, Psalm 51. The baby born to David and Bathsheba dies, but they have another son, Solomon, whom the Lord loves.

Chapters 13 through 21 fulfill God's prophecy through Nathan promising that calamity would come upon David's house as a result of his sin with Bathsheba. David's family experiences incest, rape, murder, revenge killings, and rebellion. In chapter 15 David and his family have to leave Jerusalem when his son Absalom challenges the throne. Ultimately, David returns to Jerusalem as king (chapter 19) and is greeted by Mephibosheth, Jonathan's son, who remained loyal to him even in his absence.

In chapter 22, David offers a thanksgiving psalm of praise to God for his faithfulness and deliverance. With little variation, the same song of praise is found as Psalm 18, also attributed to David.

1 KINGS 1 – 11
SOLOMON'S REIGN

David Dies

Solomon is King

Wisdom and Wealth

Temple Built

Queen of Sheba

Foreign Wives

Other Gods

Kingdom Divided

As the book begins, David is old and his son Adonijah is planning to take over the throne, based on his position as the oldest living heir. Bathsheba and Nathan, however, conspire to remind David that he promised Solomon the throne. In chapter 2 Solomon is, indeed, anointed king. And, now we see that the fourth woman in the lineage of Jesus is Bathsheba, referenced in Matthew's gospel, interestingly, as "Uriah's wife" (Matthew 1:6). This helps us understand even more the "upside down" nature of the kingdom that Jesus will bring, a kingdom where the last— deceivers (Jacob), prostitutes (Rahab), pretend-prostitutes (Tamar), foreigners (Ruth), adulterers (David and Bathsheba)—are first. What does this tell us about who Christ came for? Not just the saints, but the sinners. Not the religious elite, but the ones who have been forgiven much. Not just his chosen people the Israelites, but everyone.

In chapter 3 the Lord appears to King Solomon in a dream and offers to give him whatever he would like. Solomon replies "wisdom", which pleases God. Solomon subsequently becomes the wisest man in the land. A thought-provoking tale of Solomon's wisdom can be found in 1 Kings 3:16-28. This story of two prostitutes who come to Solomon to solve a dispute over who is a child's mother has become an exemplar of Solomon's great wisdom.

In chapters 4 through 9 Solomon establishes a kingdom of immense wealth, as evident in the building of the temple (the one God would not allow David to build) and several palaces. Solomon's reign is a time of peace for Israel, allowing him to focus his energy on building projects and amassing great wealth. He also entertains many foreign dignitaries, including the Queen of Sheba (chapter 10).

Unfortunately, establishing alliances with foreign powers often means taking on foreign wives. In chapter 11 we learn that Solomon has more than one thousand wives and concubines (*yes, over 1000---999 too many for most men, I'm guessing!*) Most of these are from foreign nations with whom God had warned about intermarrying. Solomon pays no heed, however, and allows his wives to erect altars and 'high places of worship' for their pagan gods.

God becomes angry and tells Solomon that he will tear the kingdom from Solomon's son and give ten tribes to another king, leaving Solomon's son, Rehoboam, with only the tribes of Judah and Benjamin.

1 KINGS 12 – 22
A KINGDOM DIVIDED

These chapters begin the story of Israel as a divided kingdom. After a little over one hundred years as a united kingdom, civil war ensues upon Solomon's death. What emerges is a

Northern Kingdom Israel
Southern Kingdom Judah
Kings and Prophets
Jerusalem and Samaria
Ahab and Jezebel
Elijah on Mt. Carmel

northern kingdom (Israel) and a southern kingdom (Judah). The period of the divided kingdom is one of upheaval and spiritual decline, not unlike the earlier period of the judges in this way. The two kingdoms are sometimes allies, as they fight against neighboring countries and world empires. More often, they are at war with each other. Their relationship is always competitive, contentious, and distrustful.

A look at the Kings and Prophets table on page 266 is a helpful way to get the big picture of this time in the life of Israel. Note the use of asterisks to indicate "good" kings—kings that the Bible describes as following in the footsteps of King David. How many do you find for the southern kingdom, Judah? How about the northern kingdom, Israel? This is important to remember as we continue to move through history toward the fall of both kingdoms and the writings of the prophets that lived during these tumultuous times.

More important things to remember: The capital of the southern kingdom of Judah remains Jerusalem, the City of David. The northern kingdom of Israel establishes its capital in Samaria. Thus begin the bad feelings between Jerusalem and Samaria, which will remain even as Jesus comes to change the world.

In chapter 16, we meet the "most evil couple" award winners of the OT—King Ahab and his not-so-lovely bride Jezebel. Ahab and Jezebel rule Israel, the northern kingdom, and worship the pagan god Baal. They live at the same time as King Asa of Judah, who is one of the "good kings" of the southern kingdom. The books of 1 Kings and 2 Kings continuously remind the reader of the conflict between the two kingdoms as they alternate narratives between the events happening in Israel and the events happening in Judah. This gives you a good understanding of how the two kingdoms remain a part of each other's history.

In chapter 18, Elijah—the first great prophet of the OT and the name that comes to symbolize all the prophets—comes on the scene. He prophesies in the northern kingdom and, in fact, is one of a few of the

Lord's prophets still left during the reign of Ahab and Jezebel. Elijah is a thorn in their sides and they would like nothing better than to be rid of him. So, Elijah challenges all of the "prophets" of the pagan god Baal—the god of Ahab and Jezebel—on Mount Carmel. See the *ScriptureScope* below for one of the great scenes of the OT.

The book of 1 Kings ends with the death of Ahab.

RE-TURNING TO GOD

In 1 Kings 18:37 we read Elijah's call to God: *Answer me, O Lord, answer me, so these people will know that you, O Lord, are God, and that you are turning their hearts back again.*

Here's the scene: It's 450 pagan 'prophets' versus one true prophet of the Lord, Elijah. Elijah challenges Baal's 450 prophets to light the fire under a sacrificial bull by calling on their god, Baal. They try for hours, even hopping around the altar and cutting themselves. Elijah has some fun with them, too, asking if Baal is asleep or out for a walk, perhaps? They finally give up. Now it's Elijah's turn.

First he makes the task even harder by setting stones around the altar and building a trench. Then he pours water on the wood so that it runs off into the trench, creating a moat around the bull. He does this three times, until the people are begging him to call on his God to light the fire. You can just imagine the excitement of this spectacle—with Ahab looking on.

Finally, Elijah calls on God to light the fire and make himself known, concluding with the words above. Of course, God's fire falls from the heavens—and consumes not just the bull but the wood, the stones, the dust, and even the water in the trench. But the part of this story I like best is the reason that Elijah gives God for wanting him to do this. We read it above—*so that the people, who had forsaken God for Baal, would know that God has not forsaken them.*

I once heard someone speak on 'turning', or more specifically,'re-turning.' We typically use the word 'returning' lightly—meaning, we'll be back soon from our trip, our errands, our day at work. But here, Elijah doesn't use it lightly at all. He wants the Israelite Baalworshippers to know that God is aware that they have turned away from him. More importantly, God is at work 're-turning' them to him.

God is many things, but perhaps of most value to us, he is omniscient and persistent—always aware of what is happening with his children. When we turn away, he notices. And he immediately initiates the process of our re-turn. It may take weeks, months, years, even a lifetime. But he does not give up. As the old hymn describes him:

> Oh Love that will not let me go,
> I rest my weary soul in thee,
> I give thee back the life I owe,
> That in thine ocean depths
> Its flow may richer, fuller be.

Oh Love that will not let me go…

2 KINGS 1 – 17
THE FALL OF ISRAEL

Elijah to Heaven

Elisha

Jehu

Joash

Israel Falls to Assyria

Samaria Resettled

In chapter 2 of the second volume of Kings, Elijah is taken up into heaven in a whirlwind (the story that gave us the wonderful old spiritual "Swing Low, Sweet Chariot"). One of his disciples, Elisha, receives his spirit and becomes his successor. Both Elijah and Elisha have many similarities with Jesus: numerous disciples who travel with them, the healing of sick people, performing many miracles similar to Jesus' miracles, and even raising the dead.

The lineage of kings in both Judah and Israel continues (see the Kings and Prophets table) with the leaders of both countries following in the ways of Ahab, not King David. In chapter 9, God speaks through Elisha to call Jehu, son of Judah's good king Jehoshaphat, to become king of the northern kingdom of Israel. He exterminates the remnants of

Ahab's family including Jezebel, as well as all the ministers and prophets of the pagan god Baal. The reign of Jehu is Israel's spiritual high point, but he also ultimately does 'evil in the sight of the Lord', walking in the ways of Jeroboam, the first of Israel's many evil kings.

In chapters 11 and 12 we meet Joash, one of Judah's kings who walked in the ways of David. The story of Joash is one of the most intriguing stories of the OT. In it, we meet Judah's only queen, Athaliah, as well as the great priest Jehoiada. Most importantly, it includes one of our major themes as Jehoiada leads the people in renewing their covenant with the God (chapter 11).

God's patience with Israel is running thin, and he begins to decrease the size of the northern kingdom. More and more tribes and their territories fall to conquering armies (chapter 15). Finally, God can no longer abide the sins of Israel, and in the mid-8th c. BC the capital Samaria is captured by the Assyrians. As is their practice, the Assyrians take most of the conquered people back to Assyria. To further prevent any possibility of uprising, the Assyrians also typically send people from other countries they had conquered into a newly conquered area to inhabit it. This is what happens in Samaria, which leads to intermarriage with the few Israelites left there, resulting in a hybrid religion based on Judaism but laced with paganism. The history between Israel and Judah combined with this impure worship of Yahweh forms the foundation of the relationship between Jews and Samaritans in Jesus' day. Keep this in mind for our discussion of Jesus' life and ministry in Days Seven and Eight.

2 KINGS 18 – 25
THE FALL OF JUDAH

Chapters 18 through 20 tell the story of Judah's King Hezekiah, one of the southern kingdom's greatest kings. Hezekiah is described as 'holding fast to the Lord' and keeping his commandments. Hezekiah rules for twenty-nine years and is known for

Hezekiah

Josiah

Book of the Law

Covenant Renewal

Nebuchadnezzar

Fall of Jerusalem

Temple Destroyed

destroying the 'high places' of pagan worship, withstanding a siege of Jerusalem by the Assyrians (yes, the ones who just took Samaria to the north), and surviving a life-threatening illness because of his faith. We also meet the great prophet Isaiah in Hezekiah's story, as the king calls upon him for spiritual guidance. Hezekiah and Isaiah effectively demonstrate the king/prophet relationship discussed earlier in this chapter.

Hezekiah's grandson, Josiah, also rules in Hezekiah's ways. His story can be found in chapters 22 and 23 and includes the story of his priest finding the Book of the Law as renovations are being done to the temple. The priest brings the book to Josiah, who knows nothing of its contents. The spiritual decline of the Israelites is so extreme that the law given to Moses by God is no longer being taught. Josiah consults the prophetess Huldah (one of the few women prophets mentioned by name) and learns the contents of the scrolls. He calls the people together, reads the Book of the Law to them, and leads them in a renewal of their covenant with God.

Josiah's sons succeed him and become puppet kings of Babylon, the world power that has conquered the Assyrians. Babylon's king,

Nebuchadnezzar, takes over more and more of Judah (chapter 24), deporting the Jewish scholars, leaders, and artisans to Babylon as he goes. Many scholars believe that The Great Deportation (occurring around 609 BC) included the prophets Daniel and Ezekiel, who will prophesy during the Babylonian exile to come.

In chapter 25 we read that, after a long and merciless siege, Jerusalem falls to Nebuchadnezzar. Most Biblical historians date this event to mid-6th c. BC, 150-200 years after the fall of the northern kingdom. Solomon's temple is destroyed and the remaining military, craftsmen, and artisans are exiled to Babylon. Only the poorest people are left in Judah, and they ultimately flee to Egypt after rebelling against their Babylonian rulers.

1 CHRONICLES 1 – 29
ADAM TO DAVID'S DEATH

Important Genealogies

David the Architect

Temple Building Fund

Focus on Judah

Different Perspective

Preparation to Rebuild

Take a look at the Bible Chronology found on page 264. You will see that the events of 1 Chronicles coincide chronologically with the events recorded in 1 and 2 Samuel. Likewise, 2 Chronicles matches up with 1 and 2 Kings. This means that the two volumes of Chronicles cover what we have already discussed but in half the reading. In truth, 1 and 2 Chronicles include some new information as well but focus almost exclusively on the southern kingdom of Judah. 1 and 2 Chronicles typically reference people and events in the northern kingdom of Israel only when they impact Judah.

Chapters 1 thru 9 of 1 Chronicles provide genealogies of the tribes of Israel, beginning with Adam. So, in a sense, this is a review of everything that has happened so far, all the way back to Genesis. More detailed genealogies are given for Saul, David, the kings of Judah and—notably—the first people who return to Judah after the Babylonian exile. (We have not yet read about this return [see Day 4] but it is included here.)

For what purpose? To establish that the tribal lines (particularly the line of Judah) remained intact during the exile and returned as part of the 'remnant' to repopulate Judah. Remember the Davidic Covenant, when God promised that David's line would forever reign over Israel? This shows that this covenant is in place, even after the exile. Essentially, these genealogies set the stage for the coming of the Messiah—Jesus—through David's line, as promised by God.

Chapter 10 begins with Saul's death and then retells the story of David's reign over the united kingdom of Israel (previously found in 2 Samuel). Much is a repeat, but there is some new information as well. The book ends with plans for the building of the temple. In chapter 28 we learn that David was essentially the architect and Solomon was the contractor and interior designer.

In chapter 29 David challenges the people of Israel to donate to the "building fund" for the temple. We have participated in many church building projects over the years. The plan always seems to be for the prominent members and church leaders to donate first, as an example for everyone else. This is exactly what David does, asking the leaders of the tribes and clans and the commanders of the army to give their gold and silver first. Who knew? Right here in 1 Chronicles: the "capital campaign" prototype!

2 CHRONICLES 1 – 36
SOLOMON TO EXILE

As the second volume of Chronicles begins, Solomon is king and builds, furnishes, and dedicates the temple (a reiteration of 1 Kings 5-9). In chapter 10, the story of the divided kingdom begins, focusing primarily on Judah. Unlike before, there is no see-saw narrative between the northern kingdom and the southern kingdom.

Note also that this time the story is told from the perspective of a people who have been exiled and are now recommitted to Israel's covenant with the Lord. As a result, the roles of priests such as Jehoiada who anointed Joash as king and prophets such as Isaiah are given more emphasis here than previously in 2 Kings. We also read for the first time references to Jeremiah, who prophesied during the siege and fall of Jerusalem.

Left out are references to the decay and destruction so prevalent in the northern kingdom. And, interestingly, even the story of David and Bathsheba's adultery is omitted. Instead, the writer of Chronicles focuses on the spiritual history and renewal of the people. Remember in Day Two when we discussed that Moses' speeches in Deuteronomy were designed to teach the history and law to the new generation? This is a similar scenario. 1 and 2 Chronicles were written for the returning exiles, who have been in Babylon for 70 years. Many of them do not know the history of Israel, both as a united and divided kingdom. Back in Deuteronomy, Moses' purpose was to prepare a new generation to inhabit the Promised Land and live as a nation under God's leadership. The purpose here is to prepare a new generation to reestablish Jerusalem and the nation of Israel after the exile.

And, in keeping with this purpose, the last chapter of 2 Chronicles does not end with the fall of Jerusalem as did the last chapter of 2 Kings. Instead, the last two verses of 2 Chronicles foreshadow the return of the exiles and rebuilding of the temple that will be our focus in Day Four.

REFLECTING FORWARD

Use these questions to guide your discussion of Day Three and lead you into Day Four.

1. The book of Judges focuses on a pattern of unfaithfulness as the Israelites reject God, God delivers them, they worship Him, and then fall away again. What recurring cycles do we see in our world today? Have you experienced anything like this in your life, related to faith, healthy habits, or relationships, perhaps? Did you, like the Israelites, turn to God for help?

2. How have you, like Gideon, "over-prepared" in your partnership with God? What have you learned about "letting go and letting God"?

3. King David experienced spiritual mountaintops and moral failures, committing adultery and murder. Yet, the Bible refers to David as "a man after God's own heart", in part because of his willingness to repent, admitting his sin and asking for forgiveness. Repentance is difficult for most people, requiring humility and obedience. What other examples do you see in the Bible of David-like repentance? What has been your own experience with repentance? When you have repented, how has God responded?

4. Elijah on Mt. Carmel is one of the classic scenes of the Old Testament, demonstrating the power and majesty of God. There are many great moments, but a favorite for me is the way that God answers Elijah's prayer. God did not just give Elijah what he asked for—the lighting of the altar—but much more. How has God answered your prayers in ways you could not have imagined? How has he surprised you with his faithfulness, generosity, and blessing?

5. Read 2 Kings 22-23 for the complete story of King Josiah and his reaction to finding the Book of the Law during the temple renovation. Do you find it hard to believe that this scroll, God's Word as

delivered in Exodus, Leviticus, Numbers, and Deuteronomy, had been lost for centuries? Has God's Word ever been lost to you? How might your life have been different if you had read the Bible and obeyed its teachings earlier in your journey?

6. On the Bible Chronology on page 264 notice the number of prophetic and wisdom books that were written during the period of the divided kingdom (2 Kings/2 Chronicles). What does this say about God's relationship with Israel during this difficult time? Looking back at your life, can you identify a time when God was trying to speak to you? Do you see any similarities between your life at that time and Israel during the divided kingdom years?

7. The genealogical lists throughout the Bible are notorious for putting even the most dedicated reader to sleep. Look at the genealogies at the beginning of 1 Chronicles. Knowing their purpose now, how might you read them differently? What key characters might you look for?

8. Looking at the last verses of 2 Chronicles, we get a "hint" about what lies ahead—the Israelites will return to Jerusalem. We see a stark contrast to the world view and the God-view. In the world here below, when utter, complete defeat comes, and the victors claim the spoils, the only sliver of hope centers on revenge. In God's world, the hope is reconciliation and restoration. How has God created reconciliation and restoration in your life, when—in the world's view—there was only defeat and hopelessness?

DAY FOUR

EZRA, NEHEMIAH,
ESTHER, JOB,
PSALMS, PROVERBS,
ECCLESIASTES, SONG OF SONGS

As we begin Day Four, let's first reflect on Day Three. We covered around 850 years (according to some scholars, 1390 to 535BC) from the time of the judges, through the unified kingdom under Saul, David, and Solomon, through civil war, the fall of the divided kingdom, and exile to Babylon. We even got a hint of some restoration to come at the very end of 2 Chronicles. Whew!

I am always reminded at this point in the study of my grandson Carter. About fifteen years ago, Keith and I began to spend a week each summer with our grandchildren, playing, traveling, and studying the Bible. Over the years, the scenery has changed, the older ones have gotten bigger, and we've added new little ones to our trip as they have "qualified." (*Translation: At least 3 years old and potty-trained—Daddy Keith and Nana Pam are smarter than we look.*) Carter is one of the younger ones in the group but always ready to answer any question Nana Pam asks about the Bible, thanks to his inquisitive mind and some good training at home. But, even Carter gets a little confused by all the many names, places, and events in the Bible.

On a recent trip, we were making a sprint through the entire Bible—hitting the "highlights of the highlights" as Keith would say— and Carter wanted to answer every question with his favorite character, Jonah. So, on that particular day, it was Jonah's Ark, Jonah's coat of many colors, Jonah in the basket in the Nile, Jonah at the battle of Jericho—you get the idea. The point is: He may have had the names wrong, but he knew the stories and they meant something to him, even at five years old.

So, don't feel overwhelmed with the many judges, kings, and prophets we discussed in Day Three—they do tend to run together. The important thing to remember is the story: the ongoing saga of God and his work to redeem humanity and restore us to perfect relationship, as it was in the beginning. In Day Three we saw the Israelites, as a people, fall away from their covenant with God, even as some individual leaders would re-turn them back to Yahweh. As a big picture, however, the sins of Israel were so great that, ultimately, they suffered God's judgment at the hands of their enemies, the Assyrians and later the Babylonians.

But...God will keep his part of the covenant, as we will see in Day Four.

EZRA 1 – 10
RETURN FROM EXILE

King Cyrus of Persia
Return of Remnant
King Darius
Temple Rebuilt
Covenant Renewal
Rebuilding the Wall
Book of the Law
Celebration
Esther and Mordecai

Ezra was a priest, living among the exiles in Babylon. When the book of Ezra opens, it has been seventy years since the first deportation around 609 BC. During that time, the Persians have conquered the Babylonians and become the current world power. The Persian king, Cyrus, fulfills Isaiah's prophecy (see Day Five) and allows a remnant of Israel—a small group of the people—to return to Jerusalem to rebuild the temple and the city. In chapter 2 the returning exiles are listed by family and temple role (priests, servants, singers, gatekeepers). They total 42,360 and are led back to Jerusalem by Zerubbabel and Jeshua.

Beginning in chapter 3, we read about the rebuilding of the temple altar, then the temple foundation. It's not long until the locals, who fear they will lose control of "their" land, write a letter to Cyrus' successor, Artaxerxes, asking him to order the Jews to stop working—and he does (chapter 4). In time, however, work begins again, despite the opposition. (Note: We will learn in Day Six that this is due in large part to the exhortations of the prophets Haggai and Zechariah).

In chapter 5 the renewed building effort incites further opposition and results in another letter, this time to the new king, Darius. Darius throws his support behind the project in an amusing, but meaningful, way.

MAKE AN IMPACT

In Ezra 6:8-10 CEB we read the words of Darius: *I also issue a decree about what you should do to help these elders of the Jews as they rebuild this house of God. The total cost is to be paid to these people, and without delay, from the royal revenue that is made up of the tribute of the province Beyond the River. And whatever is needed—young bulls, rams, or sheep for entirely burned offerings to the God of heaven, wheat, salt, wine, or oil, as requested by the priests in Jerusalem—let that be given to them day by day without fail so that they may offer pleasing sacrifices to the God of heaven and pray for the lives of the king and his sons.*

Bob Hope was once asked why he did so many benefits for a variety of religions and religious causes. His response: "I've done benefits for ALL religions. I'd hate to blow the hereafter on a technicality."

It seems that King Darius felt the same way. There's always an angle, isn't there? King Darius paved the way for the work on the temple to be completed by paying for it out of the royal treasury, much to the dislike of his other officials in the region. Moreover, he made sure the Jews had all they needed to offer sacrifices and keep 'the God of heaven' pleased—not entirely out of the goodness of his heart, it seems, but so that the Israelites could pray to Yahweh for him and his sons.

God even works through politicians! And, perhaps Darius was a believer—we read later that God 'changed his attitude'. One thing was sure, however…he was not taking any chances that these Israelites might really be on to something, like maybe the only true God.

What's really interesting about this passage is that somehow, during their seventy years in captivity, the Israelites' captors saw something different in them. Even as strangers in a foreign land, they made an impact.

May it ever be with us today. We are strangers in this place. Our culture of ME-focus, celebrity worship, and constantly-changing standards is not God's way. We are here in a foreign land, trying to live out our faith. May we make an impact by living in such a way that others take notice and want to learn more about God's way from us.

The last chapters of Ezra tell of the completion of the temple and Ezra's return from Babylon with another group of exiles, the second remnant (chapter 9). In chapter 10, Ezra leads the people in confession, prayer, and covenant renewal, dealing with issues of division among the people.

NEHEMIAH 1 – 13
GODLY LEADERSHIP

The books of Ezra and Nehemiah were originally one book, so Nehemiah is sometimes referred to as 2 Ezra. The story of the remnant's return and the rebuilding of Jerusalem continues under the direction of one of the Bible's great leadership models, Nehemiah.

As the book opens, Nehemiah is the cupbearer of King Artaxerxes II of Persia, a successor to King Darius we met earlier. As cupbearer, he serves in a trusted position and has a close relationship with the king. Nehemiah learns from one of the Jews who has returned from Jerusalem that the temple has been rebuilt, but the city wall and gates are destroyed, leaving the temple unprotected.

Before Nehemiah responds, he prays about the situation, asking God for guidance. In chapter 2, he asks the king for permission to go to

Jerusalem, and the king sends him back as governor of the newly rebuilt city. He provides him with everything he needs to travel safely to Jerusalem and lead the wall-rebuilding effort.

When Nehemiah arrives, he enlists the aid of the people, but also draws resistance from three local leaders threatened by the possibility of Jerusalem regaining its power. In chapter 4 Nehemiah puts extra workers on guard so that they are always prepared for a fight, even as they work on rebuilding the wall.

In Nehemiah 4:8-9 we read: *They all plotted together to come and fight against Jerusalem and stir up trouble against it. But we prayed to our God and posted a guard day and night to meet this threat.* Notice Nehemiah's actions as a godly leader: prayer first, then additional precaution. (This apparently is the origin of the battle cry attributed to Oliver Cromwell: "Trust in God but keep your powder dry!") Nehemiah understood that he was God's partner in this task, so he prayed first, acknowledging his need for divine protection, but he also did what he could do as well.

By chapter 7 the wall is completed, and Ezra reads the Book of the Law to the people. They grieve about their sins and recommit to a covenant with the Lord. Note that the reading of the Book of the Law has the same effect here as it did when Josiah had it read to the people back in 2 Kings 23. In each case, after hearing God's word, the people renewed their covenant with God. *A message for us, perhaps?*

In chapter 12 the wall is dedicated with a celebration of song, praise, and worship. This concludes God's meta-narrative as told in the History books of the Old Testament. (Although Esther is typically considered one of the books of history, the events that encompass the wisdom and prophecy literature are complete in the book of Nehemiah.)

While the event-framework that shaped the Israelites' story (beginning way back with Abram in Genesis 12) is told in these sixteen books, God's story is far from complete. We will continue to see how God worked through people—like you and me—to redeem his creation as we explore the Wisdom books and the writings of the Prophets, right after we meet Esther.

ESTHER 1 – 10
STRENGTH IN SERVICE

The small book of Esther is one of two books in the Bible named for a woman (remember the other?) It is an interesting book to read and can be studied in depth in several ways. One of the most intriguing strategies is as a series of banquets or feasts, where the story unfolds.

Esther is unique among the books of the Bible in that there is no mention of God anywhere. Some scholars question its inclusion as part of the sacred canon. Most acknowledge not only its importance as an explanation of the Jewish festival of Purim but also its message for us today. Esther also contains the longest verse in the Bible (Esther 8:9). Know the shortest verse? We'll discuss that on Day Eight.

The story of Esther takes place in the Persian court. Because of this, it is thought to have possibly occurred during the exile or shortly after the remnant had returned to Jerusalem. The story begins as the Persian King Xerxes banishes his beautiful but rebellious wife, Queen Vashti. Her crime? She refused to come when the king called (*my, how things have changed...*) Now queenless, in chapter 2 the king conducts a search for a new wife and settles on Esther, a young Jewish woman of the tribe of Benjamin who has been raised by her cousin Mordecai.

Esther is made queen, and Mordecai takes up residence at the king's gate to keep an eye on her. In chapter 3, Mordecai refuses to bow down to King Xerxes' official, Haman, when he passes the gate. Haman is furious and convinces the king to exterminate all the Jews in the kingdom. A date for the mass killing is set and the clock starts ticking.

In chapter 4 Mordecai, desperate to save the Jewish people, persuades Esther that she must go to the king and stop the killing. The queen is forbidden to approach the king without an invitation (and we know what happened to the last queen who didn't follow the rules) so Esther is reluctant to do as Mordecai asks.

He convinces her, however, with the following words, from Esther 4:14: *For if you remain silent at this time, relief and deliverance for the Jews will arise from another place, but you and your father's family will perish. And who knows but that you have come to royal position for such a time as this?* As a result, Esther cleverly devises a plan that not only saves the Jews, but also convicts Haman and honors Mordecai (chapters 6 and 7.

And the message for us in Esther? God may not seem to be active in our world, but—as Methodism founder John Wesley wrote in his notes about Esther—"the finger of God" is directing our lives and the opportunities that come to us. Wherever we are, we are there for a reason and, like Esther, perhaps for a particular moment in time. Let us be watching and ready.

JOB 1 – 21
BAD THINGS, GOOD PEOPLE

The first book of wisdom, Job, is traditionally considered an ancient tale, and often thought to be included in the Bible's wisdom writings to address the timeless question "Why do bad things happen to good people?" Put in more

The Adversary

Curse God and Die

Three Friends

Job Needs Jesus

Elihu

God, the Creator

Humility, not Arrogance

theological language, Job addresses the problem of evil in the world—why it is here, why it seems to fall on "good" people as much (or more) as "bad people", and what our response to God should be about it when it happens to us.

The book opens with a behind-the-scenes look at a conversation between God and "the Adversary", typically thought of as Satan, the Evil One. We also learn in chapter 1 that Job is a man of integrity and piety, setting the stage that whatever happens to him is undeserved—he is a "good" person.

The Adversary has challenged God to let him test Job's motivation for worshipping God: Is it because God has blessed him, and he wants those blessings to keep coming? Or, if those blessings went away, would Job still feel the same about God? (*Do you know people who are "angry" with God because something bad happened in their lives? Perhaps they have now rejected God and "lost their faith" because of this anger. This is essentially the scenario in Job.*)

God agrees, and immediately Job's children and flocks are destroyed. Job continues to honor God. In chapter 2 the Adversary asks to inflict injury to Job himself. Again, God goes along, with the caveat that the Adversary cannot kill Job. The Adversary agrees to the terms and inflicts Job with painful sores over his body. His wife offers her advice in Job 2:9 when she suggests that Job "curse God and die." Admirably, Job refuses to succumb to this and is visited by three friends who try to counsel him about his woes.

Chapters 3 through 21 record the ongoing conversations between Job and his three friends. Job argues for an opportunity to defend himself before God, while his friends try to convince him that God "does not pervert justice", that his judgments are true, and that Job should welcome his discipline. Later, in the NT, we will see that, despite Jesus' denials, the people continue to believe that any pain that comes their way is because of the sins they have committed. This is the position of Job's three friends. As Job cries out to defend himself before God, he also gives us a glimpse into what lies ahead in God's plan.

JOB NEEDS JESUS

In Job 9:32-34 we read Job's complaint: *He is not a man like me that I might answer him, that we might confront each other in court. If only there were someone to arbitrate between us, to lay his hand upon us both, someone to remove God's rod from me, so that his terror would frighten me no more.*

The CEB puts it this way: *God is not a man like me—someone I could answer—so that we could come together in court. Oh, that there were a mediator between us; he would lay his hand on both of us, remove his rod from me, so his fury wouldn't frighten me.*

Here, in the middle of the Old Testament is a story of man who is presumed to have lived between 1000 and 2000 BC, perhaps pre-dating the Exodus, but whose story sets the stage for the New Testament. In the midst of the greatest crisis of his life, Job instinctively knows that he needs someone to cover for him, someone who understands what it's like to live in this world, someone to connect him to God, someone to plead his case. Job needs Jesus.

JOB 22 – 42
GOD THE ALMIGHTY

Throughout these chapters, the more Job talks, the more apparent it becomes that Job believes he is without sin and blameless because of his good works. In chapter 22 the focus shifts to Job's sins, with the friends pointing them out to him and Job defending himself. By chapter 31, Job is pointing out all the good things he has done for the poor, the orphan, the hungry, and the sick. He is also pointing out all the sins he has *not* committed (*Sound familiar? "I could be so much worse…"*)

Another voice appears on the scene, a younger friend Elihu, who brings a different perspective, preparing the way for God's appearance. Elihu suggests that Job's insistence that he is righteous is really arrogance. In chapters 36 and 37, Elihu reminds Job of God's power through a vivid description of creation and God as Creator. Note the connection to one of our three themes. For the Israelites, God's power over creation was his defining characteristic. Here, Elihu uses this understanding to remind Job who God really is. Later, we will see how Jesus does the same thing.

In chapter 38, God arrives in a whirlwind and speaks directly to Job. God demonstrates his power over creation, reminding Job of Job's place in the universe, and demanding that Job respond to him. He has come as Job requested; now Job can petition before him as he asked. But Job has no answer. God challenges Job's desire to justify himself before God, describing in vivid detail the power of the Almighty. Finally, Job responds in Job 42:3 CEB: *I have indeed spoken about things I didn't understand, wonders beyond my comprehension.*

Once God enters the conversation, Job's position shifts from "I don't deserve this" to "I don't deserve anything"; in other words, from arrogance to humility. In the final verses, God reprimands the three friends for their bad advice and blesses Job with even more than he had before.

If you find Job a bit disappointing in that you still don't have a satisfying answer to "why bad things happen to good people", consider Job's response: *I have indeed spoken about things I didn't understand.* We are not meant to understand everything that happens in this world. Our faith requires that we accept that evil does exist, but that fact does not change the order of God as creator and humanity as God's creation. Job's wife suggested the easy answer, one that many people choose when bad things happen: Curse God. This also, however, leads to death, as she noted. Despite everything that happened to him— loss of family and possessions, personal misery—Job argued, cried, and reeled against his circumstances, but he never rejected God. Perhaps that is Job's message for us.

Stability

Disruption

Restoration

Psalm 23

PSALMS 1 – 150
GOD'S PRAYER BOOK

Psalm 1

Psalm 19

Psalm 73

We now come to one of the most familiar and beloved books in the Bible. Psalms is a compilation of songs, prayers, and poetry written by many authors over hundreds of years. See the Bible Chronology on page 264 for the variety of occasions and authors represented in the

Psalm 118

Psalm 84

Psalms. The Psalms are often referred to as God's Prayer Book; many people have found great comfort and wisdom in "praying the Psalms" or using the words of the ancient psalmists as their own prayers.

From the Bible Chronology you can see many prominent themes within the Psalms: Psalms of David for Deliverance (from Saul, perhaps); Psalms of David and the Sons of Korah (temple psalms); Psalms of the Exile (written much later); Psalms of the Restoration; and even a psalm attributed to Solomon. Many scholars have offered different ways of studying, reading, and praying the Psalms.

One way to find meaning in the Psalms is to see them as they were originally written—prayers for different occasions and different circumstances in our lives. In other words, there are prayers of worship when everything is going well in our lives (Stability); prayers for deliverance when things are not going well (Disruption); and, prayers of thanksgiving and praise when God has answered our cries for help (Restoration). *(Just thinking.... during which of these times do most of us typically pray? Exactly, Disruption. Notice the number of psalms that cry out to God for deliverance.)*

A good example of the sequence Stability-Disruption-Restoration can be found in Psalms 21, 22, and 23. The 23rd Psalm, beginning "The Lord is my shepherd", is one that many people know, whether they've studied the Bible or not. Another favorite of mine is Psalm 1, where we read in verses 1-3: *Blessed is the man who does not walk in the counsel of the wicked or stand in the way of sinners or sit in the seat of mockers. But his delight is in the law of the Lord, and on his law he meditates day and night. He is like a tree planted by streams of water, which yields its fruit in season and whose leaf does not wither.   Whatever he does prospers.*

Psalm 19 focuses on God as creator, as do many of the psalms of worship and praise.   Other psalms focus on repentance and contrition, asking forgiveness.   Psalm 51, the psalm David wrote after being convicted of his sin with Bathsheba is a beautiful example.   There we read in verse 10:   *Create in me a pure heart, O God, and renew a steadfast spirit within me.* Psalm 73 reminds us a bit of Job as the writer complains to God about how the wicked seem to prosper while he suffers.   Ultimately, he ends the psalm with a song of praise for God's faithfulness, no matter the circumstances.

Psalm 117 is the shortest psalm and Psalm 119 is the longest. In between we find Psalm 118, often referred to as the Psalm of the Returning King (or Victor).   This psalm was typically sung to honor kings returning victorious from war.   The people would shout or sing the words as the king entered the city.   Several passages in Psalm 118 may be familiar to you, but one that might stand out is verse 28: *Blessed is he who comes in the name of the Lord.* Looking ahead, we will see that it is Psalm 118 that the Jewish people shout as Jesus enters Jerusalem the Sunday prior to his crucifixion.   We will discuss its significance more in Day Seven. To close this very brief discussion of the book of Psalms, see the *ScriptureScope* on the next page.

JUST LOOKING IN

In Psalm 84:10 we read: *Better is one day in your courts than a thousand elsewhere; I would rather be a doorkeeper in the house of my God than dwell in the tents of the wicked.*

My favorite translation comes from the Anglican Book of Common Prayer: *For one day in your courts is better than a thousand in my own room and to stand at the threshold of the house of my God than to dwell in the tents of the wicked.*

What could be more comfortable, safer, more peaceful than our room? And yet the Sons of Korah write that just one day in the presence of God is better than a thousand in this safest, most comfortable place. And to just be close by, just stand in the door, looking in on God's presence exceeds living in luxury among the wicked.

How can this be? Many would wonder, but the psalmist knows. Nothing on earth can compare with the one true God!

PROVERBS 1 – 31
INSTRUCTIONS FOR LIVING

Woman Wisdom

One-liners

Virtuous Woman

Teacher's Lament

Teacher's Lesson

Lover and Beloved

Note on the Bible Chronology that the last three books of wisdom in today's reading are placed during Solomon's reign. In fact, we will see that a portion of Proverbs is actually sub-titled the Proverbs of Solomon. Most scholars believe that, although they are attributed to him—as are Ecclesiastes and Song of Songs (sometimes called Song of Solomon)—it is quite possible that they were written by someone in his court, or perhaps at his direction.

Proverbs is a collection of sayings by teachers of Israel—instructions for living, we might say. As you might expect from Solomon or his court, the book begins with a discussion of the importance of wisdom. In chapter 1, wisdom is personified as a woman, calling in the streets to all who will listen. (If you have read *The Shack* by Paul Young, you may remember a character named Sophia. I heard the author speak once and he asserted that Sophia was intended to be this personification of wisdom.)

Chapters 1 through 9 present the teachings of Woman Wisdom. A familiar scripture that you may recognize is found in Proverbs 3:5-7: *Trust in the Lord with all your heart and lean not on your own understanding; in all your ways acknowledge him, and he will make your paths straight. Do not be wise in your own eyes; fear the Lord and shun evil.* In chapters 10 through 29, we find the Proverbs of Solomon, which seem to be the "one-liners" of the Bible. Each short verse instructs the reader in God's ways. An example can be found in the brief *ScriptureScope* below.

NO EXCUSES

In Proverbs 16:2 CEB we read: *All the ways of people are pure in their eyes, but the Lord tests the motives.*

"It's no big deal. I'm just..." Ever say that to your parents when you were growing up? Or maybe to your spouse? Perhaps to a co-worker or business partner? This phrase comes to mind when I read this verse. We like to ignore our own motivations, don't we? We can excuse our obsessions with material things, or pop culture, or pleasure, or ambition, or power or [you fill in the blank] by saying that they are meaningless froth...but God knows our hearts.

As we continue through Proverbs we see that the teachings center around several themes: wealth vs. righteousness; prudent speech, discipline vs. ignorance, kindness to the poor, prudence vs. folly, pride, self-control, warnings against adultery and "devious women". The many exhortations against adultery are interesting, considering what we know of Solomon's ancestry.

The last chapter of Proverbs seems to be a bookend for the beginning of the book where we met Woman Wisdom. Here, after much discussion of "devious women" the writer introduces us to the Virtuous Woman. It is a fitting conclusion to the book as it connects us back to the place we started. The virtuous woman is described as a "wife of noble character" who is "worth far more than rubies." In closing, we read in Proverbs 31:30: *Charm is deceptive, and beauty is fleeting; but a woman who fears the Lord is to be praised.*

ECCLESIASTES 1 – 12
THE TEACHER

As we discussed earlier, this book was perhaps also written by Solomon, or someone under his influence, to instruct young men of Israel. Throughout the book the Teacher is speaking, reflecting on his own life and imparting wisdom to those in the next generation.

Initially the Teacher focuses on the meaninglessness of life, since everyone—rich or poor, wise or foolish—comes to the same fate. In Ecclesiastes 1:9 we read the Teacher's lament: *What has been will be again, what has been done will be done again; there is nothing new under the sun.* In chapter 3 we find some of the Teacher's poetry (that became a hit for the rock group the Byrds back in the 1960s), the beautiful "to everything there is a season" passage. If you are not familiar with this scripture, you can read it in Ecclesiastes 3:1-8.

The theme of eating, drinking, and finding pleasure in work is repeated often, which seems to be in direct contrast with what we just read in Proverbs. What has happened? How could this be written by the same person? Then, in the final verses we see that the Teacher has been "setting us up" for the real lesson. See the *ScriptureScope* below.

Don't Delay

In Ecclesiastes 12:1a, 6 CEB we read: *Remember your creator in your prime, before the days of trouble arrive, before the silver cord snaps and the gold bowl shatters; the jar is broken at the spring and wheel is crushed at the pit; before dust returns to the earth as it was before and life-breath returns to God who gave it.*

"Remember your creator." I am reminded of one of my favorite parts of C.S. Lewis' classic *Mere Christianity*. Reflecting on the problem of evil in the world, Lewis comments on the question posed by some: *If there is a God and he loves his creation, why doesn't he intervene in all of the horrors of the world?* Lewis reminds us that when God comes, it will be the end of life as we know it. The play is over; the curtain falls.

Why doesn't God intervene, Lewis asks? Because he is giving us as long as possible to accept him, to know him, to 'come over to his side'. When God does intervene, it will be too late. Here, in Ecclesiastes, the Teacher says the same thing: Don't delay. Fear God now, in your youth, before you return to the dust from which you came.

The Teacher concludes with this culminating thought on the matter in Ecclesiastes 12:12b-13: *There is no end to the excessive production of scrolls. Studying too much wearies the body. So this is the end of the matter; all has been heard.   Worship God and keep God's commandments because this is what everyone must do.*

Amen!

SONG OF SONGS 1 – 8
A LOVE STORY

As we come to the end of the wisdom writings we find a very different kind of book, a true love story. Often attributed to Solomon, it is more likely the combination of several writings by someone in Solomon's court.

Outwardly, it is the story of love between a man and woman, a declaration of love between the Lover and the Beloved. Some scholars have suggested that it is about Solomon and one of his wives. Others have interpreted it as an analogy between God and Israel and, later, between Jesus and the church. Whatever the interpretation, it is a beautiful expression of unselfish, unconditional love, expressed as human love. For those who see it only as this—no hidden meaning—the message that human love is holy because God created it is enough.

This brings us to an important point in our journey through the Old Testament. We have studied all of the historical books and all of the wisdom writings. In Day Five we will begin our study of the Biblical prophets, which will take us back to events we've already studied while pointing us forward to the coming of the Messiah in the New Testament.

REFLECTING FORWARD

Use these questions to guide your discussion of Day Four and lead you into Day Five.

1. Call me crazy, but I love thinking and reading about the seventy years of Babylonian exile. I think it's because the idea of living as a God-worshiper in a strange, pagan land feels so much like…now. Like life as a Christ-follower in our world today. Do you ever feel like you are called to "sing the songs of the Lord while in a foreign land?" (Psalm 137) How do you respond to this call? What opportunities have come to you to "make an impact" in today's pagan world?

2. Esther is one of many men and women who were "re-purposed" for God throughout the Bible. In Esther's case, she went through many changes in her life—from beloved daughter, to orphan, to faithful young Jewish woman, to eye-candy queen, to a voice of salvation for her people. How has God repurposed you throughout your life? Is he working to repurpose you even now?

3. Crises bring out our true characters, don't they? Job is a great example. We get just a slice of his life—a period of crisis—and from that slice we see his character. Some of it is pretty—some not. What would we see if you were faced with a crisis? Ultimately, Job came to a new understanding about God and himself through that experience. Think back to a time when you faced a crisis in your life. What did God teach you about yourself and your relationship with him through that critical time?

4. Do you have a favorite Psalm? Read it and think about it as Stability, Disruption, or Restoration. Why does it mean so much to you? How has it been a part of your faith journey?

5. Many of the books we studied in Day Four are considered Wisdom Literature, and, particularly, the book of Proverbs. In Proverbs 9:10 we read: "The fear of the Lord is the beginning of wisdom." Other translations add "reverence" to "fear of the Lord." What does this mean to you? Have you always "feared the Lord"? In your life, what has "fearing the Lord" looked like? How has reverence for God increased your wisdom?

6. The conclusion of Day Four is the small, unique book Song of Songs. It seems out of place here as it is about love, not wisdom, but...God is love and God is wisdom. For me, I can see how God has been both love and wisdom in my life. Can you think of a time when it seemed that no one loved you—and yet, God did and always has? Can you think of a time when you were faced with a decision that only God's wisdom could guide? Looking ahead to Day Five, we will see both love and wisdom in the prophets' writing.

DAY FIVE

ISAIAH, JEREMIAH
LAMENTATIONS,
EZEKIEL, DANIEL

Do you know any prophets? Do we even have prophets today? In case you are thinking of those folks who put billboards on the interstate occasionally to announce the exact day and time when the world will end, yes, we have those, but…that's not what I'm talking about.

Perhaps a better understanding of the word *prophet* would help. Prophets, in Biblical terms, not only PREdict (for the future) but also CONvict (in the present). They call us to account for our unfaithfulness and turning from God so that we can repent and re-turn to God (remember Elijah on Mt. Carmel?) And, based on what I know about the world we live in, this *conviction* is needed as much now as it was in 800 to 400 BC, the time of the Biblical prophets. In fact, modern prophets can often be found in church pulpits on Sunday mornings, reminding their flocks not only of the joy of being God's children but also that God loves his children despite their unfaithfulness.

Refer to the Kings and Prophets table on page 266 for a possible timeline of the writing prophets. You'll see that this coincides with the timeline of the final years of the northern kingdom of Israel and the southern kingdom of Judah as well as the rebuilding of Jerusalem by the returning exiles. We studied these events in Days Three and Four; they can be found in 2 Kings, 2 Chronicles, Ezra, and Nehemiah. You can also see this connection on the Bible Chronology on page 264. A little background on the Biblical prophets before we jump into our study of them might be helpful.

In the Bible, God chooses certain men and women to speak for him and to deliver his message to his children. These are the prophets, including the ones we've already studied (who don't have books named after them) and the ones we refer to as *major prophets* and *minor prophets*. This naming convention is really deceptive, as God's message delivered by the "minor" prophets is just as significant as the message delivered through the "major" prophets. The difference is typically in the length of their writings. The writings of the major prophets, who we are studying today, cover significant periods of time (30 years or more) and are written with multiple purposes, addressing several issues. The writings of the minor prophets, who we will study in Day Six, are focused on one or two issues over a shorter period of time and are typically shorter in length.

The writings of the prophets, both major and minor, are not ordered by importance in the Bible, but loosely chronologically, within each category. So, the first major prophet you find in the Bible, Isaiah, lived and prophesied at the beginning of the prophetic period, before either of the divided kingdoms had fallen. The last of the major prophets, Daniel, lived and prophesied after the fall of Jerusalem, during the exile in Babylon. The minor prophets follow a similar pattern—more on that in Day Six.

One more note on Biblical prophecy: It has (and continues to be) the source of much discussion and debate among Biblical scholars and theologians. No one seems to agree on what many of the prophecies mean. Are they talking about the fall of Rome or the fall of Hitler's Germany or the end of the world? Is this event literal or symbolic? Near future or apocalyptic (end of the world)? The people of every generation since Jesus, in fact, have found events in Biblical prophecy that they believed were speaking to their particular time in history.

Part of the problem is that prophecies often are written to both convict and predict at the same time, sometimes in multiple ways. So, a prophetic word or vision might have as many as three levels of meaning. The meaning for the current time might be the revealing of truth, the conviction of the people to see themselves clearly in God's light. The meaning also might be in the near future, predicting things that will happen in days, years, or decades. And, the meaning might also be in the distant future, for example, the coming of the Messiah or the end of the world.

The first book of Biblical prophecy we will discuss is Isaiah, with 66 chapters easily the longest prophetic book in the OT. It is often divided into three sections, based on the style and setting of the writing. The book appears to have been written over several generations, with the latter portions being written by other unknown prophets in the tradition of Isaiah, but not necessarily reflecting his personal ministry.

ISAIAH 1 – 39
FIRST ISAIAH: CONVICTION AND CONSEQUENCES

Isaiah lived and prophesied during the time recorded in 2 Chronicles 26 through 32, specifically the reigns of the following kings of the southern kingdom of Judah: Uzziah (also called Azariah), Jotham, Ahaz, and Hezekiah. Note from the Kings and Prophets table that the northern kingdom of Israel falls to Assyria during this time. You

Social Standing

Here Am I, Send Me

Judgment on Nations

Messianic Prophecy

Returning Remnant

Prophetic Pattern

King Hezekiah

may also recall from Day Three that the Assyrians attempted to take

Jerusalem also, but King Hezekiah—with Isaiah's help—withstood the siege.

This first section of Isaiah was written over at least forty years during a time of spiritual decadence in Judah as well as brief periods of renewal, particularly during Hezekiah's reign. Isaiah was married, had at least two sons, and seems to have had a high social standing. This gave him ready access to the king and his court (much to the irritation of some of those kings!)

In the opening chapters Isaiah warns the people of Judah of the wrath of God toward their sinful and rebellious behavior. He foretells God's judgment through vivid imagery of the coming destruction of Jerusalem. He also emphasizes that, when God's kingdom is restored, all will come to God's mountain to learn of him. He speaks of this future time of peace in Isaiah 2:4b: *They will beat their swords into plowshares and their spears into pruning hooks. Nation will not take up sword against nation, nor will they train for war anymore.*

In chapter 6, we read of Isaiah's calling to prophecy, including his vision of God. This is just the first vision of God we will read about among the prophets, but it is one that has inspired many people over the centuries to serve God. In Isaiah 6:1-3, 8 we read: *In the year that King Uzziah died, I saw the Lord seated on a throne, high and exalted, and the train of his robe filled the temple. Above him were seraphs, each with six wings: With two wings they covered their faces, with two they covered their feet, and with two they were flying. And they were calling to one another: "Holy, holy, holy is the Lord Almighty; the whole earth is full of his glory." Then I heard the voice of the Lord saying, "Whom shall I send? And who will go for us?" And I said, "Here am I. Send me!"*

In chapter 7, God speaks through Isaiah to King Ahaz (Hezekiah's father and an evil king) telling him to ask for a sign that God's word is true. Ahaz refuses, but Isaiah gives him a sign anyway, with these words: *Therefore the Lord himself will give you a sign: The virgin will be with child and will give birth to a son and will call him Immanuel.* Here we find perhaps the first Messianic prophecy (prophecy about the coming Messiah, Jesus) in Isaiah, but there are many more to come.

In chapters 8 through 35, the writer intertwines prophecies of judgment on Judah and Jerusalem with prophecies of woe to all nations, including Assyria and Babylon—the world powers God will use as instruments of judgment on Israel and Judah. Interspersed are prophecies about the 'returning remnant' (the exiles who returned in Ezra and Nehemiah) and the ultimate joy of the redeemed.

Throughout these chapters we also find more prophecies about the Messiah. Some of these may be familiar to you even if you've never read Isaiah. They were used by the Baroque composer G. F. Handel in the libretto of the oratorio *Messiah*, most often heard performed during Advent and Christmas. For example, Isaiah 9:6 reads: *For to us a child is born, to us a son is given, and the government will be on his shoulder. And he will be called wonderful Counselor, Mighty God, Everlasting Father, Prince of Peace.* This section also introduces the Messiah as the Branch of the Lord and the shoot from the stump of Jesse (chapter 11). (Reminder: Jesse was the father of King David, so this is a reference to the Davidic covenant. The Messiah will be a descendant of David.)

Through these chapters Isaiah introduces the "prophetic pattern" of *conviction, call to repentance, consequences,* and *comfort,* a pattern we will see throughout the Biblical prophets' writings. First, the prophet *convicts* the people of their sins and unfaithfulness to God. Often these words are directed at the religious leaders of the day (see Isaiah 28: 7-10) as God holds them accountable for failing to shepherd their flocks. Then the people are *called to repent* (confess their sins and change their ways), which they do not do. As a result, the prophet pronounces *consequences* in the form of God's judgment on them, using conquering nations as his instrument of destruction. Finally, after judgment, the prophet offers *comfort* through God's forgiveness and reconciliation.

Chapters 36 through 39 are a retelling of the story we read in 2 Kings of Hezekiah's illness, Isaiah's intervention, and the unsuccessful Assyrian siege of Jerusalem.

ISAIAH 40 – 66
SECOND AND THIRD ISAIAH: COMFORT AND HOPE

At this point the setting shifts to the Babylonian exile, after the fall of Jerusalem. Here the prophecies focus on the restoration of the remnant of Israel and a hope beyond that to the coming Messiah.

Chapter 40 begins immediately with words to counterbalance the warnings of judgment and destruction in the first 39 chapters.

After Jerusalem's Fall

Words of Hope

Restoration of Remnant

King Cyrus

Post-Exile

Isaiah 61

In Isaiah 40:1, 3-5 we read these words of reassurance and hope, also found in Handel's *Messiah*: *Comfort, comfort my people, says your God. A voice of one calling: "In the desert prepare the way for the*

Lord; make straight in the wilderness a highway for our God. Every valley shall be raised up, every mountain and hill made low; the rough ground shall become level, the rugged places a plain. And the glory of the Lord will be revealed, and all mankind together will see it. For the mouth of the Lord has spoken."

Later, in this same chapter, the prophet gives encouragement to those in exile with these words: *Do you not know? Have you not heard? The Lord is the everlasting God, the Creator of the ends of the earth. He will not grow tired or weary, and his understanding no one can fathom. He gives strength to the weary and increases the power of the weak. Even youths grow tired and weary, and young men stumble and fall; but those who hope in the Lord will renew their strength. They will soar on wings like eagles; they will run and not grow weary, they will walk and not be faint.* (Isaiah 40:28-31)

Again, more words of hope and restoration are found in Isaiah 43:1b-3a: *Fear not, for I have redeemed you; I have summoned you by name; you are mine. When you pass through the waters, I will be with you; and when you pass through the rivers, they will not sweep over you. When you walk through fire, you will not be burned; the flames will not set you ablaze. For I am the Lord, your God, the Holy One of Israel, your Savior.*

Remember back in Day Four when I mentioned Isaiah's prophecy about King Cyrus? See the *ScriptureScope* on the next page.

As The Heavens

In Isaiah 46:11 we read: *From the east I summon a bird of prey; from a far-off land, a man to fulfill my purpose. What I have said, that will I bring about; what I have planned, that will I do.*

What must Babylonian exile have been like for the Israelites? We know some of their sorrow from the poignant Psalm 137. We know they felt like they could not sing the Lord's song in a strange land. Quite likely, they could not see their future either. Would this exile last forever? How could they know that seemingly indestructible Babylon would soon be conquered by the Persians?

Here we find the prophecy which is fulfilled in the last of 2 Chronicles and first of Ezra. God uses Cyrus, a pagan king—not an Israelite—to accomplish his purpose. Through Cyrus, the first remnant returns, and the temple rebuilding project begins. Dare we question God's ways?

Imagine how this might have been worked out today, without God's direction. A committee of church leaders is in charge of devising a plan for deliverance. Who will be the leader—the pastor, or perhaps the chair of the administrative board, the head deacon, or the biggest tither? Certainly not a non-member—how could we possibly count on such a person?

The last chapter of this section of Isaiah, thought to have been written during the exile, tries to explain God's mysterious ways. In Isaiah 55:8 we read: *"For my thoughts are not your thoughts, neither are your ways my ways," declares the Lord. "As the heavens are higher than the earth, so are my ways higher than your ways and my thoughts than your thoughts."*

Indeed.

The third section of Isaiah, which encompasses chapters 56 through 66, is thought to have been written after the return of the remnant. It focuses on the challenges facing the Israelites during that period and gives them hope for the future through the promised Messiah. Of particular importance here is Isaiah 61:1-2a: *The Lord God's spirit is upon me, because the Lord has anointed me. He has sent me to bring good news to the poor, to bind up the brokenhearted, to proclaim release for captives, and liberation for prisoners, to proclaim the year of the Lord's favor.* As we noted in the beginning of our discussion, often the words of the prophets have several levels of meaning. In this case, the prophet might be referring to himself as well as the coming Messiah. Keep this passage in mind for Day Eight, when we will encounter it again.

JEREMIAH 1 – 29
GOD'S COMPLAINING PROPHET

> *Last Days of Jerusalem*
> *God's Displeasure*
> *Jeremiah's Complaint*
> *Acting Out Prophecy*
> *Letter to Exiles*

Jeremiah presents an interesting contrast to Isaiah and also gives us an "inside look" at the life of a prophet. Unlike Isaiah and most of the other prophets, we learn a great deal about Jeremiah's life through his writings. The book of Jeremiah, while undoubtedly prophecy, also contains a lot of action, making it sometimes read like one of the history books.

Jeremiah is often referred to as the "weeping prophet" or "complaining prophet". He is frequently unhappy in his prophetic role. Other prophets may have felt the same way, although no one else seems to complain quite like Jeremiah. You can see his point—he definitely has a thankless job by the world's standards. How many people want to hang around with someone who is always pointing out their faults? *(Ok, spouses and parents excluded...smile)*

Jeremiah is called to prophesy as a young man, when Josiah is King of Judah. (Reminder: Josiah is Hezekiah's grandson and it was his priest that found the Book of the Law in 2 Kings 22. As a result, Josiah led the people to recommit to their covenant with God.) According to some scholars, we are now between 722 BC and 587 BC, after the fall of the northern kingdom and in the final century of the southern kingdom. Jeremiah prophesies until the fall of Jerusalem and the Babylonian exile in mid-6th c. BC, about 40-50 years. This makes the book of Jeremiah coincide chronologically with 2 Chronicles 34 through 36.

The themes we find in this first section of Jeremiah are similar to those in Isaiah: God's displeasure and amazement with Judah and Israel's 'changing gods', abandoning Yahweh for pagan gods such as Baal. In addition, since Israel's judgment has already come at this point, Jeremiah emphasizes that Israel was faithless but Judah perhaps more so. Judah saw what happened to Israel and continues in her faithless ways. Thus, Judah will suffer a similar fate.

In chapter 8, the prophet laments the depth of Judah's wrongdoing, saying that not one righteous person can be found. In Jeremiah 9:23-24 we read these words of instruction: *This is what the Lord says: "Let not the wise man boast of his wisdom or the strong man boast of his strength or the rich man boast of his riches, but let him who boasts boast about this: that he understands and knows me."* In chapter 11, God laments the broken covenant with Israel, taking us all the way back to Mt. Sinai in Genesis. Even after all this time, God directs Jeremiah to remind everyone of the covenant they made with him and call them back to faithfulness.

In chapters 11 and 12 we are introduced to Jeremiah's frustration with the prophet role, typically referred to as Jeremiah's Complaint or Jeremiah's Lament. In Jeremiah 12:11, we read Jeremiah's words to

God: *If I took you to court, Lord, you would win. But I still have questions about your justice. Why do guilty persons enjoy success? Why are evildoers so happy?* (Echoes of Psalm 73 and Job.) God listens but responds to Jeremiah with a question of his own a few verses later: *If you have raced with people and are worn out, how will you compete with horses? If you fall down in an open field, how will you survive in the forest along the Jordan?* In other words, I have only asked small things of you so far. How will you handle the big stuff?

As we continue to read, we soon learn that the "big stuff" God has in mind for Jeremiah is acting out, not just speaking, God's message. He directs Jeremiah to bury a linen garment and later dig it up to demonstrate his judgment on Judah's pride (chapter 13). He has him buy a clay pot and shatter it in front of the people to show that God will destroy Jerusalem beyond repair (chapter 19). Jeremiah is arrested, beaten and put in stocks (chapter 20) and threatened with death (chapter 26). In chapter 27, God requires Jeremiah to make a yoke to wear around his neck, symbolizing how Judah will serve King Nebuchadnezzar of Babylon.

In chapter 29, God directs Jeremiah to write a letter to those who are already in exile in Babylon (Reminder: There were multiple deportations. Since Jerusalem was the last part of Judah to fall, many Israelites are already in Babylon during the siege.) God encourages the exiles with these words from Jeremiah 29:10–14: *This is what the Lord says: "When seventy years are completed for Babylon, I will come to you and fulfill my gracious promise to bring you back to this place. For I know the plans I have for you," declares the Lord, "plans to prosper you and not to harm you, plans to give you hope and a future. Then you will call upon me and come and pray to me, and I will listen to you. You will seek me and find me when you seek me with all your heart. I will be found by you,"* declares the Lord, *"and will bring you back from captivity."* We know from the end of 2 Chronicles and Ezra that, indeed, the exiles remained in Babylon for seventy years.

JEREMIAH 30 – 52
THE NEW COVENANT

Return to God

Access to God for All

Baruch's Scroll

Fall of Jerusalem

Significance of Temple

This section continues the focus on the restoration of Israel after the exile but moves beyond that to the time when God will be worshipped by all of Israel, not just the returning remnant. Through Jeremiah, God encourages the people to be ready to come back to him.

BREADCRUMBS

In Jeremiah 31:21 we read: *Set up road signs; put up guideposts. Take note of the highway, the road that you take. Return, O Virgin Israel, return to your towns.*

One lesson seems to jump out at me throughout Jeremiah: God disciplines his children, but he never stops loving us and never forgets us, although in times of difficult circumstances it may seem otherwise. He always wants to restore us to a relationship with him.

I can't help but think of breadcrumbs when I read this passage. Yes, Hansel and Gretel breadcrumbs. I hear my Father saying: *Pam, you may be separated from me because of your own actions, your own choices, your own sin. But, never forget the way back. In fact, as you leave, drop a few breadcrumbs and set up a few guideposts so that, even in the dark, you'll know the way home.*

What might these breadcrumbs have been for the scattered people of Israel? Prayer, keeping the Sabbath, remembering their salvation story of deliverance from Egypt. And for Christ-followers, when we separate ourselves from God? Prayer, staying connected to a fellowship of believers, remembering our salvation story through Jesus, reading the Bible.

Ultimately in this passage, I hear God saying: *I know that there will be times of darkness in your life, so here is a plan. Keep praying, going to church, and reading my word—even when you feel like I'm not there—and I will lead you home through these practices.*

Later in Jeremiah 31, God introduces the new covenant, one that will complete and replace the old covenant from Mt. Sinai that was based on an elaborate priest hierarchy and repeated sin and guilt offerings. The new covenant will make the knowledge of God available to everyone and provide forgiveness of sins once, and for all time, through Jesus (see Day Seven). Here, it is presented in Jeremiah 31:31-34 CEB: *"The time is coming," declares the Lord, "when I will make a new covenant with the people of Israel and Judah. It won't be like the covenant I made with their ancestors when I took them by the hand to lead them out of the land of Egypt. They broke that covenant with me even though I was their husband," declares the Lord. "No, this is the covenant that I will make with the people of Israel after that time," declares the Lord. "I will put my law in their minds and write it on their hearts. I will be their God and they will be my people. No longer will a man teach his neighbor, or a man his brother, saying, 'Know the Lord,' because they will all know me, from the least of them to the greatest," declares the Lord. "For I will forgive their wickedness and will remember their sins no more."*

In chapter 36, God directs Jeremiah to create a scroll with all of God's words to the people on it, so that no one can claim they did not know of the coming judgment. Jeremiah dictates everything to the scribe, Baruch. They deliver it to King Jehoiakim, one of the last of Judah's kings, and he promptly throws it into the fire. (*You can imagine how this went over with Jeremiah, the complaining prophet.*) Nevertheless, he and the persevering Baruch write everything down again in another scroll, adding even more to it.

In the last days before the fall of Jerusalem, Jeremiah is imprisoned and later thrown in a cistern by King Zedekiah, Judah's last king. Nebuchadnezzar takes Jerusalem and frees Jeremiah. After the aristocracy and army have been taken to Babylon in exile, only a small remnant of Israelites is left in Judah. They inquire of Jeremiah what they should do. Jeremiah prays for guidance and God tells them to remain there, that he will take care of them. To no one's surprise, they do not listen to Jeremiah, but go to Egypt anyway, once again demonstrating their disobedience and lack of faith in Yahweh.

LAMENTATIONS 1 – 5
GOD'S TEMPLE DESTROYED

The short book of Lamentations is aptly named, as it is a lament over the fall of Jerusalem, a post-script to the book of Jeremiah. Although often attributed to Jeremiah, many scholars now believe that it was probably written by someone else who witnessed the destruction. Lamentations is recited every year by the Jewish people on the Day of Mourning for the destruction of the temple. [Note that this recitation is not for the destruction of the temple here, by Nebuchadnezzar, for the temple will be rebuilt by the remnant (as we know). Later, another temple (the one Jesus visits) will be built by the Roman-appointed governor of Judah, Herod the Great. It is the final destruction of this temple in AD 70 by the Roman emperor Titus that is specifically remembered by the Jewish people each year on the Day of Mourning.]

Here in Lamentations, however, the focus is on the destruction of Jerusalem and the temple by Nebuchadnezzar in the mid-6th c. BC, the climax (at least for now) to the story of God's relationship with the Israelites. This relationship is dependent upon God's presence with them, first in the traveling tabernacle and then in Solomon's temple. The destruction of the temple is an indication that God cannot and will not reside with them again. This is why the rebuilding of the temple (recorded in Ezra) takes on such great meaning for the returning remnant. If the temple is not rebuilt, God will not return to dwell among them.

The lament also contains words of hope, just as in the prophetic pattern we have seen throughout Isaiah and Jeremiah. In Lamentations 3:22-23 we read: *Because of the Lord's great love we are not consumed, for his compassions never fail. They are new every morning; great is your faithfulness.* I can remember as a young person times when I might go to bed upset or worried about something. My mother would tell me that everything would look better in the morning. Even in their darkest hour, the writer of Lamentations offers the same wisdom to the people of Israel.

EZEKIEL 1 – 23
PROPHECIES FROM EXILE

Priestly Heritage

Age at Calling

Temple Idolatry

New Covenant Hope

Upside-Down Kingdom

Note from the Kings and Prophets table that Ezekiel's prophecies occur during some of the same period as Jeremiah, specifically the last days of Jerusalem. There is a significant difference, however. Ezekiel is already in exile, 'watching' the events in Jerusalem through visions and speaking to his fellow exiles in Babylon.

Ezekiel has a priestly heritage and probably was exiled in the first Great Deportation along with other religious and political leaders. Coming from a priestly lineage, Ezekiel is closely acquainted with not only worship and temple practices, but the responsibilities of the priesthood. As such, much of the prophecy in Ezekiel is related to the actions (or, more often, inactions) of the priests leading the people.

Ezekiel is called to prophesy when he is thirty years old. (Note of connection: Saul was anointed as king at the age of thirty, David became king at the age of thirty, and in Day Seven we will see that Jesus' ministry begins around the age of thirty as well.) As mentioned earlier, several of the prophets have vivid encounters with God through visions and record these "calling experiences." We saw this in Isaiah 6 and now we read of Ezekiel's calling in chapters 1 and 2.

This first section of Ezekiel focuses almost exclusively on warnings and judgment on Judah, the siege of Jerusalem, and its ultimate destruction. With each message of impending doom, God concludes his word to Ezekiel with: "Then they will know that I am the Lord."

In chapters 8 through 11, Ezekiel is taken in a vision to see the idolatry present in the current temple in Jerusalem. As noted above, his priestly heritage gives him a particular insight into temple activities. Chapters 12 through 22 are full of rich images of the sin and unfaithfulness of Jerusalem and the impending destruction, so much so that we read Ezekiel's complaint (a la Jeremiah) in Ezekiel 20:49: *They say of me, 'Isn't he just telling parables?'* Chapter 16 also reminds us of

Jeremiah, as God claims that Jerusalem (capital of Judah) is much worse than Samaria (capital of Israel). Nevertheless, he adds a word of hope in Ezekiel 16:60: *Yet I will remember the covenant I made with you in the days of your youth, and I will establish an everlasting covenant with you.* Here again, as in Jeremiah 31, God is introducing the new covenant to come with the Messiah. See more about the new kingdom in the *ScriptureScope* below.

NOT AS IT WAS

In Ezekiel 21:25b CEB we read: *This is what the Lord God says: "Remove the turban, take off the crown! Nothing will be as it was. Bring down the exalted and exalt the lowly."*

Does this sound familiar? You may have heard of Jesus' words in Matthew 19:30 that *"many who are first will be last, and many who are last will be first"* and in Matthew 20:16 *"so the last will be first, and the first will be last."*

We will read in Day Seven that many who heard Jesus' words rejected them, including the most learned men of the Law, the Pharisees and Sadducees. Perhaps these words reminded them of the stories they had heard of the prophet Ezekiel's words during the Babylonian exile. No wonder they feared Jesus and saw him as a threat to their way of life.

And we still struggle with these words today, along with other revolutionary statements from Jesus like: *"Blessed are you who are poor, for yours is the kingdom of God"* and *"Woe to you who are rich, for you have already received your comfort"* (Luke 6). Jesus brought an "upside down kingdom", and here Ezekiel gives the exiles a hint of what it will be like. Nothing will be as it was.

EZEKIEL 24 – 48
THE GOOD SHEPHERD

Death of Wife

Shepherd Imagery

Dry Bones

River of Life

The Lord is There

As we have already seen with Jeremiah, prophets are often called upon not only to speak but to live out God's word for the people. In Ezekiel 24, Ezekiel's wife dies. God directs Ezekiel to demonstrate through his lack of mourning the same stunned silence that the people will experience when Jerusalem falls. After this event, the prophecies turn quickly to doom and laments for the nations surrounding Judah who have taken joy in her downfall.

In chapter 34, Ezekiel's focus shifts to shepherd imagery. God describes his relationship as shepherd to his sheep, the people of Israel. We are reminded of Psalm 23, where David wrote centuries earlier "The Lord is my shepherd". God as shepherd of his people is not a new image, but Ezekiel uses it to pronounce judgment on the religious leaders of the day.

First, he gives a description of the shepherds of Judah, in Ezekiel 34:2, 4: *This is what the Sovereign Lord says: Woe to the shepherds of Israel who only take care of themselves! Should not shepherds take care of the flock? You have not strengthened the weak or healed the sick or bound up the injured. You have not brought back the strays or searched for the lost. You have ruled them harshly and brutally.* A few verses later God describes the Good Shepherd in the *ScriptureScope* on the next page.

THE GOOD SHEPHERD

In Ezekiel 34:23 we read: *I will place over them one shepherd, my servant David, and he will tend them; he will tend them and be their shepherd. I the Lord will be their God, and my servant David will be prince among them.*

This passage refers to Jesus, of course, as a descendant of the house of David. I particularly like the description of him as a shepherd, servant, and prince. But it makes me wonder: What does God think of us? We are all shepherds. Some among us may shepherd diverse and sometimes unwieldy congregations of parishioners. Others shepherd smaller flocks, perhaps a Sunday School class, Bible study, or small group. Most of us have had some kind of experience shepherding diverse and sometimes unwieldy families.

What does God think of our shepherding? Do we extend the same care to our flocks that we do to ourselves? Do we encourage the weak ones, pray for the healing of the sick ones, and comfort the broken ones? How carefully do we search for the strays and lost?

Lord, make me an instrument of your salvation for the people entrusted to my care, that by my life and teaching I may set forth your true and living Word. Amen.

Chapter 37 shifts focus to the restoration of Israel, again following the prophetic pattern of conviction/judgment/restoration. Here we find the imagery of the valley of dry bones which inspired the words of the great spiritual "Dem bones, dem bones gonna rise again!"

In chapters 40 through 48, after twenty-five years in exile, Ezekiel is given a vision of the new temple, a vision which has great similarity to the new Jerusalem described in Revelation 21 (see Day Ten). The river of life runs through the middle of the temple in Ezekiel's vision, symbolizing that life is found in God and only in God. Ezekiel ends on a note of hope, proclaiming of this new vision of the temple: *The Lord is There.*

DANIEL 1 – 13
FAITH UNDER FIRE

In the King's Court

Daniel in Charge

The Fiery Furnace

Writing on the Wall

The Lion's Den

Visions

The prophet Daniel, like Ezekiel, lived and prophesied during the Babylonian Exile. There is a major difference in their writings, however. Whereas Ezekiel's prophecy shared similar themes with Jeremiah, following the prophetic pattern of conviction/judgment/restoration for Judah, the book of Daniel focuses on the life of the exiles under Nebuchadnezzar and times beyond the restoration. You can see this indicated on the Kings and Prophets table where Ezekiel and Daniel are both listed among the prophets who prophesied during the last days of Judah, but only Daniel is listed as a prophet to the kings of Babylon.

The book of Daniel is divided into two sections, with the first six chapters written as a narrative of faith, much like the history books. The second half of the book is a series of visions similar to many found in the book of Revelation (Day Ten) and the minor prophet, Zechariah (Day Six).

As chapter 1 begins we learn that a young man, Daniel, and his three friends have been taken as exiles from Jerusalem and are training to be in King Nebuchadnezzar's service. They demonstrate their steadfast commitment to the God of Israel by refusing to eat the king's food or drink the king's wine—and end up healthier than those that do. Daniel also interprets a dream for Nebuchadnezzar that the king's other sages cannot. The dream of the statue of gold, silver, bronze, iron, and clay is explained as the coming empires that will rule the world. Nebuchadnezzar rewards Daniel for his wisdom by making him ruler over the provinces of Babylon (Sound familiar? Remember Joseph in Egypt back in Genesis?)

Because of the attention Daniel and his friends receive, some of the others in the king's court find ways to challenge them. David's friends, Shadrach, Meshach, and Abednego, are brought before the king because they refuse to bow down and worship the image of gold Nebuchadnezzar has created. Nebuchadnezzar threatens to throw them into the furnace of fire if they do not worship the idol. For their response, see the *ScriptureScope* below.

BUT IF NOT

In Daniel 3:16-18 we read: *Shadrach, Meshach and Abednego replied to the king, "O Nebuchadnezzar, we do not need to defend ourselves before you in this matter. If we are thrown into the blazing furnace, the God we serve is able to save us from it, and he will rescue us from your hand, O king. But even if he does not, we want you to know, O king, that we will not serve your gods or worship the image of gold you have set up."*

"But even if he does not..." These words are the difference between Daniel's three friends' prayer and many of our prayers. We pray to God for healing for a loved one, or deliverance from our woes, or for a particular blessing. And, if God answers our prayers as we desire, we may remember to praise his name. We will surely remember, however, if God does not answer as we wish. More than once Keith and I have been approached by people who are angry with God, abandoning God, because he did not heal their loved one or remove a trial from their lives as they asked.

But listen to the difference here.

Shadrach, Meshach, and Abednego know that God can save them from the fire, but they also understand that God may not do that. It is God's will that will be done, or, as I heard a cowboy preacher say once, "God will have his way." Their faithfulness to God did not depend on what God did or did not do for them—and neither should ours.

In fact, as we will see in Day Seven, God has already done for us all we need—through the ultimate sacrifice of Jesus he has loved us, forgiven us, saved us. Anything else is just gravy at this point!

The end of the fiery furnace story is that God does save the three friends. In fact, when Nebuchadnezzar looks in, he sees not only three unscathed men, but a fourth walking among them. As a result, the king proclaims his faith in the Israelite God and begins to experience visions which will ultimately lead to his conversion.

In chapter 5, the new king Belshazzar has a dinner party that turns out a little differently than he expected. A hand appears to write on the wall, which Daniel interprets as a prophecy about Belshazzar's death. When Darius the Mede takes over the kingdom after the death of Belshazzar (as Daniel prophesied), jealousy among the court officials leads to Daniel being thrown in the lion's den for disobeying an edict against prayer. The lions do not touch him, and King Darius proclaims his own faith in Daniel's God.

Beginning in chapter 7, the action shifts to prophecies in the form of visions. Like many prophecies, they have multiple levels of meaning, from near future to end of days. Among some Bible scholars, the visions of Daniel work together with the visions in Revelation and Zechariah to create a clear picture of what the end of the world will be like. These are the visions upon which many apocalyptic predictions in our own time are based.

Before we leave Daniel, see the *ScriptureScope* on the next page for some thoughts on one vision that connects to God's ultimate victory portrayed later in Revelation (Day Ten).

ANCIENT OF DAYS

In Daniel 7:13-14 we read: *In my vision at night I looked, and there before me was one like a son of man, coming with the clouds of heaven. He approached the Ancient of Days and was led into his presence. He was given authority, glory and sovereign power; all peoples, nations and men of every language worshiped him. His dominion is an everlasting dominion that will not pass away, and his kingdom is one that will never be destroyed.*

A few verses earlier we read that a river of fire runs before the Ancient of Days, sitting on the throne. "Thousands upon thousands" worship him and before him, the beast is slain and thrown into the fiery river. Then, the son of man (or, as the CEB translates it, "one like a human being") appears to share the throne.

For a moment, in Daniel's vision, the curtain that separates heaven and earth parted and he saw the other side, God's side. And in this vision, he saw God—the Ancient of Days—seated on the throne. As we noted earlier, many of the prophets report seeing God in their visions—this is Daniel's experience. In previous verses, he describes the river of fire before him, the hundreds of thousands of worshipers, and the slaying of the beast. Then comes Jesus to take his seat next to the Father. All peoples worship him, and his kingdom is everlasting; it will never be destroyed like the kingdoms of this world.

Now, maybe that's what it looks like and maybe that's just the picture that Daniel could handle. Either way, it gives me peace. The Ancient of Days is still on the throne. My Savior sits beside him. And, no matter what it may look like at times down here, the beast is slain. Hallelujah!

REFLECTING FORWARD

Use these questions to guide your discussion of Day Five and lead you into Day Six, our last day in the Old Testament.

1. Read Isaiah 6:1-8 for Isaiah's call to prophecy. This was Isaiah's "burning bush" moment, reminding us of Moses' call to be God's instrument of salvation for the Hebrew slaves in Egypt. Have you been called to ministry? I'm not talking about being a pastor or priest,

necessarily, but serving God in some way. Perhaps teaching Sunday School or working at the soup kitchen or teaching your children or grandchildren about Jesus. What was your calling like? How did you know that you were hearing God's voice? Did you respond like Isaiah, with immediate enthusiasm, or more like Moses, with reluctance and fear? Or maybe something in between?

2. Jeremiah, the complaining prophet, shows us that God's work is not always easy. If you have found yourself serving God in some way— either in the church or in the world—has it been rewarding, challenging, or both? How have you grown because you answered God's call?

3. We began this chapter considering whether we have prophets today and what their role might be. Think about the prophetic pattern, specifically conviction of sin. How has God convicted you of your sin? Through Bible study? Through prayer? Through another person? How did you respond? What was God's response to you?

4. Ezekiel often focuses on the shepherds of Israel, the temple leaders, and their unfaithfulness. Do you think of yourself as a shepherd? Or are you, more often, looking to be shepherded, or led, by others? For Christ-followers, which is it? Or, is it both? Who are your shepherds? Who do *you* shepherd?

5. Daniel and his three friends demonstrated an unwavering faith while in captivity in Babylon. Because of it, they not only thrived but influenced the conversion of both Nebuchadnezzar and Belshazzar, two pagan kings. Think about your world—family, friends, work, church, hobbies, travel, whatever and wherever you spend your time. Have you ever found yourself needing to reject the ways of the world and demonstrate "Daniel faith" in those situations? If you succeeded, how did you do it? Do you know if your actions influenced anyone else?

6. As we leave the major prophets in Day Five and focus on the minor prophets in Day Six, think back again on the prophetic pattern. This time focus on comfort, the promised hope and restoration. Have you ever been without hope? If so, where did you turn? Looking back, how was God part of the restoration of hope to your life?

DAY SIX

HOSEA, JOEL, AMOS,
OBADIAH, JONAH, MICAH
NAHUM, HABAKKUK, ZEPHANIAH,
HAGGAI, ZECHARIAH, MALACHI
INTERTESTAMENT PERIOD

A friend of mine was driving home from a business trade show alone across a desolate stretch of highway in Arizona. She noticed an elderly Navajo woman standing on the side of the road. The woman looked like she could barely walk as she hobbled along the pavement. My friend, Lucy, longed for some company on the long drive, so she stopped to offer the woman a ride. She got in the car without a word and sat silently in the passenger seat as they began their journey. Lucy began to make conversation, talking about the weather, the road, anything she could think of. The woman never responded, but just looked straight ahead, motionless.

Lucy told her that she had been at a trade show for her business and that was why she was traveling home alone. She talked and talked until, exhausted from the one-way conversation, she fell silent. They rode along for a few more miles with nothing but the road noise. Finally, the old woman turned her head and looked down in the seat between them. On the seat was a paper sack Lucy had placed there as she had left the trade show for home.

"What in bag?" asked the woman. Lucy jumped at the unexpected question and took a moment to respond. Then she answered casually, "Oh, that's a bottle of wine. I got it for my husband." Again, the woman looked ahead of her down the road for several minutes. Finally, she spoke quietly, as if lost in her thoughts. With the wisdom of the ages in her voice, she said, "Good trade." (*smile*)

Communication is a funny thing, isn't it? What seems perfectly clear to us is often misunderstood by others. The minor prophets are a great example. As I mentioned in Day Five, they are categorized as "minor", but not minor at all. Here, in print, at least we have spelling to assist with understanding. That was not the case with the little girl who innocently asked the preacher during a children's sermon on the minor prophets: What were they mining for?

Charles Feinberg, a 20th century Jewish historian and Biblical scholar, wrote that the minor prophets are often the "clean pages" of our Bibles. By that he meant that they are seldom the texts of sermons—with a few notable exceptions—and even less often the subject of intense Bible study. Thus, even the most studious Bible reader has rarely taken notes on those pages. If this describes you, I hope to change your mind about these twelve little books.

The Hebrew Bible actually keeps the minor prophets together in one book, entitled the Book of the Twelve. This indicates the importance of each writing. If they are separated into individual books, one of the smaller ones might get overlooked. They are related, each with its own importance to the Biblical story, so they are kept together. They are ordered in the Bible in a loosely chronological fashion, as you can see from your Bible Chronology.

HOSEA 1 – 14
GOD'S REDEEMING LOVE

You may remember from the introduction to Day Five that the books assigned to the minor prophets are typically shorter than those of the major prophets. The key word is, of course, "typically."

> *Contemporary of Isaiah*
>
> *Prostitute-wife Gomer*
>
> *Children's Names*
>
> *Redemption*
>
> *God—Hosea*
>
> *Israel—Gomer*

Hosea is not typical of the other minor prophets in many ways, and one of them is its length. Because of its length as well as its content, Hosea can be seen as a bridge between the major prophets and the minor prophets. It can also be seen as an Overture for the Book of the Twelve. If you attend an opera or musical theater production, the first piece the orchestra will play is the Overture. The Overture contains the major themes heard throughout the entire musical work, played in small pieces and sometimes intertwined to demonstrate how they are connected. Here, in Hosea, we see a similar process.

Hosea was a prophet to Israel, the northern kingdom, shortly before its fall to Assyria. Here is one difference from the major prophets. None of the major prophets lived and prophesied in the northern kingdom. Their focus was Judah, Jerusalem, and the Exile. They sometimes reference Israel and its capital Samaria in their prophecies, but they lived in Judah.

Hosea was a contemporary of Isaiah and the minor prophets Micah and Amos. He prophesied during the reign of Jeroboam II, a time of great prosperity and growth in Israel. His prophecies cover 60 to 65 years—another atypical aspect for a minor prophet. Hosea also takes the prophet's acting out of God's words to a new level, as you will see. This is important—Hosea's story is not an analogy or parable, but a lived experience.

The book opens with God directing Hosea to take a prostitute, Gomer, as his wife. God directs Hosea to give their children names which demonstrate his displeasure with and separation from the people of Israel and Judah. Names like "No Compassion" and "Not My

People", while certainly not pleasant to live with as a child, make it abundantly clear that God's judgment is coming.

Hosea and his prostitute-wife become the literal version of the imagery of God and prostitute-Israel used throughout the book. The image of Israel as a prostitute who has been unfaithful to her husband God was introduced in the major prophets but is made vividly clear in Hosea. The writer explains the connection to the reader between Gomer and Israel and between Hosea and God.

In chapter 3, it seems that Gomer has left Hosea and returned to her life of prostitution. God directs Hosea to buy her back, a representation of God's redemption (buying back) of his people. The remainder of the book, like Isaiah and Jeremiah, focuses on Israel's sins, impending punishment, and God's redeeming love that restores his people to him. (Remember the prophetic pattern?)

In Hosea 6:1-2, we read these words of hope: *Come, let us return to the Lord. He has torn us to pieces but he will heal us; he has injured us but he will bind up our wounds. After two days he will revive us; on the third day he will restore us, that we may live in his presence.* Keep this timeframe—three days to restoration—in mind as we move into the New Testament in Day Seven.

JOEL 1 – 3
THE DAY OF THE LORD

Unlike some of the other prophets, both major and minor, we do not know much about Joel. He was perhaps the earliest of the minor prophets and may have lived during the reign of Joash in the

Army of Locusts

Day of the Lord

Joel 2:28-29

Amos, Judean Shepherd

Worship without Justice

southern kingdom. Where he lived (northern or southern kingdom) is not known, as his message could be for either kingdom.

The book of Joel begins with images of an invading "army" of locusts. Literal or symbolic? We don't know but it's possible that this was a real event and God seizes the opportunity to draw a parallel to the impending Day of the Lord. (What we call in the field of education "a teachable moment".)

Joel has several areas of significance for us. One is the introduction of the terminology "Day of the Lord" to represent the day of judgment. The second significant piece is Joel's emphasis on returning to God. See the *ScriptureScope* below.

EVEN NOW

In Joel 2:12-13 we read: *"Even now," declares the Lord, "return to me with all your heart, with fasting and weeping and mourning. Rend your heart and not your garments. Return to the Lord your God, for he is gracious and compassionate, slow to anger and abounding in love, and he relents from sending calamity."* [Did you catch the connection back to God's description of himself given to Moses in Exodus 34?]

I bet you are wondering what makes these two verses so significant in today's reading, especially when there are pleas from God to return to him throughout the prophetic writings. What makes this one special?

It's in the first two words: "Even now."

What do these words say to you? To me, they say everything. Even now—when I've blown other chances, I can still return to God. Even now—when I've made so many mistakes along the way, I can still return to God. Even now—when I've rejected him and his love over and over, I can still return to God. Even now—no matter what I've done or who I've been, I can still return to God.

Even now.

Finally, we find significance in this passage, found in Joel 2:28-29: *After that I will pour out my spirit upon everyone; your sons and daughters will prophesy, your old men will dream dreams, and your young men will see visions. In those days, I will also pour out my spirit on the male and female slaves.* Here, in Joel—a seemingly insignificant "minor" prophet—we find the words that will inspire Peter to preach his first sermon on Pentecost, recorded in Acts 2:17-21. That's way over in Day Eight, so keep this tucked away until then.

AMOS 1 – 9
HYPOCRITICAL WORSHIP

Amos was a shepherd and farmer, living in the southern kingdom of Judah. God called him to prophesy in the northern kingdom of Israel. While we don't know for sure, most scholars believe that Amos may have been the first of the writing prophets.

The timeframe is the period just before the fall of Israel, like Hosea, and during a time of great prosperity and military success in Israel. So…which do you think would be easier—to awaken the people to what's wrong in their culture when they are down and out or when everything seems to be going well? Think about your world. In a time of peace, with a strong economy, most people feel good about things. The last thing they want to hear is "gloom and doom"—especially from a foreigner.

This is exactly the position Amos was in. The northern kingdom was enjoying some peace after many years of war, experiencing the fruits of a strong economy. Then, here comes Amos, a Judean shepherd from the southern kingdom, convicting them of their meaningless and hypocritical worship practices.

The book of Amos follows the prophetic pattern—charges against Israel, coming judgment on Israel, and ultimately restoration, but it's interesting to see how Amos approaches it. First, in chapter 1 he begins by pronouncing God's judgment on the surrounding nations, such as Damascus, Edom, and Moab. You can imagine that this went over very well in the northern kingdom—these were their enemies. Then, in chapter 2, he pronounces judgment on the southern kingdom of Judah—even better! So far, Amos' message is well-received—he is saying all the right things. Imagine their surprise and anger, then, when Amos turns his attention to them.

The rest of the book addresses the sins of the northern kingdom, focusing on misplaced priorities, complacency, and hypocrisy among the religious leaders. He preaches against worship without justice—not an uncommon complaint against the church today. In Amos 2: 6-7 we read: *They sell the righteous for silver, and the needy for a pair of sandals. They trample on the heads of the poor as upon the dust of the ground and deny justice to the oppressed.*

A recurring theme is the lament of God declaring that, in spite of everything done for the Israelites throughout history, "…yet you have not returned to me."

OBADIAH
THE SIN OF PRIDE

Justice for Edom

Jonah and the Whale

Jonah's Anger

God's Compassion

Obadiah is the shortest book in the Old Testament (one chapter). The prophet's message is exclusively for the nation of Edom. God's punishment is coming for their actions toward Judah as Jerusalem fell to the conquering Babylonians.

Surely many of the neighboring nations—Egypt, Moab, Damascus—took some joy in a former enemy's demise. Why would Edom be singled out for God's judgment? Reminder: The nation of Edom descended from Esau (see Day One and Day Two). And the nation of Israel descended from? Jacob, Esau's conniving twin brother, whose name was later changed to Israel. Edom's actions are particularly appalling to God because Edom is, essentially, family.

God, speaking through Obadiah, charges Edom with not only failing to help Judah as Babylon attacked, but also taking pleasure in Judah's downfall. And, he makes it clear that the reason underlying it all is Edom's pride. In the introduction of Obadiah, we read: *"Your proud heart has tricked you…Though you soar like the eagle, though your nest is set among the stars, I will bring you down from there,"* says the Lord.

JONAH 1 – 4
ISRAEL'S MISSIONARY

Remember my grandson Carter and his obsession with Jonah? Well, we have finally found him. Here in this short book, we meet the minor prophet with whom most people are familiar (even Carter). In fact, the story told in the first part of Jonah is one of many Biblical stories that have become part of the secular culture of our world as well. But, there is much more to Jonah than just that piece, as we will see.

Jonah is a unique book among the prophetic literature in that it focuses more on the prophet than the message. In fact, it only contains one verse of "prophecy", found in Jonah 3:4 when Jonah finally makes it to Nineveh: *On the first day, Jonah started into the city. He proclaimed: "Forty more days and Nineveh will be overturned."* The rest of the book of Jonah provides us some insight into the mind of the prophet, such as what we get in the book of Jeremiah, and also some insight into God's plan for the world.

In the first chapter God calls Jonah to get up and go to the ancient city of Nineveh, capital of the Assyrian empire, and pronounce God's judgment on the people because of their evil ways. Jonah gets up, all right, but runs in the opposite direction. (*Sound familiar, anyone?*) He boards a ship, where his presence brings on such a storm that he volunteers to be thrown overboard to calm the seas. In chapter 2, we read that God provides a "great fish" (traditionally, a whale) to swallow Jonah. Jonah spends three days and three nights in the belly of the whale (Connections: Back to Hosea and forward to Jesus), prays to God, and is deposited on dry land.

In chapter 3, once again God calls Jonah to go to the huge city of Nineveh and this time he does. What we see here is something unique in the Israelite story—a missionary. The vast majority of the OT story of the Israelites centers around them and their covenant with God. Any effort at converting others to worship Yahweh is incidental. The conversion of Rahab in the book of Joshua, for example, occurs because of the faithfulness of the spies she hid from Jericho's army. Nebuchadnezzar and Belshazzar worship God as a result of seeing the great faith of Daniel and his friends, not by any direct efforts Daniel made to convert them.

Here, though, we see God sending Jonah to a foreign nation to let them know that he has noticed their evil ways and wants them to repent. Jonah, like all prophets, convicts them of their sin and pronounces God's judgment upon them. But then, something unexpected happens. The king—and therefore the people—listen to Jonah and confess their sins and God does not destroy them. Jonah's message is heard and heeded, and lives are saved—the essence of any missionary effort.

You would think Jonah would be happy about the way things turned out, but in chapter 4 we read that he is actually angry with God over his compassion on the repentant people of Nineveh. Essentially, Jonah's response was: *Are you kidding me? Seriously? After all I've been through? I knew this would happen—that's why I ran away in the first place.* In Jonah 4: 11 we read God's response to Jonah: *But Nineveh has more than a hundred and twenty thousand people who cannot tell their right hand from their left, and many cattle as well. Should I not be concerned about that great city?* Connection: Remember God's description of himself to Moses in Exodus 34:6 – 7 (Day Two)? Here we see that God is a "compassionate and gracious God", just as he described himself there.

So then, what is the message of the little book of Jonah? Don't resist God's call because ultimately he will have his way? Yes. Have faith even when in the belly of a whale? Apparently. God's forgiveness and grace is for the whole world? Definitely!

MICAH 1 – 7
JUSTICE, MERCY, AND HUMILITY

You can see from the Kings and Prophets table that Micah was a contemporary of Isaiah. In fact, we can find some striking similarities in their writing (see Micah 4:3). Like Isaiah,

Capital Condemnation

Bethlehem

God's Justice for Nineveh

God's Timing for Justice

Avoid Complacency

Micah prophesied to the southern kingdom of Judah during the time of

Kings Jotham, Ahaz, and Hezekiah. This places him in the final days of the northern kingdom and the height of the Assyrian empire's power.

Micah's prophetic message also has similarities to that of Amos, the Judean called to prophesy in Israel prior to its fall. Amos focused on the misplaced priorities and lack of social justice in Israel's capital of Samaria. Likewise, Micah's prophecy condemns Jerusalem, the capital of Judah. God uses Micah to charge the religious leadership of both kingdoms—located in their respective capitals—with the responsibility for the sins of the rest of the people.

In chapter 1, Micah begins with the destruction of Samaria, then pronounces judgment on each nation geographically located between Samaria and Jerusalem, indicating the Assyrian army's march toward Jerusalem. From 2 Kings 18 and 19 we know that this is exactly what happened during the reign of Hezekiah.

God speaks through Micah demanding social justice and proclaiming Israel's hope of restoration in Zion (Jerusalem, the Holy City). This hope also lies in the coming Messiah. Micah is known for a particular Messianic prophecy, found in Micah 5:2: *But you, Bethlehem Ephrathah, though you are small among the clans of Judah, out of you will come for me one who will be ruler over Israel, whose origins are from of old, from ancient times.*

In Micah 6:8, we read God's expectations on the people: *He has showed you, O man, what is good. And what does the Lord require of you? To act justly and to love mercy and to walk humbly with your God.* And, finally, we read God's words of hope in Micah 7:15: *As in the days when you came out of the land of Egypt, I will show Israel wonderful things.*

NAHUM 1 – 3
JUDGMENT FOR THE NATIONS

Like Joel, we do not know much about the prophet Nahum. Some Biblical scholars have suggested that he might have lived near the Sea of Galilee, in the city of Capernaum. (Capernaum will play a prominent role in Day Seven.) "Caper" is a Greek transliteration of the Hebrew "kapar", meaning "village", so Capernaum could be "village of Nahum." At the same time, the first verse of the book of Nahum identifies Nahum as an Elkoshite, so his origins remain uncertain.

The book of Nahum focuses on God's punishment of Assyria and the great city of Nineveh. Wait! This is the same thing Jonah did, right? And the people repented, right? True, but over one hundred years have passed, and things have gone downhill again. In fact, the Assyrians are now worse than ever. We know from ancient texts that they were ruthless toward their enemies, maiming, boiling, and skinning their victims alive. Nahum is not a book for the weak-stomached or faint of heart.

So, what is the point of this short book? The message, for the people of Israel and for us, is actually encouragement. As we read in Psalm 73 and the books of Job and Jeremiah, it sometimes seems that evil people are not punished for their actions. This was particularly true for the people of Israel as they saw God use the wicked Assyrian empire as his instrument to exact judgment on his chosen people. The people of Judah would feel the same way about Babylon.

God makes his judgment on all the nations clear throughout the prophetic writings. The book of Nahum, however, focuses exclusively on this. In doing so, it provides hope to the Israelites that God's justice will be served.

HABAKKUK 1 – 3
QUESTIONING GOD'S WAYS

Habakkuk was a contemporary of Jeremiah, and the book of Habakkuk reflects Jeremiah's style. Habakkuk complains to God, just as Jeremiah did. His central complaint, or question, is: *How could God use a wicked nation such as Babylon for his divine purpose?* Broadened, that question becomes one we've seen before in the Bible: Why does God allow the wicked to prosper while the righteous (or, at least, those trying to be righteous) suffer?

The first two chapters of the book are written as a dialogue between Habakkuk and God. Habakkuk poses questions and the Lord responds. For example, in Habakkuk 1:13, the prophet asks: *Why, then, do you tolerate the treacherous? Why are you silent while the wicked swallow up those more righteous than themselves?* The Lord responds in 2:2: *Write down the revelation and make plain on tablets so that a herald may run with it. For the revelation awaits an appointed time; it speaks of the end and will not prove false. Though it linger, wait for it; it will certainly come and will not delay.*

What is this revelation that "awaits an appointed time"? The message from Habakkuk is one not just for ancient times, but for all times. Even though evil seems to be winning right now (the Babylonians, African-American slavery, the Holocaust, civil war, oppression, genocide) God will prevail. The revelation of his justice is worth waiting upon, and it will come in the appointed time.

Habakkuk concludes with a psalm of praise to God, much as Psalm 73 concludes with the psalmist's words of praise for God's deliverance.

ZEPHANIAH 1 – 3
THE DAY OF THE LORD

Zephaniah was a relative of King Josiah. If you recall from 2 Kings, Josiah became king of Judah at age eight. Both Josiah and Zephaniah were descendants of the great King Hezekiah. Many scholars believe Zephaniah was likely called into service as a prophet to advise his cousin the king. Like Habakkuk, Zephaniah was a contemporary of Jeremiah.

Zephaniah's prophetic word focuses on God's judgment against Judah and the nations surrounding her. He uses the term "Day of the Lord", which we first encountered in Joel, more than all the other minor prophets combined. In an attempt to rouse the people from their complacency and spiritual arrogance, he preaches that the Day of the Lord will be a day of judgment for their smug self-satisfaction and refusal to accept correction. We might think of Zephaniah's message as "what goes around comes around." See the *ScriptureScope* below for more.

OVERRATED

In Zephaniah 1:12 we read: *At that time I will search Jerusalem with lamps and punish those who are complacent, who are like wine left on its dregs, who think, 'The Lord will do nothing, either good or bad.'*

Comfort is overrated. When we get comfortable, we get complacent. Thesarus.com lists the following synonyms for 'complacent': conceited, egotistical, self-assured, self-contented, self-pleased, self-possessed, self-righteous, self-satisfied, smug, and unconcerned. Hmmm…that's a whole lotta SELF.

When we get complacent, we are not at our best. We need to be slightly uncomfortable, somewhat concerned, a little less assured, contented, pleased, and satisfied with ourselves. That's why we need prophets—they rattle our cages and remind us that it is God who is righteous, faithful, and divine—not us. As the great New Testament missionary Paul will remind us in his letter to the Romans, "…all have sinned and fall short of the glory of God." (Romans 3:23)

HAGGAI 1 – 2
PRIORITIES AND OBEDIENCE

Post-exile Prophets

Priorities

Holiness

Night Visions

Where is the Messiah?

We move forward in time now, past the exile to the return of the remnant and the rebuilding of the temple, which we read about in the book of Ezra, the priest. [Note: The major prophets Ezekiel and Daniel were the only prophets who prophesied during the exile.] The rebuilding effort was led by Zerubbabel and Jeshua, and among the returning exiles is Haggai.

You may recall that the rebuilding of the temple stopped for fifteen years after King Artaxerxes of Persia halts the work in response to pressure from the local people. During that time, a drought comes; the returning exiles' crops cannot be harvested. The people are hungry and thirsty. Haggai tells the people to remember their priorities and begin work again. In Haggai 1:7, 9 we read: *This is what the Lord Almighty says: "Give careful thought to your ways. You expected much, but see, it turned out to be little. What you brought home, I blew away. Why?" declares the Lord Almighty. "Because of my house, which remains a ruin, while each of you is busy with his own house."*

The book of Haggai is written over a period of four months, and a very specific timeline is included. The message is essentially a call to holiness (remember Leviticus 11:44-45). Haggai's message might be paraphrased: *God called you to rebuild the temple, his place of dwelling. Now you have stopped because of fear and misplaced priorities. Remember that you are God's holy people.*

ZECHARIAH 1 – 14
CALL TO HOLINESS

In many ways, Zechariah picks up where Haggai left off. Zechariah was a younger contemporary of Haggai with the exiles during the rebuilding of the temple. Zechariah takes the theme of returning to holiness that Haggai introduces and extends it beyond the physical temple to spiritual renewal. By way of comparison, Haggai's message might be more like the OT Ten Commandments; Zechariah's message is more akin to the NT Beatitudes presented by Jesus (Matthew 5:3-12).

In terms of size and significance among the minor prophets, the book of Zechariah compares closely with Hosea, and the two can be seen as bookends for the Twelve. Malachi, the remaining minor prophet, may be seen as a post script. We'll discuss why in the next section.

Zechariah's prophecy consists of eight night visions, many of which are similar to the second half of Daniel. Included also are Messianic prophecies such as Zechariah 9:9 where we read: *Rejoice greatly, O Daughter of Zion! Shout, Daughter of Jerusalem! See, your king comes to you, righteous and having salvation, gentle and riding on a donkey, on a colt, the foal of a donkey.* Keep this in mind as we study the Gospel of Matthew in Day Seven.

The final chapters of Zechariah return to a theme throughout the minor prophets, the Day of the Lord. Zechariah describes in vivid imagery what will happen "on that day." Like other prophecies we have studied, these words can refer to the near future, to end-times, or to both. Zechariah's prophecies are often included with those of Daniel, Ezekiel, and Revelation as scholars try to understand what will happen in the final days of the world. The book concludes with the assurance that, whatever the details are, God will ultimately prevail.

MALACHI 1 – 4
LOOKING FORWARD

Malachi is the third of the minor prophets who lived and prophesied to the returning remnant in Jerusalem, serving soon after Haggai and Zechariah. Malachi was a contemporary of Nehemiah, the cupbearer-turned-governor who led the rebuilding of the Jerusalem wall. Malachi's prophecy continues the theme of holiness and obedience to God, exhorting and encouraging the people.

Malachi employs a unique literary device in which Malachi presents God's accusation to the people. Then God speaks for the people and offers their defense in the form of a question. This is followed with God's answer. We can read an example of one complete exchange in Malachi 2:17 CEB, beginning with God's accusation: *You have made the Lord tired with your words. You say, "How have we made him tired?" When you say: "Anyone doing evil is good in the Lord's eyes," Or "He delights in those doing evil," or "Where is the God of justice?"*

Later, Malachi focuses on the coming Day of the Lord and begins to set the stage for the coming of the Messiah. In Malachi 3:1 CEB we read: *Look, I am sending my messenger who will clear the path before me; suddenly the Lord whom you are seeking will come to his temple. The messenger of the covenant in whom you take delight is coming, says the Lord of heavenly forces.* Nevertheless, the book seems to end on a somewhat hopeless note. Where is the promised Messiah?

In conclusion, God challenges the people to look forward in Malachi 4:4-5 CEB: *Remember the Instruction from Moses, my servant, to whom I gave Instruction and rules for all Israel at Horeb. Look, I am sending Elijah the prophet to you, before the great and terrifying day of the Lord arrives.*

INTERTESTAMENT PERIOD

Before we move forward, let's take a moment to reflect on the Old Testament. Our focus on the meta-narrative of creation, covenant, and salvation has revealed a divine master plan designed to teach humanity about the nature of God and prepare the world for a savior. It is the story of that savior and his followers that will be the focus of the New Testament.

Reviewing the Bible Chronology on page 264 you see that the last events of the OT occurred around 425 BC. While the specific years on this chronology may be debated, most scholars agree that a period of 400 years or so elapsed before the birth of Jesus.

Why this 400-year historical interlude in the story?

Biblical and religious scholars have proposed several reasons for God's timing. Some have suggested that the 400-year gap in the Bible's story allows time for the coming Messiah to be disassociated from the Hebrew nation. As we will see in Day Seven, although Jesus was a Jew, he comes as a king for all nations and a savior for all peoples, not just the

Israelites. Nevertheless, his significance as the Jewish Messiah is critical to everything we've been studying in the Old Testament. So, there are many New Testament scholars who disagree with this position.

A second theory is that the historical events that occurred during the period between the testaments worked together to create a political and cultural climate conducive to the creation of a new religion. Although Jesus came as the Jewish Messiah, the resulting Christ-follower movement quickly became distinct from Judaism in many ways. Between 425 BC, when the Jerusalem wall was completed, and around AD 30 when Jesus was crucified and resurrected, the Persian empire gave way to the Greeks and then to the Romans. The Romans, although merciless toward their enemies, prided themselves on being a "free religion" society. They were very focused on their pantheon of gods, allowing citizens and slaves alike to worship any god(s) of their choosing--as long as that worship did not conflict with allegiance to Rome.

Another factor that evolved from these events was the proliferation of one language throughout the civilized world. Although the Greeks were no longer in power, Rome adopted many aspects of the Greek culture as their own. One of these, the Greek language, became the language of the people throughout the majority of the Roman Empire.

Finally, but certainly not of least importance, the Roman highway system throughout the Mediterranean and Asia Minor created a way for Jesus' followers to spread the good news of the Messiah. The Romans were great road builders and, while they used them primarily for commerce and military maneuvers, they also were available to missionaries such as Paul, Silas, and Barnabas.

Again, it should be noted that these are just a few of the theories that have been suggested. There are many others.

The intertestament period, while notably "blank" in most Protestant Bibles, was not a silent period. The writing of the period, referred to as the Apocrypha or "hidden" writing, is not accepted as divinely-inspired scripture by many believers. It was, however, included in most Bibles from AD 382 through the first King James Bible in 1611. Most Protestant versions dropped the Apocryphal writings by 1629, although they are still included in Roman Catholic and Greek Orthodox versions. They are not part of the Hebrew Scriptures of the Jewish faith. The Apocrypha typically includes fourteen books written between 300 BC and AD 100. Of familiarity to you may be 1 and 2 Maccabees, Judith, and Ecclesiasticus.

In addition to the rise of the Roman Empire and the writings of the Apocrypha, significant changes were happening within the Jewish religion. During the exile, the Jewish people were relocated throughout the Mediterranean. This diaspora meant that, even after the rebuilding of the temple during the restoration, many people could no longer worship at the temple in Jerusalem. As a result, local synagogues emerged with rabbis (teachers) as leaders. This also led to written interpretations of the Law and less emphasis on the priesthood.

During this period Jewish sects also arose, formed along political, cultural, and religious lines. The Pharisees became the keepers of the oral traditions which they considered the Law. The Sadducees rejected the oral tradition and adopted more Hellenistic (Greek-influenced) practices, including forsaking belief in resurrection from the dead. Essenes were monk-like and often lived in the desert, removing themselves from cultural influences. Many scholars believe that the Essenes were the keepers of the documents discovered as the Dead Sea Scrolls.

Zealots were militaristic, believing that the only way to get out from under Rome's rule was through revolt. It was from the zealots that many "messiahs" arose during this period. These would-be leaders typically gathered followers for a while but were ultimately killed by Rome. You can see how this history might cause some who witnessed Jesus' crucifixion to wonder if he had been the real Messiah.

The Herodians were Jews who sought to ingratiate themselves to Rome, typically through the Judean governor, Herod—hence their name. We might think of them as the "if you can't beat 'em, join 'em" sect. And finally, we can't forget the Samaritans. The Samaritans lived in Samaria—no longer just a city, but an area north of Jerusalem—and practiced the blended religion that evolved after Assyria's conquest of the northern kingdom around 722 BC. They were despised by the religious leaders in Jerusalem. Most faithful Jews in first century Palestine would go out of their way to avoid going through Samaria or having anything to do with Samaritans.

Into this world of Roman domination, fractured Jewish religion, and centuries of waiting for the next word from God's prophets comes.... Jesus. We begin his story in Day Seven.

REFLECTING FORWARD

We have come to the end of the Old Testament. Use these questions to discuss what you've learned and think about what comes next.

1. Joel uses a natural disaster, the invasion of an "army of locusts" on the land, to lead into his prophetic message. He tells the people that this is a time they should reflect on their lives. Do we see that in our world today? Can times of crisis sometimes lead people to God? Have you experienced anything similar in your own life?

2. The people of Israel and Judah could not understand how God could use evil Assyria and Babylon as his instruments of judgment. In their minds, they were "holier" than these other countries and God's use of them seemed like a "bitter pill". Have you ever experienced God's discipline? How did it come to you? Were you surprised by the source of God's corrective message to you?

3. Zephaniah focused on complacency and the common belief that God had distanced himself from the people and would not take any action against the unfaithful. Or, in today's language, God is really not involved in our world, so don't waste your time with him or his church. Have you ever felt that way? Has God, from your perspective, abandoned you? Looking back, can you see ways that he was "working behind the scenes" out of love for you? What message would you give to others who believe as Zephaniah wrote?

4. Haggai and Zechariah called upon the people to get their priorities straight. They were there to rebuild the temple and that's what they needed to do, no matter what the locals did to try and stop them. Zechariah explained that, for God's people, the priority must be holiness. But, that's a high standard, isn't it? How have you focused on being holy, as God has called us to be holy? Or, have you seen that as "spiritual arrogance" or something that others would see that way? How can we "work on" holiness without our humanity getting in the way?

5. Imagine yourself as a Jewish scholar during the Intertestament Period. It's been 400 years and no savior has come to deliver God's people. Has God forgotten his promise? You have read the scrolls of the prophets. God kept his covenant with Abraham and Israel. Surely,

God will keep his promise to send a savior. Based on what you've read, how will you recognize the Messiah when he comes? What are you looking for?

6. The story of Hosea and Gomer vividly demonstrates God's love for his people. Not only did Hosea take on a wife he knew would be unfaithful to him, but he repeatedly bought her back when she left him. Sound familiar? It's the story of Israel that comprises all of the Old Testament. But that's not all we find in Hosea. This minor prophet also demonstrates the unheard-of love we will read about in the New Testament when we read the story of Jesus. In anticipation, think about how God has loved you. How have you, personally, experienced God's radical, unrelenting, redeeming love?

DAY SEVEN

MATTHEW, MARK

A few years ago, we were sharing lunch with our older son, his wife, and our grandson, Harry. Harry was between two and three years old at the time. When it came time to say grace over the food, Harry volunteered.

He clasped his little hands in front of his heart and said with genuine two-year-old fervor, "Thank you, God, for this food. Thank you, God, for Mommy and Daddy. Thank you, God, for Nana Pam and Daddy Keith. And thank you most of all for Jesus!" After a heart-felt "Amen!" he broke into a big smile, formed a "touchdown" signal with his fists closed, then opened his hands suddenly as if sharing a surprise, and cried out "Bon Appetit!"

I turned to our daughter-in-law and asked, "Did he just say Bon Appetit? How precious! (*yes, I am his grandmother*) Did you teach him to do that?" She replied yes, but that it had some unexpected consequences. Now, Harry thinks that any time you say "Amen!" it should be followed by "Bon Appetit!" This adds a new dimension to his recitation of the Lord's Prayer, as you can imagine. She seemed a bit disturbed by this, but after thinking about it, I decided that it's just perfect.

As I hope you are seeing by now, God has prepared quite a feast for us in his Word, the Bible. Indeed, "Bon Appetit" seems appropriate. And, if we look at God's Word as a feast, we have come to the main course as we begin our study of the New Testament today. Let's dig in!

Day Seven presents two of the five history books in the New Testament. These two books, Matthew and Mark, along with Luke and John (Day Eight) are referred to as the four Gospels. The word "gospel" means "good news", specifically the good news that God sent his Son, Jesus, as the fulfillment of the OT promises of the coming of the Messiah, to save not only the Jewish people but all people from the consequences of their sinful lives. The good news Jesus brings is the offer of an eternal life of perfect relationship with God, just as humanity had with God in the beginning, before sin entered the world.

The Gospels introduce us not only to Jesus, the man who lived in Palestine (Judea, Judah, Israel) in the first century AD, but to Jesus, the divine Son of God, whose gift of salvation brings a new way of living in relationship with God and with others. This "new way" is not really new at all, but a re-creation of the original relationship God created with humanity back in Genesis.

This new covenant based on grace fulfills God's promise that we saw earlier in Jeremiah (Day Five). Jesus brings not only a new way to live but a new path to forgiveness of sins, salvation from death, and reconciliation with God. Jesus's life, death, resurrection, and promised return perfectly, and finally, connect the three themes of our study—creation, covenant, and salvation.

The gospels are not meant to be complete historical biographies of Jesus' life. Rather, they were written with different readers in mind but with a single purpose: to convince all people, both Jews and Gentiles (non-Jews), to believe in Jesus as the Son of God and accept his gift of forgiveness and grace. They did this by telling the story of Jesus' life, death, and resurrection.

The gospels are designed to be "evangelistic", meaning their goal is to convert others to Christianity and to provide a way for Christ-followers to confirm their understanding of their faith. Consequently, a significant portion of all four books is devoted to the last week of Jesus' life on earth and what it means for all people—more on this to come.

Three of the gospels—Matthew, Mark, and Luke—are often called the "synoptic" gospels. The adjective "synoptic"—meaning literally "one [syn] eye [optic]"—reminds us that these three gospels share many of the same stories and teachings of Jesus. This has led Biblical scholars over the years to suggest that the writers either borrowed from each other and/or drew from another earlier source to guide their writing. The fourth gospel, John, shares much of the same information, but also includes significant material that is not found in the synoptic gospels.

It's important to understand that the gospels were not written during Jesus' lifetime. Three of the gospels—Matthew, Mark, and John—have traditionally been attributed to individuals who were quite likely with Jesus during much of his ministry. This does not mean, however, that they were taking notes and writing things down as Jesus spoke like a journalist would do today.

We will see as we study the gospels that most of his followers had no idea who Jesus really was and what his ministry would mean until after his crucifixion and resurrection. For at least twenty-five years and possibly much longer, the accounts of Jesus were only shared orally, passed down through families and circulated through letters. When the gospels were finally written down, they were each written with a specific purpose and audience in mind.

At this point, it would be helpful to take a look at the Christ's Life and Ministry table on page 268. Here you will find not only one possible chronology of Jesus' life (according to some scholars) but also specific scriptures from the four gospels that support these events. Note that not all sources are listed for each event, especially when concerning the synoptic gospels. Only one synoptic source may be given, but because of the similarities between the three, you can often find the story or teaching in the others as well. When you find John as a source, however, this is typically an event recorded only in John's gospel. It will be helpful to refer to this table throughout today's reading.

MATTHEW 1 – 11
JESUS' MINISTRY BEGINS

These first chapters of Matthew introduce the reader to *who* Jesus is, *how* he lived, *what* he taught, and *the people's response* to him. Matthew's gospel was written to convince educated Jews that Jesus was the long-awaited Messiah, the one described in the Psalms and the prophecies of Isaiah, Jeremiah, Malachi,

Jesus' Lineage

Visit of the Magi

Jesus' Baptism

Temptation of Jesus

Calling of Disciples

Sermon on the Mount

Healings and Miracles

Storm on Galilee

Reassurance for John

and others. With this purpose in mind, this gospel contains more references to OT passages than any of the others.

Keeping in mind that the OT—what we just spent six days studying—was (and is) the Hebrew Bible. If the writer of Matthew wants to convince his readers that Jesus is the Jewish Messiah—not a false messiah or would-be messiah like so many others over the previous four hundred years—then connecting him to the Hebrew scriptures is critical.

Of primary importance in this connection is Jesus' genealogy. Remember the Davidic covenant (Day Three), when God promised King David that his line, the line of Judah would reign forever? This means that the Messiah, the Savior, must be a descendant of David. So, Matthew begins with the genealogy of Joseph, Jesus' earthly father. We will learn that Jesus' true father is God, but Jewish custom assigns lineage to the father, so Joseph must come from the line of Judah and David.

Through our study of the OT, we discussed four women found in the lineage of Jesus—Tamar (Day One), Rahab (Day Two), and Ruth and Bathsheba (Day Three). Here we find them in Matthew 1, along with the fifth woman in Jesus' lineage, his mother Mary. Matthew traces Jesus's lineage back to Abraham, indicating an unbroken line of Jewish heritage. The stage is set to convince the Jewish reader that Jesus is the prophesied Messiah.

In 1:18 through 2: 23, we read Matthew's only scriptures related to Jesus' birth and life prior to the start of his ministry at around the age of 30. This is not the "Christmas story" with which you are probably most familiar—that's coming in Luke. Matthew's account is presented differently but is consistent with that narrative.

It is also the only place we read of the visit from the magi (wise men or kings) who followed a bright star from the East to Bethlehem to worship "the newborn king". Notice that I did not say "three kings", as there is no evidence in Matthew that there were three kings—just that they brought three gifts. (*Who knows? Maybe there were actually four kings and one accidentally left his gift at the last oasis stop...smile*)

This is followed by the story of Herod, the Roman governor of Judea, requiring that all the children in Bethlehem be killed to get rid of this new "king of the Jews". An angel warns Joseph in a dream to escape with Jesus and Mary to Egypt. They return to Palestine once they learn of Herod's death and live in Nazareth, so that Jesus is referred to as a Nazarene. (Note: This is not the same as being a Nazarite [Numbers 6]. A parent's commitment to raise a child as a Nazarite indicates a dedication to the Lord's service and was most notably made by the parents of Samson and Samuel.)

In chapter 3, Jesus is baptized in the Jordan River by John the Baptist, the one sent to announce the coming Messiah. As confirmation to his readers that Jesus is the Son of God and the Messiah, Matthew 3:16-17 reports: *As soon as Jesus was baptized, he went up out of the water. At that moment heaven was opened, and he saw the Spirit of God descending like a dove and lighting on him. And a voice from heaven said, "This is my Son, whom I love; with him I am well pleased."*

Immediately, Jesus goes to the wilderness of Palestine and fasts for 40 days and 40 nights (Connection: These numbers should sound familiar. Moses spent 40 days on Mt. Sinai receiving the law from Yahweh. The spies, including Caleb and Joshua, surveyed the Promise Land for 40 days. The Israelites wandered in the desert for 40 years. Numbers can be symbolic in the Bible but are also used to remind the reader of these connections.) After 40 days, Jesus is tempted three times by Satan, the Evil One. Satan offers him food, wealth, and power if Jesus will worship him. Jesus rejects them all, each time quoting the OT and choosing instead to worship God, his heavenly Father.

Note that Jesus' baptism is recorded or referenced in all four gospels, and the temptation is recorded in all three synoptic gospels. While some of the details are different, the essence of the stories is the same, indicating their importance to understanding that Jesus was the Son of God, not just another rabbi, teacher, or prophet.

As Jesus begins his ministry, he surrounds himself with twelve disciples who know him as teacher and friend. Each gospel tells the story of the calling of these men differently, and Matthew's includes a particularly important piece. The first four disciples called—James, John, Peter, and Andrew—are fishermen on the Sea of Galilee. We find Jesus' invitation to them in Matthew 4:19: *"Come, follow me," Jesus said, "and I will make you fishers of men."*

Jesus begins his ministry, then, in Galilee. His home base is often Capernaum, a city on the shores of the Sea of Galilee. This is the city we discussed in Day Six as a possible home of the minor prophet Nahum. See the *ScriptureScope* below for Matthew's description of Jesus' Galilean ministry.

PAST, PRESENT, AND FUTURE

In Matthew 4:23 CEB we read: *Jesus traveled throughout Galilee, teaching in their synagogues. He announced the good news of the kingdom and healed every disease and sickness among the people.*

This is the first of several times in Matthew's gospel where we read Jesus' ministry described in this way. Let's look closely at the three things that Jesus did.

First, he taught in their synagogues. What would he have taught? The law and prophets—the Old Testament we just finished studying, including the Books of Moses, the Psalms, and the writings of both the major and minor prophets. In his synagogue teaching, he talked to the people about things with which they were familiar, and he reminded them of their history with Yahweh as well as their covenant with him. Remember—Jesus was a well-trained, first-born Jewish son. We know from the times he quotes the OT throughout all four gospels that he knew the scriptures by heart.

Second, Jesus announced the good news of the kingdom of God. Here was unfamiliar territory for his listeners, but his preaching gave the people hope, even if many of them misunderstood the nature of the kingdom or when it was available to them.

Finally, he healed their diseases. In other words, he dealt with their most pressing issues of here and now.

Jesus did not just reflect on the past through the familiar Hebrew scriptures. He did not just focus on the future with his talk of a coming kingdom and eternal life. He also enriched their lives in the present, just as he does for each of us today. Our God and Savior is a God of the past, the future, and the present.

In chapter 5, we get our first glimpse of how the people respond to Jesus' teachings. Here, we see that large crowds are following him, eager to hear his teachings. Chapters 5 through 7 present what has come to be known as the Sermon on the Mount. These teachings include the Beatitudes, which we have discussed previously as being the "Ten Commandments of the New Testament." Unlike the commandments God gave the Israelites from Mt. Sinai, these words of Jesus focus not on outward physical treatment of others, but inward expressions of holiness through meekness (or humility), hunger for righteousness, mercy, peacemaking, and purity of heart.

The Sermon on the Mount also contains what has become known as the Lord's Prayer as Jesus teaches his disciples how to pray (*Bon Appetit!*). Jesus gives warnings about worry, assuring that God will provide for his children as he does for the lilies of the field (6:28). In

Matthew 6:33 we read more words of promise: *"But seek first his kingdom and his righteousness, and all these things will be given to you as well."* Note the connection back to the first of the Ten Commandments in Exodus 20:1: *You shall have no other gods before me.*

He also instructs his listeners to refrain from judging others, so that they will not be judged as well (7:1). His message is that the "eternal life" he brings is not just life after death but abundant life here and now. See the *ScriptureScope* below for more on how to find this abundant life.

TWO ROADS

In Matthew 7:13 we read Jesus' words: *"Enter through the narrow gate. For wide is the gate and broad is the road that leads to destruction, and many enter through it. But small is the gate and narrow the road that leads to life, and only a few find it."*

This is perhaps my favorite directive from Jesus, as it seems to sum up the challenges of this world in which we are placed. I think of the words of Robert Frost, who described himself as an "Old Testament Christian" because of his Puritan upbringing: "Two roads diverged in a yellow wood…and I took the one less traveled by, and that has made all the difference." With Frost the implication is that the fork in the road presents the choice between right and wrong, work and sloth, love and hate, accomplishment and worthlessness, knowledge and ignorance, individuality and following the crowd.

This is all good stuff, but it isn't original with Frost. Jesus made it clear over 2000 years ago.

We always have a choice with Jesus. God's road is narrow, and his gate is small. It is the true road less traveled, as the other road—the world's road—is broad and the gate is wide. Anyone can travel it, and anyone can pass through the gate—it's easy, comfortable, no challenge.

Not so with God's road of obedience, faithfulness, and holiness. Choosing God's road, however, offers rewards that far outweigh any sacrifice we might make, as the sacrifice has already been made through Jesus the Son.

Like Frost said in the secular version, our choice makes all the difference. And the choice Jesus gives us here in Matthew is much more important than the choices presented by Frost's two roads. Indeed, the choice Jesus presents is the choice between death and life—abundant life in the here and now as well as eternal life after death with God.

In chapters 8 through 11 we learn more of the people's amazement at Jesus' teaching and his response to them. He begins to perform healing miracles, including a man with leprosy, the centurion's servant, a paralyzed man, two demon-possessed men, the blind, the mute, and the woman with a lingering blood disorder who reached out in faith to touch the hem of Jesus' robe. Jesus' compassion for the poor, the sick, the widow, the orphan, and the foreigner mirror not only the laws given to the Israelites by Moses, but the four women in his own lineage.

In chapter 8 Jesus and his disciples are on the Sea of Galilee when a storm comes up quickly. Jesus is sleeping below deck, but his friends awaken him in fear. Jesus arises and calms the winds and the rolling lake. The disciples ask in Matthew 8:27: *"What kind of man is this? Even the winds and the waves obey him!"* Connection: Remember that Yahweh as Creator is perhaps Israel's greatest image of God. In the book of Job (Day Four) God called Job into account by demonstrating his power over creation. In many Psalms, God's role as Creator takes center stage. The disciples had seen other rabbis, healers, and would-be messiahs come and go—but this was different. This rabbi—Jesus—held power over Creation.

In chapter 11, we learn that John the Baptist (who baptized Jesus earlier) is imprisoned and now wonders if Jesus is indeed the true

Messiah. He sends his disciples to Jesus to ask this question. Jesus answers by quoting Isaiah 35 and 61, saying in verses 4-5: *"Go back and report to John what you hear and see: The blind receive sight, the lame walk, those who have leprosy are cured, the deaf hear, the dead or raised, and the good news is preached to the poor."* Jesus was telling John—and Matthew is telling his readers—that Jesus is the fulfillment of the prophecies about the coming Messiah.

MATTHEW 12 – 20
RESPONSE FROM JEWISH LEADERS

The Pharisees Question
The Kingdom of Heaven
John Beheaded
Feeding the 5000
Walking on Water
Jesus' Transfiguration

In these chapters, Jesus begins to encounter the Pharisees regularly. As a reminder, the Pharisees were one of the religious sects that evolved during the Intertestament Period (Day Six). The Pharisees considered themselves the keepers of the oral tradition of the law, much of which was not in the Law of Moses. They were typically highly educated Jews, often from aristocratic families, and held themselves and their "wisdom" in high regard. As such, they were suspicious and threatened by this new rabbi on the scene, who was attracting such attention from the masses.

The Pharisees question Jesus about his actions on the Sabbath (the weekly day of rest and strict worship practices). They also question him about the fasting practices of his disciples and their adherence to the laws regarding the clean and the unclean. Jesus consistently responds to their questions by frustrating their efforts to discredit him in front of his followers.

In chapter 13, we find Jesus teaching the people using parables, or stories that use familiar examples or symbolism to teach a spiritual truth. Jesus teaches about the kingdom of heaven (or God) by comparing it to a sower, a mustard seed, a pearl, and a fisherman's net. Many of the parables are included in all of the gospels with minor differences, but some are included only in Luke (the longest gospel) and John (the non-synoptic gospel).

In chapter 14, Jesus learns that John the Baptist has been beheaded by Herod. Although he is grieving for his friend, over 5,000 people have gathered to hear him teach. (Note: Most scholars believe this number was only the count of the men, meaning a true count of closer to 15,000 – 20,000 including women and children.) Jesus not only teaches them but miraculously feeds them all (with leftovers!) from the five loaves of bread and two fish a young boy offers.

Later, when the Twelve (his closest disciples, also called *apostles,* meaning "messengers") are on the Sea of Galilee, Jesus walks from the shore on the water to join them. The apostle Peter, who has emerged as the leader of the group of twelve, professes his faith and attempts to walk out to greet Jesus—but fails when he takes his eyes off Jesus. Jesus rescues him from drowning.

Note in Matthew 14:27, when the disciples ask who approaches their boat, Jesus' reply is typically translated as "It is I" or in the CEB "It's me". The original Greek, however, translates as "I AM". Remember when Moses asked God his name at the burning bush in Exodus 3:14? God replied, "I AM". This connection is not lost on his disciples. Because of this understanding and this second demonstration of Jesus' power over creation, they here—for the first time—proclaim him the "Son of God."

Jesus continues to heal, preach, and teach, trying to help the people as well as his closest disciples understand the upside-down nature of his kingdom. His kingdom will not be one of power and dominion over others as the Assyrians, Babylonians, Greeks, and Romans have dominated the Israelites for centuries.

Instead, Jesus comes to establish a kingdom where his followers experience lives of joy and peace through humility, love, grace, and hope, putting others' needs ahead of their own. In Matthew 16:24-25, Jesus explains the cost of being his disciple: *Then Jesus said to his disciples, "If anyone would come after me, he must deny himself and take up his cross and follow me. For whoever wants to save his life will lose it, but whoever loses his life for me will find it."*

Jesus is transfigured in chapter 17. Transfiguration in the Bible is a physical transformation indicating a glorification of the person and a renewed dedication to the Lord. Moses—the savior in the OT salvation story—was transfigured on his second trip up the mountain to speak with God. From then on, his faced glowed and he wore a veil over it. Here Jesus, the savior of the NT salvation story, is transfigured to demonstrate that God is preparing him to be glorified through the coming ordeal of crucifixion and resurrection.

Jesus takes Peter, James, and John (the inner circle of the disciples) with him up a mountain. They are joined there by Moses, representing the Law, and Elijah, representing the Prophets (see connection in Malachi 4:4-5 at the end of Day Six). Typically-impetuous Peter suggests that they build three shelters on the mountain—presumably so they can hang out for a while—but his plan is, thankfully, ignored. Instead, Jesus' face and robe glow and God speaks, declaring in verse 5: *"This is my Son, whom I love; with him I am well pleased. Listen to him!"* Compare this verse to the words of the "voice from heaven" at Jesus' baptism, recorded in Matthew 3:17.

When Jesus comes down from the mountain, the Pharisees continue to test him with questions and accusations, all the while plotting his death. Jesus speaks to his disciples more and more about his impending death and resurrection. In chapter 18 he teaches the people on the importance of being least and childlike in their faith. By contrast, he talks about how difficult it is for the rich man to give up his importance and wealth, saying in 19:24: *"Again I tell you, it is easier for a camel to go through the eye of a needle than for a rich man to enter the kingdom of God."*

Triumphal Entry

Temple Cleansing

The Great Commandment

Final Judgment

The Last Supper

Garden of Gethsemane

Jesus' Trials

Crucifixion

Resurrection

The Great Commission

MATTHEW 21 – 28
HOLY WEEK

The Church has traditionally referred to the final week of Jesus' life on earth as Holy Week. The events of this week are critical to the gospel writers' mission of evangelism-- convincing non-believers that Jesus was the Christ (Messiah) and that his death and resurrection created an opportunity for all people to have abundant and eternal life. As a result, while the gospels cover between 3 and 33 years depending on the author, the percentage of each book devoted to this one week may surprise you. Thirty percent of Matthew is devoted to Holy Week. In Mark, Holy Week comprises 40%; it is 62% of Luke and 47% of John.

Chapter 21 of Matthew begins with Jesus and his disciples entering Jerusalem for Passover week, the annual celebration of the Israelites' delivery from Egypt under Moses (Day Two). Jesus has asked his disciples to bring him the colt of a donkey to ride into the city, fulfilling the prophecy found in Zechariah 9:9 (see Day Six). As he enters, the people wave palm branches and cry out words from Psalm 118, the Psalm of the Returning Victor: *"Blessed is he who comes in the name of the Lord!"* As we noted in Day Four, this designation of Jesus as king by the people is not lost on the Pharisees, Sadducees, and temple authorities. They continue to plot his death, seeing Jesus as a threat to their spiritual power.

Jesus immediately goes to the Temple (not Solomon's temple or the one rebuilt in Ezra, but one built by Herod to establish his rule over Palestine.) There, in what might be described as "righteous anger", Jesus clears the temple of "money-changers" and vendors who are cheating poor pilgrims trying to purchase a dove or pigeon for a Passover sacrifice.

While the Roman denarii were used everywhere else in Palestine as currency, the temple required the archaic temple shekel as currency. The temple priests and leaders were making money not only with the inflated price of the sacrificial birds, but also on the currency exchange rate. This is what enrages Jesus and prompts his accusation in Matthew 21:13 that combines Isaiah 56:7 and Jeremiah 7:11: *"It is written,"* he said to them, *"'My house will be called a house of prayer,' but you are making it a 'den of robbers.'"*

Jesus then begins to teach daily in the temple, challenging the chief priests and elders (the Sanhedrin), many of whom are Pharisees and Sadducees. Jesus accuses all of these groups of hypocritical worship and blind leadership. In chapter 22:37-40, a Pharisee in the crowd attempts to trap him by asking Jesus which commandment in the law is the greatest. Jesus quotes Deuteronomy and Leviticus in his response: *"'Love the Lord your God with all your heart and with all your soul and with all your mind. This is the first and greatest commandment. And the second is like it: 'Love your neighbor as yourself.' All the Law and the Prophets hang on these two commandments."* Look back to Day Two for several connections to these particular scriptures.

In chapter 24, Jesus teaches about "signs of the end of the age", including his return. He makes it clear that no one knows the day or hour of his return but God the Father, saying: *"Therefore keep watch, because you do not know on what day your Lord will come"* (verse 42) and *"So you also must be ready, because the Son of Man will come at an hour when you do not expect him"* (verse 44).

In chapter 25, Jesus describes a vivid scene of the final judgment after his return to earth. Jesus judges the people, separating the sheep from the goats. When the sheep (the righteous) ask why they are blessed to come into his kingdom, he replies in Matthew 25: 35 – 36, 40: *"For I was hungry and you gave me something to eat. I was thirsty and you gave me something to drink, I was a stranger and you invited me in. I needed clothes and you clothed me, I was sick and you looked after me, I was in prison and you came to visit me. I tell you the truth, whatever you did for one of the least of these brothers of mine, you did for me."* This definition of "righteousness" is a clear affront to the temple authorities' positions of self-importance and power.

Chapter 26 is full of action, beginning with the chief priests and elders assembling in the home of the high priest, Caiaphas, to plan their arrest of Jesus. One of the Twelve, Judas Iscariot, agrees to betray Jesus to them for thirty pieces of silver.

On Thursday evening, the disciples join Jesus for a Passover meal in a room on an upper floor in Jerusalem. Here, in the upper room, Jesus radically reinterprets this most important of the Jewish feasts and institutes the sacrament or ordinance of Holy Communion, also called the Eucharist and the Lord's Supper. Using bread to symbolize his body and wine to symbolize his blood, he directs the disciples to eat and drink as a remembrance of him. He refers to the bread and blood as symbols of the new covenant—the covenant foretold in Jeremiah 31.

He announces that one of the disciples will betray him to the authorities. He also tells Peter that he will deny that he knows Jesus to protect himself. Peter, nothing if not confident, vows that he will never deny Jesus.

After the supper, Jesus and the disciples go to the Garden of Gethsemane, a grove of olive trees east of the temple. Leaving the rest of the disciples at the entrance, Jesus takes Peter, James, and John deeper into the garden with him to pray, but they fall asleep. Jesus cries out to God the Father, asking that the cup of death might be removed from him. Despite his anguish about what lies ahead, he lovingly yields to the

Father's will. Judas shows up with the temple guards sent from the chief priests, and Jesus is arrested.

Jesus is brought before the temple ruling body, the Sanhedrin, for a makeshift trial in the early hours of Friday morning. Jesus is accused of blasphemy when he finally, and for the first time, claims to be the Son of God. Meanwhile, Peter, despite his faith, denies that he knows Jesus three times—just as Jesus told him he would.

As chapter 27 opens, Judas returns the money to the temple authorities and hangs himself. After being spat upon and beaten by the temple guards, Jesus is taken to Pontius Pilate, the Roman governor who is in Jerusalem to keep the peace during Passover. While the temple leaders could pronounce a verdict of guilty upon Jesus, only the Roman governor can assign the death sentence.

Jesus does not offer defense of himself before Pilate, which arouses Pilate's curiosity. Pilate's wife has had a dream about Jesus and warns Pilate not to crucify him. Wary, Pilate tries to release a murderer, Barabbas, to the people in Jesus' place, but they cry for Jesus to be crucified. Pilate literally washes his hands in front of the crowd, claiming that he is not responsible. He releases Jesus to the Roman soldiers to be flogged and crucified.

As is the Roman crucifixion practice, Jesus is required to carry his cross to the hill of Golgotha, where he will be crucified between two thieves. Because of the flogging he has received and his weakened state, he repeatedly falls. A bystander, Simon of Cyrene, is enlisted to help him carry the cross.

While on the cross, the soldiers, teachers of the law, chief priests, and elders mock Jesus. They taunt him, telling him to save himself if he is, indeed, the Son of God. Around noon on Friday, darkness covers the earth until Jesus dies around 3:00 pm. At that moment, the curtain in the temple separating the Holy of Holies (where only the high priest could enter) is ripped apart from the top to bottom. Although the people who witness Jesus' death do not see the possibility at this point, the new covenant has come! Humanity is no longer required to go through the high priest to access God and his forgiving grace. Now, because of Jesus, men and women have direct access to God's presence, forgiveness, and grace, as in the beginning.

At the moment of Jesus' death, an earthquake shakes the world. The dead come walking out of their tombs, prompting some of those watching to exclaim that Jesus was, indeed, the Son of God. Jesus' body is taken by Joseph of Arimathea, a wealthy member of the Sanhedrin who also believed Jesus was the Son of God, and he is buried in Joseph's family tomb. The chief priests and elders request that Pilate assign Roman soldiers to guard the tomb and he does.

The last chapter of Matthew opens on Sunday morning, following the crucifixion on Friday. Women followers of Jesus who have come to the tomb discover that the stone has been rolled away. They are greeted by an angel. The angel announces that Jesus has risen from the dead and will meet the disciples in Galilee. Suddenly, Jesus himself appears to them and directs them to tell the others.

When the remaining eleven disciples meet Jesus in Galilee, he commissions them to share the story throughout the world. We read the following in Matthew 28:18-20: *Then Jesus came to them and said, "All authority in heaven and on earth has been given to me. Therefore, go and make disciples of all nations, baptizing them in the name of the Father and of the Son and of the Holy Spirit, and teaching them to obey everything I have commanded you. And surely I am with you always, to the very end of the age."*

A couple of notes before we leave Matthew: This last passage, typically called the Great Commission, includes the words used in the Holy Baptism of believers throughout Christendom. The words *"baptizing them in the name of the Father and of the Son and of the Holy Spirit"* emphasize the triune nature of God and are found nowhere else in the scriptures. And, finally, note that the passage translated "go and make disciples" is literally translated *"as you go* make disciples". This may seem insignificant, but it changes the meaning of evangelism for Christ-followers. Mission and witness are not something that you must "go" somewhere to do. Instead, they are to be done "as you go", wherever you go…at work, at play, at home, as you travel. God's mission field is everywhere, and Jesus challenges us to tell the gospel story anytime, anywhere.

MARK 1 – 16
THE ACTION GOSPEL

| Customs Explained |
| Young Man in Garden |
| Pilate Surprised |
| Original and Edited Endings |

Mark's gospel is the second of the synoptic gospels found in the Bible but thought by most scholars to have been the first one written. When I read Mark, I am reminded of reading my father's *Reader's Digest Condensed Books* when I was a child. The same gospel story is presented in Mark as in Matthew, but shorter and more action-oriented. The writing moves quickly from event to event with less details and discussion.

It's generally thought that Mark decided to write his gospel— perhaps the first gospel—primarily to encourage early persecuted Christians in Rome in the second half of the first century. It has fewer references to the old testament than Matthew (although quoting Isaiah in the first three verses.) Instead, it includes more explanation of Jewish customs. This would have been necessary for a less Jewish, more Gentile readership.

Mark offers no birth narrative for Jesus and no genealogy but begins by introducing us to John the Baptist. Immediately, we read about Jesus' baptism and temptation, similar to Matthew but more concisely told. By the end of chapter 1, Jesus has been baptized, tempted, called his first disciples, performed numerous healings, and begun his ministry in Galilee.

By the end of chapter 3, the Pharisees have begun to question and challenge Jesus. In chapters 4 and 5, Jesus teaches through parables and calms the storm on the Sea of Galilee. In Mark 5:21-43 you will find two wonderful stories of faith that result in healing, one of the woman with the bleeding disorder and one of the synagogue ruler Jairus' daughter.

Chapter 6 includes the story of the beheading of John the Baptist, the feeding of the 5,000 (or, more likely 15,000), and Jesus walking on the water—but no mention of Peter's attempt here. In Mark 7:2-3, we find a good example of the additional explanation the writer gives of Jewish customs and law. The Pharisees question Jesus about the disciples eating food with "unclean" hands. By way of explanation, Mark adds in parentheses in verse 3: (*The Pharisees and all the Jews do not eat unless they give their hands a ceremonial washing, holding to the tradition of the elders.*)

Mark records Jesus' transfiguration in chapter 9, and Jesus begins to talk more about his impending death throughout chapter 10. The events of Holy Week begin in chapter 11 with Jesus' triumphal entry into Jerusalem on what has become known as Palm Sunday.

Mark's fast-moving, action-packed version of the Holy Week events gives the reader a better sense of the passage of time between the triumphal entry on Sunday and the crucifixion on Friday. Once again, we read of Jesus clearing the temple of dishonest money changers, the plotting of his death by the temple authorities, Jesus' Last Supper with the disciples, Judas' betrayal, and Jesus' arrest in the Garden of Gethsemane.

One interesting piece is added that is not in any of the other three gospels. In chapter 14, after Jesus is led away under arrest, we read: *A young man, wearing nothing but a linen garment, was following Jesus. When they seized him, he fled naked, leaving his garment behind.* More than one Biblical scholar has suggested that the young man might be Mark—John Mark as we will know him later—to whom this gospel is attributed.

Jesus' trial before the Sanhedrin and Pilate are consistent with Matthew's version, as is the crucifixion narrative. An additional detail is added, however, regarding the release of Jesus' body to Joseph of Arimathea for burial. See the *ScriptureScope* on the next page.

NOT ONE SECOND

In Mark 15:43-45 we read: *Joseph of Arimathea, a prominent member of the Council, who was himself waiting for the kingdom of God, went boldly to Pilate and asked for Jesus' body. Pilate was surprised to hear that he was already dead. Summoning the centurion, he asked him if Jesus had already died. When he learned from the centurion that it was so, he gave the body to Joseph.*

This insight into Pilate's thoughts is not included Matthew. Only in Mark do we read that Pilate was surprised that Jesus was already dead. Why was he surprised? A little research into crucifixion as it was administered by the Roman Empire reveals that it often took days, not hours, for the one being crucified to die, even after being flogged as Jesus had been. Typically, the soldiers would break the legs of the man on the tree to speed up the death.

According to Mark, Jesus was nailed to the cross around 9:00 am and breathed his last shortly after 3:00 pm. It makes sense, then, that Pilate was surprised that Jesus was dead after a mere six hours on the cross.

What does this tell us about our loving God? The same thing we read over and over in the prophets' message: There will be judgment, but only what is absolutely necessary. God loved the Israelites so much that, even in his anger and disappointment, he could not bear to punish them any longer than he had to. They were in exile only 70 years and then returned to the Promised Land.

And, no, the cup could not pass from innocent Jesus as he took the sins of a guilty world upon himself in one final act of atonement…but the Son of God would not suffer one second longer than was necessary.

And, what about us? Speaking for myself, I have to say this is very good news. My God loves me so much that, yes, he will discipline me when I need it, but only as long as is necessary to accomplish his purpose in my life. Hallelujah? Hallelujah!

Chapter 16 begins with a very brief account of the women finding an angel at the empty tomb on Sunday. The book originally concluded with a statement about the women's fear to tell anyone what they had seen (16:8). Most Biblical scholars believe that Mark 16:9-19 was added by a second century editor to complete the story. The final verses add consistency with the narratives found in Matthew, Luke, and John.

We conclude Day Seven after reading just two of the gospels. If you are unfamiliar with the story of Jesus, you may be wondering—what more could there be? Get ready for Day Eight—our feast has just begun!

REFLECTING FORWARD

Use these questions to discuss what you've learned and think about what comes next, keeping in mind the context of the Old Testament and projecting forward to the remainder of the New Testament.

1. It has been said that Jesus was a "different kind of messiah"—not what the Jewish people expected. They thought the Messiah would be someone like King David, who militarily restored the nation of Israel to its place of power in the world. Jesus surprised them. How has Jesus surprised you in your life? How has he been a "different kind of savior" to you?

2. All three synoptic gospels record Jesus' temptation in the wilderness following his baptism. Satan tempts Jesus with food, wealth, and power. What evidence do you see of these temptations in our world today? How about in your own life? Read Jesus' responses to Satan in Matthew 4:1-11. How do you respond to temptation?

3. Compare the Ten Commandments found in Exodus 20 to the Beatitudes found in Matthew 5:3-12. Which are easier for you to follow? Which do you struggle with the most? Where do you turn for help?

4. Review the *ScriptureScope* on page 166 and think back. If you were to map out your life, can you see crossroads—decision points— where you chose the broad way, the way of the world? How about times you took the narrow road, God's road? What differences do you see in your life based on those choices?

5. We have said that Jesus introduced an "upside-down kingdom", where the first would be last and the last would be first—a kingdom that was counter-cultural and not accepted by those in power. The church of Jesus Christ—the 21st century community of Christians— is called to be counter-cultural as well. What does that look like in your life? In what ways are you living out an "upside-down kingdom? How does your faith separate you from the world?

6. In our study of the Old Testament, we talked about God's character and what we learned about God through those 39 books. (Review Exodus 34:6 as an example.) Jesus is God incarnate, living among us, showing us what God is really like. How are Jesus and the God we met in the OT alike? Do they seem different in some ways? When you think of God, do you see the God of the Old Testament or do you see Jesus?

7. Review the Christ's Life and Ministry table on page 268. What questions do you have as we continue our study of the four gospels? What are you looking forward to in Day Eight?

DAY EIGHT

LUKE, JOHN, ACTS

Our reading today will complete the five books of historical narrative found in the New Testament. We begin first with the third synoptic gospel, Luke. Then we will explore John's gospel. In both books we will find events and teachings not found in Matthew or Mark that further help us understand why Jesus came and what his mission was. Finally, we will find out what happened *after* Jesus in the Acts of the Apostles, or more commonly, just Acts.

LUKE 1 – 9
MORE OF THE STORY

Elizabeth and Zechariah

Gabriel

Mary and Joseph

Angel's Announcement

Upside-down Nativity

Jesus in His Father's House

Jesus at the Synagogue

Luke, a doctor and scholar, was not an eye-witness to Jesus' life on earth. Unlike Matthew, John, and possibly Mark, Luke could not write anything about Jesus based on memory. Instead, Luke tells the reader up front that he has written what we might call a "research paper" on Jesus. He has visited with eye witnesses and verified the oral tradition that has been passed along to him.

We might, in the 21st century, consider this to be a "vetting" of Jesus. Can his story be believed? Are his teachings trustworthy? Was he really the Son of God? Did he really rise from the dead after a very public execution and burial?

Luke's gospel is unique in that it is addressed to a specific name. Luke's audience, Theophilus, is believed by some scholars to be a Roman official who has become a believer. Others have asserted that Theophilus was a well-known Jew from Alexandria. The word "Theophilus" means in the Greek "friend of God" or "loved by God", which some take to mean that there was no person named Theophilus. Rather, Luke's gospel is directed to anyone and everyone who fits that description.

Whatever the meaning, the result of Luke's research is the longest of the four gospels. It is written in the tradition of the synoptic gospels of Matthew and Mark but with additional information, much of which may have come from another ancient source known simply as Q. In these first chapters, the added information serves to provide background and context to the events of Matthew and Mark, hence the subtitle for this section, "More of the Story."

Luke begins earlier than either Matthew or Mark, with the story of John the Baptist's parents, Elizabeth and Zechariah. We learn that Zechariah and Elizabeth are Levites, that Zechariah serves as a priest, and Elizabeth is barren. Remember Sarai, Rachel, and Hannah (Samuel's mother)? In the Bible, a woman's inability to conceive provides an avenue for God to be glorified through a "miraculous" birth.

Zechariah is doing his priestly duties one day when the angel Gabriel appears and tells him that Elizabeth will have a son and they are to name him John. He will precede Jesus and announce the coming kingdom, as was foretold in Isaiah 40. Zechariah wonders how this can happen and reminds Gabriel that he and Elizabeth are old. An indignant Gabriel reminds him that he, Gabriel, is God's messenger and then promptly seals Zechariah's mouth shut until the baby is born.

When Elizabeth is about six months pregnant, Gabriel shows up again, this time to a young Jewish girl named Mary. He announces to her that she will have a child, even though she is a virgin and betrothed to Joseph. Mary wonders how this will be and asks Gabriel the same question Zechariah did. Based on Gabriel's response, apparently she did it in a gentler way. (Or maybe Gabriel attended Angel Anger Management classes after the Zechariah incident?) Whatever the reason, this time he patiently explains that the Holy Spirit will descend on her, and she will bear God's Son. She will name him Jesus. Mary is pleased to be the Lord's servant. Everything happens just as Gabriel said, and Mary becomes pregnant.

Mary is a relative of Elizabeth and goes to visit her. Elizabeth's baby jumps in her womb when she sees Mary, and Elizabeth identifies her as "the mother of my Lord." Mary sings a song of praise and obedience to God's plan for her. Elizabeth gives birth to her baby, and Zechariah passes her a note to name him John. Immediately he can speak again. Chapter 1 ends with Zechariah's song of praise.

The second chapter of Luke provides the traditional Christmas story most often read in churches and homes on Christmas Eve—and even in public schools back when I was growing up. Luke dates the story of Jesus' birth by placing it during the reigns of Caesar Augustus and Quirinius of Syria. Joseph and Mary must go to Bethlehem to register for taxation. Mary is very pregnant and gives birth while they are there staying in a stable (or possibly a cave) due to the crowded conditions in town. To the casual observer, it is an unimportant event, ordinary in every way. Not hardly! See the *ScriptureScope* for what happens next.

THE STIRRING

In Luke 2: 8, 10, 13-14 KJV we read: *And there were in the same country shepherds abiding in the fields, keeping watch over their flocks by night. And the angel said unto them, "Fear not: for behold, I bring*

*you good tidings of great joy which shall be to all people. For unto you
is born this day in the City of David a Savior which is Christ the Lord."
And suddenly, there was with the angel a multitude of the heavenly host,
praising God and saying: "Glory to God in the highest and on earth
peace, good will toward men."*

On this far from ordinary night, the heavens opened, and God's angelic
choir sang to…shepherds.   And note that in this—Jesus' birth
announcement—he is not described as a teacher, or healer, or prophet, or
even a great role model. He is given the name "Savior", making his
mission perfectly clear.

The shepherds go to find the baby in Bethlehem and worship Jesus in the
stable. No doubt you've seen a nativity scene or two in your lifetime.
Typically, they include Mary, Joseph, Jesus, an angel or two, some
animals, the shepherds, and the wise men we read about in Matthew.
Biblical historians are fairly certain that the magi were not actually there
on that first night, but that's the way nativities are typically depicted.
And, while they may not be historically correct, they are a perfect visual
representation of the "upside down kingdom" Jesus brings.

Think about it: Jesus' birth was not announced to kings or rulers or even
the magi. It was announced in glorious fashion to shepherds, a low rung
on the first century social ladder. The magi, in fact, had to find the baby
by following a star and stopping to ask for directions. Still, they all
ended up there together, on their knees in worship and in wonderment at
the star—and, indeed, the stir—this tiny king had brought to their very
different worlds.

What does this say about who Jesus came to save?

Luke's chapter 2 includes more information about Jesus' early life.
As good Jewish parents, Mary and Joseph take him as a baby to be
dedicated at the temple. He is acclaimed the Messiah there, even as an
infant.

The action moves forward to Jesus at the age of 12, when he is
accidentally left behind by his parents in Jerusalem after Passover.

When they find him three days later—notice the three-day symbolism—he is sitting with the temple teachers, listening and asking questions. When questioned by Mary, he responds that she should have known he *"would be in my Father's house."* In Luke 2:52, we read: *And Jesus grew in wisdom and stature, and in favor with God and men.* Connection: We read the same description of Samuel in 1 Samuel 2:26.

Chapter 3 presents the baptism of Jesus by John the Baptist, followed by Luke's genealogy of Jesus. If you recall, Matthew's genealogy connected Jesus back to Abraham, as was fitting for Matthew's Jewish audience. Luke connects Jesus all the way back to Adam and therefore to his place as the Son of God and a savior for all people.

Chapter 4 presents the temptation of Jesus, then follows it with a story of Jesus returning to his home synagogue in Nazareth to read the scriptures. He stands and reads Isaiah 61: 1, 2, a scripture we discussed in Day Five: *"The Spirit of the Lord is upon me, because he has anointed me to preach good news to the poor. He has sent me to proclaim freedom for the prisoner and recovery of sight for the blind, to release the oppressed, to proclaim the year of the Lord's favor."*

Then he folds up the scroll, returns it to its place, sits down and adds: *"Today this scripture is fulfilled in your hearing"* (Luke 4:21). What a dramatic moment! Can't you imagine the hushed whispers? *Isn't this Joseph the carpenter's son?* Jesus responds by chastising them for rejecting a prophet in his hometown. Ultimately, they run him out of Nazareth, but the message is clear: Jesus' ministry has begun.

Chapters 5 through 9 include many of the same events found in Matthew and Mark, with some notable exceptions. For some insight into Jesus' compassionate heart, read the story of the raising of the Nain widow's son in Luke 7:11 – 17.

LUKE 10 – 18
PARABLES AND WARNINGS

The Good Samaritan

Ask and Receive

The Prodigal Son

The Pharisee and the Tax Collector

This section of Luke contains many parables and teachings of Jesus found only in Luke. In fact, some of these are perhaps the most familiar of his words, common to both the sacred and secular communities. For example, in Luke 10:25 -37, Jesus is questioned by a lawyer in the crowd about what he must do to obtain eternal life. As Jesus so often did, he answered the man with another question, *"What is written in the law?"*

The man responded by reciting the same verses Matthew reports Jesus quoting as the Great Commandment (Day Seven). He cites Deuteronomy 6:5 (*Love the Lord your God with all your heart and with all your soul and with all your strength and with all your mind*) and Leviticus 19:18 (*Love your neighbor as yourself.*) Jesus told him that he was correct and added *"Do this and you will live."*

The lawyer pushed, however, and asked then: *And who is my neighbor?*

Well, that's all it took. Jesus launched into a story of a man who was robbed on the road to Jericho. Three people passed by: A priest moved over to the other side of the road so as not to become unclean. A Levite did the same. But a Samaritan—a descendant of Samaria, the capital of the northern kingdom of Israel, detested by the people of Judah to the south—bandaged him and even paid for lodging and care for him.

Jesus finished by asking the lawyer which one he thought was a good neighbor. Thus, the parable of the Good Samaritan has become the epitome of unexpected mercy and undeserved grace, just as Esau offered Jacob way back in Genesis.

In chapter 11, Jesus continues this theme of grace with a parable about a friend who needs bread in the night. See the *ScriptureScope* below for the lesson.

THE OPEN DOOR

In Luke 11:9-10 CEB we read Jesus' words: *"And I tell you: Ask and you will receive. Seek and you will find. Knock and the door will be opened to you. Everyone who asks, receives. Whoever seeks, finds. To everyone who knocks, the door is opened."*

There are many amazing things about Jesus and his story as recorded in the Gospels. But what separates Jesus' story from every other story of a god, a prophet, or a king is found in two words in this passage: *Everyone. Whoever.*

What Jesus offers is unqualified and unconditional. No expiration date, no shelf life. It's not *transactional*—you do something for me and I'll do this for you—but *transformational*. This open door is available nowhere else, from no other religion, no other god, no other prophet, no other king.

Think back again to Luke 2:10—the angel's announcement. The messengers to the shepherds made it clear: This child is your *Savior*.

C.S. Lewis, an atheist intellectual turned Christian intellectual gave a series of radio speeches during the dark days of World War II to the people of Britain. In his effort to explain "Mere Christianity", he boldly stated that Jesus did not leave the option of considering him just a great human teacher open to us.

What he did leave open is the opportunity to accept his love, his grace, his salvation. Indeed, to accept *his* acceptance of *you*, however and whoever you may be—to knock on that door that is waiting for you.

In chapter 15 of Luke we find another of Jesus' most familiar parables. In fact, chapter 15 contains three parables, all with the same message. We've already encountered one in Matthew and Mark, that of the lost sheep. The shepherd leaves the 99 sheep that are safe to search for and bring home the one who is lost. We are reminded of the good shepherd imagery from the Psalms and from Ezekiel.

Here in Luke 15 we also find parables of the lost coin and the lost, or prodigal, son. When the son who left home and lost his inheritance returns to his waiting father, he is greeted with open arms. The father kills the fatted calf, puts a robe and ring on his son, and calls for a celebration. The child who was lost has been found!

Perhaps the greatest visual image of this story is Rembrandt's painting, *The Return of the Prodigal Son*. It hangs in a far corner of the Hermitage Museum in St. Petersburg, almost begging you to make a special trip to find it and then to linger before you move on. The light of the father's love speaks clearly of God's love for his children and his unending wait for the lost ones' return. If a trip to Russia is not on your bucket list, look for it online. It won't be quite the same, but you can linger as long as you would like.

Jesus also gives warnings in this section about the challenges of being his disciple, about being ready for his return—like a faithful servant awaiting his master—and about the dangers of spiritual pride. In Luke 18:9-14 Jesus compares the prayer of the boastful Pharisee thanking God that he is better than everyone else with that of the lowly tax collector quietly asking God's mercy on him, a sinner. In verse 14, Jesus reminds his listeners of the revolutionary nature of his kingdom: *"All who lift themselves up will be brought low, and those who make themselves low will be lifted up."*

LUKE 19 – 24
HOLY WEEK AND ASCENSION

Herod Antipas

Words from the Cross

Called to be Witnesses

Ascension

Kingdom Life

The scriptures found in Luke 19:29 through Luke 24:12 present the synoptic narrative of Holy Week with some additional details. One new piece that is included here is Jesus' additional trial before Herod Antipas, the Roman-appointed tetrarch (ruler) of Galilee. (Note: This is not the Herod who was living when Jesus was born. You may remember that it was his death that prompted Mary, Joseph, and Jesus to return from Egypt to Nazareth. This is one of his sons, and it is the same Herod who imprisoned and then beheaded John the Baptist.)

After a brief encounter, Antipas returns Jesus to Pilate, and the trial and sentencing continue as found in Matthew and Mark. In the crucifixion narrative, Luke gives more attention to Jesus' words from the cross.

Both Matthew (27:48) and Mark (15:34) report Jesus quoting Psalm 22:1 *("My God, my God, why have you forsaken me?")* around 3:00. Luke 23:34 adds that soon after being nailed to the tree Jesus forgives his executioners, saying, *"Father, forgive them, for they do not know what they are doing."* Later, when one of the thieves being crucified with him asks to be remembered in his kingdom, Jesus replies, *"I tell you the truth, today you will be with me in paradise."* Then, at the time of his death, Luke 23:46 reads: *Jesus called out with a loud voice, "Father, into your hands I commit my spirit." When he had said this, he breathed his last.* We will see that John adds even more words of Jesus from the cross.

In Luke's gospel, after the women discover the empty tomb on Sunday morning they return to tell the others. Peter runs to the tomb himself to see. Then, Luke reports several appearances of Jesus after his resurrection. First, the risen Jesus explains the week's events to two men walking on the road to Emmaus.

Later, he appears to the disciples and tells him they are his witnesses to the world (Luke 24:48). Note the use of the word "witnesses"—not attorney, judge, or jury. They—and we, as Christ-followers today—are not called to convince, convict, judge, or sentence anyone. We are called to do what witnesses do—tell what we have seen, what we have experienced, and what we know to be true.

Jesus also tells them that they are to stay in Jerusalem until they *"have been clothed with power from on high."* We will see just what Jesus means in the book of Acts.

In the last verses of Luke, we read that Jesus *"left them and was taken up into heaven."* More attention is given to this event, the Ascension, in Acts. Nevertheless, it is important to note that even though this is mentioned briefly here, Jesus' ascension into heaven is critical to understanding the uniqueness of Jesus' resurrection.

As you may remember, the great OT prophets Elijah and Elisha both brought people back to life after they had died. Jesus did the same on many occasions. In Acts we will read of the apostles doing this as well.

So, what makes Jesus' resurrection unique?

It's just this: In each of these other cases, the person brought back to life will ultimately die again. Their life on earth has been extended but sooner or later their bodies will give out and they will die a physical death.

When Jesus ascended into heaven, he ascended to live forever there. He will never die—his resurrection from the dead to eternal life is just that—eternal. And ascending into heaven as a living being is evidence of that. Jesus' ascension into heaven is also evidence that the "living" Jesus is Lord over all creation, now and forever.

This is the "kingdom life"—now and eternally—that Jesus offers all who believe in him. It's not an easy concept to understand, but fortunately we have some great books of NT wisdom to help us as we will see in Days Nine and Ten.

JOHN 1 – 12
JESUS, THE SON OF GOD

John's gospel, the gospel least like the other three, is also perhaps the best loved. It presents events of Jesus' life and aspects of his character that are emphasized less—or not mentioned at all—in Matthew, Mark, and Luke.

Jesus, the Word

Simon to Peter

Wedding in Cana

Nicodemus

Born Again

John 3:16

Woman at the Well

I AM

Raising of Lazarus

John's gospel was written to convince all people not just to believe in the fully human Jesus but to believe specifically in his divine nature, his oneness with God as his Son. John takes us back to where we began in Genesis 1:26 when God says: "Let us make man in *our* image to resemble *us*…"

John incorporates the Greek belief in logos—literally "word"—as he describes Jesus, attempting to connect with readers in the Greco-Roman world. John 1:1-18 presents a prologue to the gospel and begins dramatically with John 1:1: *In the beginning was the Word, and the Word was with God, and the Word was God.* Where have we read the phrase "in the beginning" before? In Genesis, of course, as God created the world. John begins his gospel by connecting Jesus—the Word—with God and even says that he was with God as God created, in the beginning. (Connect to our first *ScriptureScope* on Genesis 1:26.)

Like Mark, John presents no birth narrative or genealogy for Jesus, but moves straight from the prologue into the baptism of Jesus by John the Baptist. John the Baptist's testimony is given great importance, indicating his belief in Jesus as the Son of God, the Messiah, the Christ. In John 1:36 we read: *When he [John the Baptist] saw Jesus walking along he said, "Look! The Lamb of God!"*

Why would John use this metaphor for Jesus? Remember the Passover lamb, whose blood shielded the Israelite children from death the night before they left Egypt. And recall the lambs sacrificed as sin and guilt offerings in the laws of the old covenant. The gospel writer uses John the Baptist's exclamation to further his purpose of proclaiming Jesus as the Savior of the world.

The remainder of the first chapter of John focuses on the calling of Jesus' first disciples. In John's version, some of the disciples immediately believe they have found the Messiah, presumably because of John the Baptist's testimony as he baptized Jesus. When Jesus first meets Peter in John 1:42, he changes his name from Simon to Cephas (Peter), which means "rock". Although Peter is far from transformed at this point, this name-changing foreshadows what Jesus already knows about Peter's role in the early church.

If you take a look at the Christ's Life and Ministry table on page 268, you will see that after the baptism and the temptation, John reports several incidents most scholars think occurred before the Galilean ministry reported in the synoptics. If this is correct, Jesus' first "official" miracle occurred at a wedding in Cana. He saves the wedding host from embarrassment when, at his mother Mary's request, Jesus turns several large jugs of water into wine (better than the brand the host had run out of). This, of course, means that his ministry has officially begun, as no ordinary carpenter's son can do that!

In chapter 2 we also see Jesus attending Passover in Jerusalem much earlier in his ministry than the synoptics report. During this Passover Jesus also encounters a member of the Jewish ruling council, perhaps a Pharisee, by the name of Nicodemus. Nicodemus comes to him by night with questions, curious but careful not to be seen by his colleagues from the Temple. He greets Jesus with respect, but Jesus quickly turns the focus on his visitor's own salvation, saying in John 3:3: *"I tell you the truth, no one can see the kingdom of God unless he is born again."*

Later in the same conversation, Jesus explains it again in perhaps the most familiar verse from the New Testament, John 3:16-17: *"For God so loved the world that he gave his one and only Son, that whoever believes in him shall not perish but have eternal life. For God did not send his Son into the world to condemn the world, but to save the world through him."*

Jesus returns to Galilee from Passover by way of Samaria—a very unusual thing for a Jewish teacher to do, as we have already seen from the parable of the Good Samaritan in Luke 10. There he stops for water at one of the wells dug by Jacob centuries earlier and meets a Samaritan woman. He offers her "living water" of salvation, and she returns to her village to tell everyone she has met the Messiah. Thus, in this upside-down, revolutionary kingdom that Jesus brings, a Samaritan woman becomes one of the first missionaries!

In chapters 5 through 8 we read many familiar stories, but important additions as well. In chapter 6, Jesus begins to explain himself through a prolonged series of analogies that continues through chapter 15. Each analogy begins with "I am", connecting back to God's name for himself in Exodus—I AM. Jesus says that he is: the bread of the world; the light of the world; the gate for the sheep; the good shepherd; the resurrection and the life; the way, the truth, and the life; and, the vine supporting the branches. In chapter 9 Jesus heals a man who was blind from birth, leading Jesus to compare physical blindness to the spiritual blindness of the Pharisees (9:39-41).

In chapter 11, Jesus raises his friend Lazarus who has been dead for four days. It is here that is recorded what has traditionally been considered the shortest verse in the Bible: John 11:35 *Jesus wept.*

(Of course, it all depends on the translation. In the newer Common English Bible (CEB) the verse is translated *Jesus began to cry,* which confounds the issue. A further complication comes when you consider the original Greek, as a friend attending one of our cruise studies pointed out. But, I digress. By the way, do you remember where we found the longest verse in the Bible? Right, the little book of Esther.)

Back to Lazarus. Before Jesus calls him to come out of the tomb, he prays to his Father, giving the glory to him. This not only glorifies God, but also reinforces the Father/Son connection so prominent in John's gospel. Jesus also brings some negative attention upon himself by alarming the temple leaders. After the raising of Lazarus, they begin to plot a way to rid themselves of the teacher from Galilee.

Chapter 12 begins the Holy Week narrative, with Jesus's triumphal entry into Jerusalem. The chapter concludes with Jesus providing a summary of his teachings and connecting himself again to God as his Son. In John 12:44 – 50 CEB we read:

Jesus shouted, "Whoever believes in me doesn't believe in me but in the one who sent me. Whoever sees me sees the one who sent me. I have come as a light into the world so that everyone who believes in me won't live in darkness. If people hear my words and don't keep them, I don't judge them. I didn't come to judge the world but to save it. Whoever rejects me and doesn't receive my words will be judged at the last day by the word I have spoken. I don't speak on my own, but the Father who sent me commanded me regarding what I should speak and say. I know that his commandment is eternal life. Therefore, whatever I say is just as the Father has said to me."

JOHN 13 – 21
THE HOLY SPIRIT

In these chapters we find perhaps the most striking differences between John's

Foot Washing

A New Commandment

A Promised Comforter

Women at the Cross

Breakfast in Galilee

Peter, the Rock

gospel and the other three. The backdrop is Holy Week, specifically the Last Supper, Garden of Gethsemane, arrest and trial, crucifixion, and resurrection—just as in Matthew, Mark, and Luke. The difference is not in the action, but in the discourse and relationships that emerge from the action.

Chapters 13 through 17 are excellent examples of this difference. Chapter 13 presents Jesus' last meal with his disciples in the upper room, but it begins with Jesus humbling himself to wash his disciples' feet. Through this act, Jesus teaches the disciples about pride, humility, and serving others and reminds them that the first will be last and the last will be first.

After the sharing of the meal (with none of the "bread and wine, new covenant" language found in the synoptics), Jesus sends Judas to do what he has to do. Then, Jesus begins to teach again. The reader gets the sense that Jesus knows his time is short, and he must make the most of what remains with his disciples. After all, as we will see in Acts, these are the men who will take Jesus' message to the world.

In John 13:34-35, Jesus teaches: *"A new command I give you: Love one another. As I have loved you, so you must love one another. By this all men will know that you are my disciples, if you love one another."* Shortly afterward, Jesus comforts them as they struggle to understand what is about to happen. John 14:1-4: *"Do not let your hearts be troubled. Trust in God; trust also in me. In my Father's house are many rooms; if it were not so, I would have told you. I am going there to prepare a place for you. And if I go and prepare a place for you, I will come back and take you to be with me that you also may be where I am. You know the way to the place where I am going."*

Later in chapter 14, Jesus promises to send the Holy Spirit (also called the Comforter or Companion or the Greek "Paraclete") as a Spirit of Truth to be with them when he has returned to his Father. The Holy Spirit will be a guide to them and a holy presence in their lives. In chapter 15 he concludes his "I am" analogies with a beautiful explanation of his role as the vine, his followers as the branches, and God the Father as the gardener. In chapter 16 he explains the work of the Holy Spirit and encourages the disciples that while they will experience grief, ultimately they will know joy.

In chapter 17, Jesus prays to the Father for himself, then his disciples, and finally all believers. This beautiful prayer offers a different insight into Jesus' heart and mind immediately prior to his arrest. Compare it to the picture presented in the synoptics of Jesus' anguished prayers in the garden.

Chapters 18 and 19 present the arrest, trial, crucifixion, and resurrection narratives. One obvious difference is the role of Nicodemus, Jesus' earlier night visitor. John reports that he protests the actions of the Sanhedrin and also assists Joseph of Arimathea in burying Jesus.

As noted earlier, John includes more words of Jesus on the cross. John mentions specifically that Jesus' mother Mary, his aunt Mary, and Mary Magdalene, one of his followers, remain near the cross during the crucifixion. He reports that Jesus speaks to "the disciple he loved" who is with them (presumably John himself) and asks him to care for his mother. Later, John records Jesus saying, *"I am thirsty"* and finally, *"It is finished."*

Note that none of the other disciples are mentioned here or in any of the gospels as witnessing the crucifixion. In each gospel, however, the writer reports that some women followers were there watching from a distance.

Chapter 21 serves as an Epilogue in John, just as much of the first chapter is a Prologue. Here, Jesus appears to the disciples at the Sea of Galilee after his resurrection, before the Ascension into heaven described at the end of Luke. Early in the morning, the disciples are fishing, just as they were when Jesus called them three years earlier but catching nothing. Jesus calls to them from the shore to try the other side of the boat. They do not recognize him until the nets are miraculously filled. Then they share breakfast on the beach.

Here Jesus calls Peter to be the foundation—the rock—of the new church that will emerge from Jesus' followers. Jesus asks Peter three times if he loves him, and Peter repeatedly professes his love for his Lord. We are reminded of the three times during Jesus' trial that Peter denied he even knew Jesus. It is fitting that the last thing John wants us to remember about Jesus is his gift of grace to Peter.

ACTS OF THE APOSTLES 1 – 15
THE EARLY CHURCH

We learn quickly as we read this last of the history narratives of the New

Luke's Second Book

Holy Spirit and Pentecost

Fellowship of Believers

Stoning of Stephen

The Church Scattered

Saul Encounters Jesus

Gentiles in the Church

Jerusalem Council

Testament, that this is a second book by Luke. It is also addressed to Theophilus and begins essentially where Luke's gospel leaves off. The disciples wait in Jerusalem as Jesus directed them.

In chapter 2, the promised Holy Spirit (Comforter, Companion) comes upon all believers during the Feast of Pentecost, around AD 30. The three Persons of the Trinity—God, Jesus, and Holy Spirit—have now been introduced into the story. Peter emerges as the leader of the believers and preaches his first sermon—yes, impetuous rough-hewn fisherman Peter. And, he begins in Acts 2:17-18 by quoting the minor prophet Joel we discussed in Day Six: *In the last days, God says, I will pour out my Spirit on all people. Your sons and daughters will prophesy. Your young will see visions. Your elders will dream dreams.*

Peter's impassioned preaching leads to thousands believing in Jesus as the Christ, but—no surprise—this does not set well with the chief priests and Pharisees. In chapter 3, Peter and John heal a well-known crippled man at the Temple gate and promptly find themselves arrested. They must defend themselves before the Sanhedrin. See the *ScriptureScope* below for the Sanhedrin's reaction to the disciples' testimony.

ONLY JESUS

In Acts 4:13 we read: *When they saw the courage of Peter and John and realized that they were unschooled, ordinary men, they were astonished and they took note that these men had been with Jesus.*

Peter and John took their roles as witnesses very seriously. In fact, as we will learn, the remainder of the New Testament is about men and women who took their witness responsibility seriously.

Here, as the two apostles have been brought before the Sanhedrin—an institution built on 'religion', but very much 'of the world'—they speak boldly of Jesus. In fact, they do not stop speaking of him despite threats of danger to themselves.

Peter and John.... who went to seminary where? Who had Ph.D.'s from where? Who studied with whom, were ordained by whom?

Only Jesus.

Peter and John were just two fishermen or, as the chief priests noted, "unschooled, ordinary men"—like you and me. But they were ordained by God through Jesus and took that ordination very seriously, even when facing the powerful Sanhedrin.

Let us seek that ordination, that courage, that commitment to serve Jesus. Let us follow the example of these two unschooled but far from ordinary men, proclaiming the witness of how Jesus has worked in our lives.

These first chapters of Acts also give us a description of the very early days of the church. We learn that this fellowship of believers meets in homes, prays, and listens to the apostles' teaching. They celebrate the new covenant through communion and share all their possessions. Like the church today, there are challenges, conflicts, and celebrations.

It's important to remember that at this point Jesus' followers are not a new religion—Christianity as we think of it does not yet exist. Rather they are a Jewish sect, specifically those Jews who believe that Jesus of Nazareth was indeed the Christ, the promised Messiah. At this point, any persecution Jesus' followers are experiencing is coming not from the Romans, but from fellow Jews who do not believe in Jesus.

This is the case with a follower of Jesus, Stephen, whose story we find in chapters 6 and 7. He is accused of blasphemy and brought before the Sanhedrin. In chapter 7, Stephen preaches a beautiful sermon that retells the story of the Israelites' rejection of God in the wilderness as a comparison to the Jews' rejection of Jesus. This is all the Sanhedrin can stand. They stone Stephen, while one of the greatest advocates for persecuting Christians, Saul of Tarsus, looks on with approval.

The stoning of the first Christian martyr, Stephen, is a tragedy, but Stephen will serve as an inspiration to Christian martyrs through the ages. This event also leads many from the fellowship of believers to flee Jerusalem to avoid persecution themselves. This scattering of Christ-followers outside of Jerusalem creates an opportunity for the apostles to obey Jesus' command at his Ascension to "be my witnesses". The result? Churches emerge throughout the Roman world.

In chapter 9 we again encounter Saul, who is continuing his violent persecution toward followers of the Way, the name given to the Jesus movement among Jews. Biblical historians tell us that Saul is a well-educated Jew, a self-proclaimed Pharisee, and also a Roman citizen. (This distinction will be especially important later in his story.) Saul's background tells him that believing in this Jesus of Nazareth as the Son of God is blasphemy. He is committed to putting an end to "the Way" through any means possible.

As Saul travels to Damascus (AD 33-35) to arrest Christ-followers there, he encounters the risen Christ himself. Jesus appears to him as a blaze of light, asks Saul why he is persecuting him, and sends Saul into Damascus to await further direction. Blinded by the light, Saul does as Jesus commands and when his blindness is relieved three days later (again, the symbolism) he is a changed man. He will now invest his energy and zeal in spreading the gospel throughout the Mediterranean region.

Chapters 10 through 12 focus primarily on Peter's missionary efforts, including healings, imprisonment, and a vision from God. The vision enables Peter to understand that Jesus came not only for the Jews, but the Gentiles as well. This understanding is key to the rest of the book of Acts, as the original apostles and newer followers such as Saul, Barnabas, Timothy, and Silas direct their evangelism less toward Jews and more toward Gentiles. As a result, Christianity emerges as a new religion, rather than a sect of Judaism. In fact, in Acts 11:26 we read: *The disciples were called Christians first in Antioch.*

In chapter 13 the church at Antioch sends Barnabas and Saul on their first missionary journey. This would be a good time to refer to the Paul's Ministry table on page 271. Based on this chronology, Paul's journeys were made, and letters were written between AD 35 and AD 67. As always, keep in mind that the dates provided are the thoughts of one scholar or group of scholars. They are not based on irrefutable evidence and are certainly up for debate. But, they do allow us to consider one possible chronology of Paul's ministry.

We learn in Acts 13:5 that "John" is with them also. You will see on the table that he is referred to as John Mark—yes, probably the "Mark" of the Gospels. A few verses later we see that Saul is now referred to as Paul. Remember the significance of name-changing in the Bible? In the Old Testament, Abram became Abraham, Sarai became Sarah, and Jacob became Israel. In the Gospels we read of Jesus changing Peter's name from Simon to Peter. In each case, the name-changing indicates a transformation, a new commitment to serve God. The same is true with Paul.

This section concludes in chapter 15 with the first church council (there will be many more!) held in Jerusalem around 49 AD. The council is called to address issues related to Gentiles becoming part of the Christian fellowship. Just as in the church today, there are differences of opinion. In this case the question is whether these new "Christians" should be required to follow all the laws of the old covenant, including circumcision. (You can imagine that requiring circumcision before Gentiles could be baptized might decrease the number of potential converts!)

Ultimately the issue is resolved (no circumcision) as the apostles work to understand the place of their Jewish traditions in this new covenant. Through this process we see the leadership of Peter, as expected, but also James, the half-brother of Jesus. As Peter has been gone on missionary journeys, James has become the leader of the church in Jerusalem.

ACTS 16 – 28
PAUL'S MISSIONARY JOURNEYS

Paul and Silas

Areopagus in Athens

Riots in Ephesus

To Jerusalem

Rights of a Roman Citizen

Shipwrecked on Malta

House Arrest in Rome

The remainder of Acts focuses almost exclusively on Paul and his missionary journeys. Following his path through the narrative of Acts helps to put his letters that we will read in Day Nine in context. Again, consider the Paul's Ministry table for one possible chronology.

Barnabas and John Mark have now separated from Paul, who is traveling with Silas. In Acts 16:10 an interesting change in the writing of Acts occurs. No longer is the action being reported in third person, but in first person. This can only mean that Luke is traveling with Paul at this point, as are many others.

Often throughout these chapters, we read of Christ-followers being imprisoned or persecuted. God uses men and women as well as angels and earthquakes to, literally, keep the gospel alive. The *ScriptureScope* below details one such incident.

SOMETHING DIFFERENT

In Acts 16:25-30 we read: *About midnight Paul and Silas were praying and singing hymns to God, and the other prisoners were listening to them. Suddenly there was such a violent earthquake that the foundations of the prison were shaken. At once all the prison doors flew open, and everybody's chains came loose. The jailer woke up, and when he saw the prison doors open, he drew his sword and was about to kill himself because he thought the prisoners had escaped. But Paul shouted, "Don't harm yourself! We are all here!" The jailer called for the lights, rushed in and fell trembling before Paul and Silas. He then brought them out and asked, "Sirs, what must I do to be saved?"*

Here, we find Paul in a familiar place—prison. Sometimes he is beaten before he is sent to prison; other times, he goes directly to jail. In this case he and Silas had been 'severely flogged' prior to being locked up. In spite of their bleeding, cut, and bruised bodies, they were still praying and singing to God late into the night. The jailer could certainly hear them as well as the other prisoners.

God sends an earthquake which opens up the jail. The jailer knows that if they escape he will be executed. Fearing the worst, he starts to take his own life. Amazingly, Paul says "Whoa! You don't need to do that. We haven't gone anywhere." The jailer can't believe it. The prisoners did not escape when they had the opportunity to? Even after being beaten nearly to death?

Surely there is something different about these men.

The question for us is: Are we that different? Would our faith in God and our actions be so different from those of the world that someone would take notice? They better be, because people are watching—our children, our grandchildren, the checker at the supermarket, the greeter at Walmart, the neighbor who needs our help. People are looking to see if Christianity makes a difference in our lives.

We might remember the directive often attributed to St. Francis of Assisi, the namesake of Pope Francis: Preach the gospel every day, and if you have to, use some words.

Paul's missionary journeys continue. In each new city or town, he always goes first to preach in the Jewish synagogue. The apostles, including Paul, still consider themselves Jews. To them, Jesus is the Christ—the Messiah—the long-awaited hope of the Jewish people. They do not think of the Way as a new religion, but rather a fulfillment of God's promises to the people of Israel.

Nevertheless, as Paul is rejected in synagogues, his ministry shifts to the Gentiles. In chapters 16 through 20, Paul spends time in many of the places he later writes to in his letters: Philippi, Corinth, Galatia, Thessalonica, and Ephesus. He also debates with the philosophers in Athens on the Areopagus, a large rock that served as the court of appeals in ancient Athens. If you ever visit the Acropolis, you can climb it and stand where Paul stood.

Paul continues to encounter problems. In chapter 19, for example, he causes a riot in Ephesus when the local craftsmen see this new Jesus movement as a threat to the economy. If people turn away from their pagan gods in favor of this Jesus, who will need the statues of the goddess Artemis they are selling the people?

Following this episode, Paul feels led by the Holy Spirit to go to Jerusalem. He makes several stops along the way, one in the ancient seaport of Troas. There, his preaching brings on an unexpected lesson. See the *ScriptureScope* below.

DETERMINED, NOT DISCOURAGED

In Acts 20:7b, 9-11 CEB we read: *Since he [Paul] was leaving the next day, he continued talking until midnight. A young man named Eutychus was sitting in the window. He was sinking into a deep sleep as Paul talked on and on. When he was sound asleep, he fell from the third floor and died. Paul went down, fell on him and embraced him, then said, "Don't be alarmed. He's alive!" Then Paul went back upstairs and ate. He talked for a long time—right up until daybreak—then he left.*

Paul was long-winded. He was leaving Troas the next day. Understandably, he wanted to say as much to the fledgling church there as he could before he left them. So, he's talking late into the night.

Eutychus is sitting in an open window, probably to get the fresh air to help him stay awake. He still drops off, then literally drops off the edge, falls to the ground, and dies. Paul rushes to his aid and raises him from the dead. You might think that an incident such as this would cause the entire gathering to break up.

But not with Paul.

He simply goes back upstairs, takes a quick snack break, and continues talking for five or six more hours. Paul was nothing if not determined. I suspect that God knew this when he chose him—this persecutor of Christ-followers, this self-proclaimed Pharisee—to be his "Man in the Mediterranean." God knew that, if channeled for good and not evil, Paul's dogged determination would serve the cause of the gospel well.

So, what's the word for us here? Not everyone we witness to will stay awake for the whole message. Let us, like Paul, not be discouraged. Let us help where we can, take a quick break to get renewed, and continue our mission!

In chapter 21 Paul arrives in Jerusalem where the Jews (non-Christ-followers) demand that he be arrested for blasphemy. Paul is put in chains until he announces that he is a Roman citizen. This initiates a series of trials (chapters 23 – 26) before the Sanhedrin, the garrison commander, two governors, and the king. Ultimately, Paul plays his "ace card" and claims his right as a Roman citizen to demand a trial before Caesar in Rome.

In chapter 27, Paul and his companions (apparently including Luke) set sail for Rome. They encounter a tremendous storm and are shipwrecked on the island of Malta. After spending the winter months there, they continue to Rome, where Paul is put under house arrest awaiting trial. The writer of Acts concludes by letting us know that Paul continues to preach from his temporary home for at least two more years.

The historical narrative of the New Testament is complete. The gospels presented the story of Jesus as the Son of God, fully divine and fully human. He came as a baby, lived as a teacher, healer, and prophet, and died a fully human and agonizing death on a cross.

Then, after three days in the tomb, Jesus conquered death and lives again. He ascended as a living being to join the Father God in heaven and promises those who believe in him this same divine, eternal life. He then sent the Holy Spirit to comfort, guide, and encourage his followers in his absence.

The Acts of the Apostles told us what his followers did with this "good news", this incredible but true story of love and grace for the world. In Days Nine and Ten we will study the writings of these same followers. And, in Day Ten, we will conclude with a vision of the future of the revolutionary kingdom of Jesus the Christ.

REFLECTING FORWARD

Use these questions to guide your discussion of Day Eight and lead you into Days Nine and Ten.

1. After studying all four gospels, do you have a favorite? Looking back over your faith journey, which one(s) have impacted you most?

2. The gospels are meant to both affirm our own beliefs and lead others to find their salvation in Jesus. Which of the gospels would you recommend to someone seeking God? Which would you suggest for a new believer?

3. Luke 2 gives us the amazing story of Jesus' birth in Bethlehem. I love to think about the angels as they gathered to make the announcement to the lowly shepherds ("Are you sure, Gabriel? Those guys?") And I love to think about the stir his birth caused, as God broke into the world of humans. We know what a stir the birth of a baby causes, right? But this baby…this stir changed everything. How has Jesus' birth in your heart transformed your world? How has it changed who you are, what you value, how you live?

4. Read John 3 and 4. Notice how Jesus explains faith to Nicodemus and how he explains it to the Samaritan woman at the well. Nicodemus is a highly educated Jewish man; the woman is an everyday person, just struggling to get by. What differences do you see in how Jesus explains himself to each one? What does this say about the gospel and how we can help others find Jesus? How does Jesus speak to you?

5. Thinking back on the book of Acts, we see that the first-century church experienced many challenges. Consider what you know of the Christian church today, both from your personal experience and from what you read in the media. How is the 21st century church like the 1st century church? How are they different? What can we learn from the church described in Acts to guide our churches today?

6. Paul was not one of the original twelve disciples. He did not live with Jesus for three years as they did, experience the agony of the crucifixion as they did, or the joy of the resurrection. In fact, he was an enemy of the kingdom that Jesus brought—until he met the risen

Jesus on the Damascus road. How does Paul's experience as a transformed follower of Jesus—one with some baggage from his former life—help you as you try to follow Jesus today?

7. Think of your own life. Did you experience a dramatic conversion experience as Paul did? Have you experienced a dramatic call to ministry, like Moses or the prophets? Or, perhaps, has your experience with Jesus been more subtle, more like a journey one step at a time? How would you describe your faith experience to others?

8. Looking ahead, how might Paul's "baggage" and dramatic conversion experience influence his understanding of Jesus and the gospel? How might these issues impact his preaching and his writing?

DAY NINE

ROMANS, 1 AND 2 CORINTHIANS,

GALATIANS, EPHESIANS, PHILIPPIANS,

COLOSSIANS, 1 AND 2 THESSALONIANS,

1 AND 2 TIMOTHY, TITUS, PHILEMON

Before we move on to the wisdom literature of the New Testament, let's reflect just a moment on the context for these writings. In the NT history books covered in Days Seven and Eight, we learned that God kept his promise to King David that one of his descendants would forever be on the throne of Israel by sending Jesus, the Messiah or Christ. Jesus lived, died, and was resurrected to provide a once-and-forever offering of love and sacrifice for the sins of humanity.

Jesus was God's Son, sent out of God's love for his creation and for the purpose of restoring it to God as in the perfect beginning. God never stopped loving his children, and Jesus' crucifixion and resurrection are evidence of just how much. As one preacher put it: *Jesus did not die on the cross to change God's mind about us. Jesus died on the cross to change our minds about God.*

While he was on earth, Jesus prepared his followers, the twelve apostles, to take on the job of evangelizing the world. We read about their early efforts in the book of Acts, and learned specifically about a new apostle, Paul. As Acts closed, Paul was under house arrest in Rome, no longer able to take the gospel to the churches established throughout the Mediterranean region. We read in the last verses that he continued to "preach and teach" for at least two more years. Based on some of his letters, most scholars believe that he continued to write letters to the churches from his temporary home during that time as well.

These were not the first letters Paul had written. Based on one suggested chronology (see the Paul's Ministry table on page 271), Paul's first letter may have been written as early as AD 50, shortly after the Jerusalem council and at least ten years prior to his imprisonment in

Rome. Paul's thirteen letters make up the majority of the NT wisdom literature.

Paul's letters are grouped in the Bible by their audience. First, we find nine epistles (letters) to various churches. Then, we find three letters to young pastors he is mentoring, Timothy and Titus. The last letter attributed to Paul is the brief epistle to the slave-owner Philemon. They are not presented in chronological order but rather in order of length.

Note that, unlike many books in the Bible, the authorship of Paul's letters appears to be clear to most Biblical scholars. Each one begins with a direct introduction by Paul, indicating that he (along with others in some cases) has written the letter. This serves much like the heading of an email would today—who it is from, who it is to, and a greeting in the subject line. The subject-line greeting is consistently something like: *"Grace and peace to all of you from God our Father and the Lord Jesus Christ."*

Paul is often considered the first Christian theologian after Jesus. A theologian is defined as an expert in the study of God. Through his letters, he analyzed and synthesized the words and teachings of Jesus to arrive at an understanding of *who* Jesus was, *why* he came, *what* he did, and *what it means* for the world. This study of Jesus is known as Christology, and Paul basically invented it. Using his Jewish scholarship and academic training, he applied the same principles of study that he had used in his study of God in the Jewish scriptures to Jesus' life and teachings. Then, he wrote down—or dictated to a scribe—what he had come to understand.

In so doing, Paul gave the Christian community a common language of the new covenant and the kingdom of heaven that Jesus spoke of. Paul also explained the atonement—Jesus' death on the cross as a way to reconcile the world to God. He explained the resurrection and the gift of eternal life Jesus offers because of it. And, he explained how Christ-followers should live individually and in community as a result of this gift.

Paul sometimes seems defensive in his letters, justifying his role as an apostle, almost attempting to compensate for his former life as Saul, the Christ-persecutor. In every letter he is driven and passionate—just as driven and passionate as he was in his life. Throughout, we will see that Paul has a unique writing style, influenced by his Jewish-scholar education, his Roman citizenship, and, most importantly, his dazzling experience with the risen Jesus on the Damascus road.

ROMANS 1 – 16
PAUL'S MASTERPIECE

Adam and Jesus

Slaves to Righteousness

How to Be Saved

How to Live Saved

The first of Paul's letters found in the Bible is Romans, his longest letter. Many Biblical scholars consider it to be Paul's masterpiece. It pulls together many of the themes he touches on in other letters and demonstrates a maturity in his understanding of the gospel.

One indication of the maturity of his writing in Romans is the enhanced greeting. In addition to his standard elements, he summarizes his understanding of Jesus in verses 2 through 6. After the greeting, he begins by expressing his wish to visit Rome. Interesting…I wonder if he found a way to get there by going to Jerusalem—where he knew he would be arrested—and requesting a trial before Caesar!

In chapters 1 through 5, Paul focuses on Jesus as Savior for the world. He says that God has called both Jew and Gentile, circumcised and uncircumcised. He compares Adam, the one man through whom sin came to every person, to Jesus—the one man through whom salvation comes to every person. In Romans 3:23 we read: *For all have sinned and fall short of the glory of God.* Then, in Romans 5:8b: *While we were still sinners, Christ died for us.*

In chapters 6 through 8, the imagery shifts to that of slavery. Paul writes that while we have been slaves to sin, we can now become slaves to righteousness and become living sacrifices to God. Read Romans 8 for some of Paul's most beautiful writing about the abundant new life Christ-followers have. For example, Romans 8:1-2: *Therefore, there is now no condemnation for those who are in Christ Jesus, because through Christ Jesus the law of the Spirit of life set me free from the law of sin and death.* Later in Romans 8:28: *And we know that in all things God works for the good of those who love him, who have been called according to his purpose.*

Finally, hear Paul's confidence in the affirmation in Romans 8:35, 37-39: *Who shall separate us from the love of Christ? Shall trouble or hardship or persecution or famine or nakedness or danger or sword? No, in all these things we are more than conquerors through him who loved us. For I am convinced that neither death nor life, neither angels nor demons, neither the present nor the future, nor any powers, neither height nor depth, nor anything else in all creation, will be able to separate us from the love of God that is in Christ Jesus our Lord.*

In chapters 9 through 15, Paul shifts his focus again to how to claim this salvation and live 'transformed lives.' Note how the letter is organized: The first section makes Jesus' invitation of salvation available to everyone, to anyone listening or reading the letter. The second section explains the gift of this salvation—what anyone who accepts it will receive. Finally, he explains how to get this gift and how to live in response to it.

Concerning his first purpose in this last section—how to get God's gift of salvation through Jesus—read Romans 10:9: *That if you confess with your mouth, "Jesus is Lord," and believe in your heart that God raised him from the dead, you will be saved.* That's it! Just believe. Jesus has done all the hard work already.

Then, regarding the second purpose—how to live in response to this gift of grace—we read Romans 12. There we find scriptures such as Romans 12:2 CEB: *Don't be conformed to the patterns of this world, but be transformed by the renewing of your minds so that you can figure out what God's will is—what is good and pleasing and mature.* Then, in the last verse of the chapter: *Don't be defeated by evil, but defeat evil with good.*

1 CORINTHIANS 1 – 16
DIRECTIONS FOR THE CHURCH

Divisions in the Church

Everything for God

Worship Practices

Spiritual Gifts

Faith, Hope, Love

Resurrection

This letter to the young church at Corinth, while listed in our Bibles as the first letter to the Corinthians, is generally believed to be Paul's second letter, making 2 Corinthians (coming up next) his third or possibly fourth letter. While the other letters are lost, he refers to previous communication as he tries to answer questions or clarify.

The city of Corinth referenced in Paul's letter was built by Julius Caesar around 44 BC to replace ancient Corinth, destroyed by other Roman generals about a century earlier. It was made the provincial capital of Greece and had a diverse population of Romans, Greeks, and Jews. Corinth was a large city, sitting at the heart of an important trade route and known for its abundant sexual immorality and paganism.

Paul begins by giving thanks for the church in Corinth but moves quickly to addressing concerns. The church is struggling with the temptations of its paganistic surroundings. In chapter 3 he cautions the Corinthians against jealousy, arrogance, immorality, and quarreling, leading to divisions in the young fellowship. In chapter 6, he encourages the church to imitate him in all that they do and tells them he is sending Timothy to remind them of Paul's way of life (1 Corinthians 4:16-17).

In chapter 7, Paul answers one of their burning questions about whether they should marry. We find no evidence in the scriptures that Paul was married, so—no surprise—he advises that it is better for a man not to marry. But, after a lengthy discussion, he concedes in verse 9 that *"it is better to marry than to burn with passion."* Apparently, from Paul's perspective, burning with passion is only a problem *before* you marry. After marriage, no more passion? Surely I misunderstood...(*smile*)

Chapters 8 through 10 focus on directives on living life as a Christ-follower, again addressing some issues specific to the Corinth church. But, as Paul addresses these specific issues he shares some profound truths. For example, one question is whether Christ-followers should eat food that has been sacrificed to idols—not an issue that comes up much today. The Corinthians were arguing about it, however, so Paul answers, concluding in 1 Corinthians 8:8 – 9, 13: *But food does not bring us near to God; we are no worse if we do not eat, and no better if we do. Be careful, however, that the exercise of your freedom does not become a stumbling block to the weak. Therefore, if what I eat causes my brother to fall into sin, I will never eat meat again, so that I will not cause him to fall.*

In 1 Corinthians 9:24 he reminds the people of God's way of life, what Jesus referred to as "the narrow gate" (Matthew 7:13): *Do you not know that in a race all the runners run, but only one gets the prize? Run in such a way as to get the prize.* Then, in 1 Corinthians 10:31, Paul summarizes: *So whether you eat or drink or whatever you do, do it all for the glory of God.*

Chapter 11 shifts to proper worship practices, including the administration of the Lord's Supper or Holy Communion. He reminds his readers of its importance in 1 Corinthians 11:23b-25: *The Lord Jesus, on the night he was betrayed, took bread, and when he had given thanks, he broke it and said, "This is my body, which is for you; do this in remembrance of me." In the same way, after supper he took the cup, saying, "This cup is the new covenant in my blood; do this, whenever you drink it, in remembrance of me."* Then, Paul reminds the people that: *A man ought to examine himself before he eats of the bread and drinks of the cup* (11:28).

Chapters 12 and 13 introduce the idea of spiritual gifts, with all gifts equally important. The gifts, such as wisdom, knowledge, faith, healing, prophecy, and speaking in tongues all come from the Holy Spirit. They should all be used for the good of the one body, Christ's church. But, Paul says, there is one gift available to everyone, the universal gift of love.

The oft-quoted 13th chapter of 1 Corinthians focuses on love, beginning in verse 1: *If I speak in the tongues of men and of angels, but have not love, I am only a resounding gong or a clanging cymbal.* The brief chapter concludes in verse 13: *And now these three remain: faith hope, and love. But the greatest of these is love.* Note that while this chapter is frequently quoted in marriage ceremonies, Paul wrote it to help a young, divided church understand that it is through their love for each other that they will be Christ's church. Remember Jesus' words to his disciples recorded in John 13:34-35: *"A new command I give you: Love one another. By this all men will know that you are my disciples, if you love one another."*

The last chapters of 1 Corinthians focus on the reality of Christ's resurrection and what our resurrection, as believers in him, might be like. In 1 Corinthians 15:20-22 we are reminded of Paul's analogy in the first section of Romans: *But Christ has indeed been raised from the dead, the firstfruits of those who have fallen asleep. For since death came through a man, the resurrection of the dead comes also through a man. For as in Adam all die, so in Christ all will be made alive.*

Later, he adds in verses 51-52: *Listen, I tell you a mystery: We will not all sleep, but we will all be changed—in a flash, in the twinkling of an eye at the last trumpet.* To make the final connection for his Jewish readers he quotes Isaiah: *Death has been swallowed up in victory (Isaiah 25:8).* And then Hosea 13:14: *Where, O death, is your victory? Where, O death, is your sting?*

Before we leave 1 Corinthians, I'll share something I heard from a lovely woman attending our cruise Bible study. She volunteered in the church nursery and said that the favorite scripture among the volunteers was from 1 Corinthians. In fact, they had it hanging over the infant changing table. The verse was 1 Corinthians 15:51: *We will not all sleep, but we will all be changed.* Indeed, the Bible has something for every occasion!

2 CORINTHIANS 1 – 13
A NEW CREATION

God's Comfort

Paul's Hardships

Transformation

Paul's second letter to the church at Corinth begins with praise to God for the comfort he gives each of us, enabling us to comfort others. Paul explains that the reason he has begun this way is because of the hardships he and his companions have experienced. Paul then explains in chapter 2 that he is not coming to visit the Corinth church as he had planned, because they upset him, and he upsets them. He is writing to them instead of coming in person out of love for them.

Much of the remainder of the letter focuses on Paul defending himself as an apostle and his hardships in that role. For example, in 2 Corinthians 4:7-10 we read: *But we have this treasure in jars of clay to show that this all-surpassing power is from God and not from us. We are hard pressed on every side, but not crushed; perplexed, but not in despair; persecuted, but not abandoned; struck down, but not destroyed.*

We always carry around in our body the death of Jesus, so that the life of Jesus may also be revealed in our body. Paul is saying that the hardships he endures are minimal compared to the death Jesus suffered on the cross. He is happy to endure what he does, in order that Jesus might be glorified through his work.

Likewise, Christ-followers should look beyond physical changes to spiritual ones. See the *ScriptureScope* below for more.

NOT I

In 2 Corinthians 5:16-17 we read: *So from now on we regard no one from a worldly point of view. Though we once regarded Christ in this way, we do so no longer. Therefore, if anyone is in Christ, he is a new creation; the old has gone, the new has come!*

One of my favorite characters from the early church is Augustine of Hippo, sometimes referred to as St. Augustine. His life is full of twists and turns. He was raised as a Christ-follower in the 4th c. AD by his Christian mother, but he rejected his upbringing for a life of pleasure and frivolity. He continued to search, however, for meaning in his life.

Ultimately that search led him to a vivid conversion experience, after which he became a pillar of the young church. As Paul says, he was a new creation. He wrote about this conversion in his multi-volume Confessions which told of his life both pre- and post-conversion.

After his conversion, Augustine truly thought of himself as a different person, a new creation. The story is told of him walking down the streets of Alexandria. A woman from his former life, one of his many consorts, repeatedly calls his name. He passes her by without stopping, so she comes to him, grabs his arm, whirls him around to face her and says, "Augustine! It is I!" Augustine looks at her and says, "I know, madam, but it is not I."

This is the kind of transformation Jesus offers—not just a fresh start, forgiveness and grace, although those gifts are amazing in themselves. But Jesus offers a completely new life. When we believe in Jesus, we are in Christ, as Paul says, and new creations: the old has gone, the new has come!

Second Corinthians concludes with Paul's warning to the church in Corinth that he is coming to see them a third time and will settle all these matters with them in person. While I would love to meet Paul (and I will someday), I'm pretty sure I would not want Paul to "settle any matters with me" in person. Yikes!

GALATIANS 1 – 5
SPIRIT, NOT LAW

Paul's letter known as Galatians was written to a group of churches in Galatia, an area which today is in the country of Turkey. It is perhaps the

Defense of Apostleship

Fruits of the Spirit

Ephesians 2:8-9

Children of Light

Submission

Full Armor of God

first of the written letters, composed shortly after the Jerusalem Council (Day Eight). Reminder: The Jerusalem Council convened to address the questions surrounding Gentiles becoming part of the Way, the fellowship of Christ-followers.

The letter to the churches in Galatia deals with these same issues, in the context of false teaching about what is required to receive Jesus' gift of salvation. In Galatians 2:16 CEB, Paul explains: *We know that a person isn't made righteous by the works of the Law but rather through the faithfulness of Jesus Christ.*

Earlier in chapter 2, Paul relates his perspective on the Jerusalem Council. In fact, the verse above is part of a speech he made to Peter about the circumcision issue, among other concerns. As in 2 Corinthians, Paul defends his own apostleship in Galatians, arguing for the churches to remember his preaching and not be swayed by false teachers among them.

In chapter 4, Paul counsels the Galatians on the difference between law and grace. He reminds them that as Christ-followers, they are no longer under the supervision of Jewish law. Read Galatians 4:21-31 for an interesting analogy built around Hagar and Sarah (mother of Ishmael and Isaac, respectively) back in Genesis. These connections to the OT remind us that Paul is a Jew and is, still at this point, writing to Jews more than Gentiles.

Chapters 5 and 6 conclude with directions for living as new creations in Christ. In Galatians 5:22-23, Paul lists the fruits that will demonstrate a life being lived in the Spirit: *But the fruit of the Spirit is love, joy, peace, patience, kindness, goodness, faithfulness, gentleness, and self-control. Against such things there is no law.* Hmmm... Anyone else challenged by self-control? See the *ScriptureScope* for more on the Spirit-filled life.

EVERYTHING MATTERS

In Galatians 6:7b-8 CEB we read: *A person will harvest what they plant. Those who plant only for their own benefit will harvest devastation from their selfishness, but those who plant for the benefit of the Spirit will harvest eternal life from the Spirit.*

In his classic *Mere Christianity*, C. S. Lewis talks about the importance of each and every decision we make. He asserts that every decision—no matter how small—either moves us closer to righteousness or to wickedness, to holiness or to sin, to God or to the world. With each choice we make, we spiral either downward toward slavery to sin and death or upward to freedom in Christ and abundant life.

Or, as Paul says here, we reap what we sow.

Do we think in these terms about every choice we make, no matter how trivial it may seem to us? The problem is, I believe, that what seems trivial to us is not trivial to God. We must guard against seeing triviality through the world's eyes, where virtually everything is trivial and very little matters at all.

Instead, through Paul's word to the Galatians, we learn that everything matters. Centuries later, Paul Young, author of *The Shack*, writes in the final chapters: "If anything matters, then everything matters." The apostle Paul, C.S. Lewis, Paul Young—three different times, one conclusion. Perhaps we should pay attention.

EPHESIANS 1 – 6
SALVATION THROUGH GRACE

Paul's tone in his letter to the church at Ephesus is softer, indicating his affection for those believers among whom he lived and suffered for many years. The primary theme of this letter is salvation through faith in God's grace rather than doing good works. In Ephesians 2:8-9 we read: *For it is by grace you have been saved, through faith— and this not from yourselves, it is the gift of God—not by works, so that no one can boast.* Looking ahead, in Day Ten we will study the letter of James, which focuses on the importance of good works in response to this saving grace.

In chapters 4 through 6 Paul focuses on how to live as "children of the light". He emphasizes living in unity in Christ, as one body of believers. (Remember this discussion back in 1 Corinthians?) Paul gets specific in these chapters, including practices to be avoided as well as practices that reflect holiness. For example, in Ephesians 4:31-32 we read: *Get rid of all bitterness, rage and anger, brawling and slander, along with every form of malice. Be kind and compassionate to one another, forgiving each other, just as in Christ God forgave you.*

In chapters 5 and 6, Paul discusses submission among believers, between wives and husbands, among children and parents, and even between slaves and masters. He sums up his teaching in Ephesians 5:21 with these words: *Submit to one another out of reverence for Christ.*

The letter to the church at Ephesus closes with encouragement in times of trials, using an image Paul's readers would have been very familiar with, the Roman soldier. We read in Ephesians 6: 13-17: *Therefore put on the full armor of God, so that when the day of evil comes, you may be able to stand your ground, and after you have done everything, to stand. Stand firm then, with the belt of truth buckled around your waist, with the breastplate of righteousness in place, and with your feet fitted with the readiness that comes from the gospel of peace. In addition to all this, take up the shield of faith, with which you can extinguish all the flaming arrows of the evil one. Take the helmet of salvation and the sword of the Spirit, which is the word of God.*

PHILIPPIANS 1 – 4
HAPPINESS IN HOLINESS

Paul's letter to the church at Philippi focuses on the joy that comes from living in Christ, no matter the circumstances. Paul states this theme early in chapter 1 when he writes to the Philippians: *In all my prayers for all of you, I always pray with joy because of your partnership in the gospel from the first day until now, being confident of this, that he who began a good work in you will carry it on to completion until the day of Christ Jesus* (1: 4 – 6).

Christ's Attitude

Transcendent Peace

Contentment

Paul's Song of Praise

Supremacy of Christ

The New Nature

Holy Living

Jesus' Return

In chapter 2, Paul encourages them to "make his joy complete" by doing *nothing out of selfish ambition or vain conceit, but in humility consider others better than yourselves* (2:3). He advises in Philippians 2:5, 10: *Your attitude should be the same as that of Christ Jesus…that at the name of Jesus every knee should bow, to heaven and on earth and under the earth and every tongue confess that Jesus Christ is Lord, to the glory of God the Father.*

In chapter 3, Paul encourages hope and faith in Christ, not in men. In Philippians 4:6-8 we read: *Do not be anxious about anything, but in everything, by prayer and petition, with thanksgiving, present your requests to God. And the peace of God, which transcends all understanding, will guard your hearts and your minds in Christ Jesus. Finally, whatever is true, whatever is noble, whatever is right, whatever is pure, whatever is lovely, whatever is admirable—if anything is excellent or praiseworthy—think about such things.*

The letter concludes with Paul's confidence in Christ when facing suffering: *I have learned to be content whatever the circumstances. I know what it is to be in need, and I know what it is to have plenty. I have learned the secret of being content in any and every situation whether well-fed or hungry, whether living in plenty or in want. I can do everything through him who gives me strength* (Philippians 4:11b-13).

COLOSSIANS 1 – 4
SUFFICIENCY OF CHRIST

Colossae was a small city located in Asia Minor (modern day Turkey) in the region of Laodicea and about one hundred miles from Ephesus. Laodicea is mentioned in chapter 2 of Paul's letter and will appear again in Revelation (Day Ten) when Jesus addresses the seven churches. In the greetings found at the end of Colossians, Paul greets many from the church in Laodicea and encourages the church at Colossae to share his letter with them (Colossians 4:16).

The authorship of the letter to the Colossians, while completely accepted as Paul by many NT scholars, has also been questioned by others. They argue that the writing style and vocabulary are not consistent with Paul's other letters, despite the standard greeting. For our discussion here, we will proceed with the assumption that Paul is the author.

One immediate example of the unique aspects of Colossians can be seen in Colossians 1:16-19, where a song of praise to Christ is found. While songs of praise are common throughout the Bible (think of Moses, Miriam, David, Mary, and Zechariah for just a few) they are not common in Paul's writing.

The subject of the song, the supremacy of Christ and Christ's work, is the subject of the entire letter as well. Chapters 1 and 2 focus on an understanding that belief in Jesus Christ is sufficient for salvation. Once again, Paul is writing to reaffirm a church that has been infiltrated with false teaching. As in Galatians, the people are questioning if they need to return to the Jewish law or if acceptance of the grace offered by Jesus because of the cross is enough. Paul encourages them in Colossians 1:22-23 CEB: *But now he has reconciled you by his physical body through death, to present you before God as a people who are holy, faultless, and without blame. But you need to remain well established and rooted in faith and not shift away from the hope given in the good news that you heard.*

In chapters 3 and 4, the letter returns to a theme common throughout Paul's writing, specifically living a holy life in response to salvation received through faith. In Colossians 3:9 -17, the readers are encouraged to "take off" their old habits and nature and "put on" the new nature they received through Christ. Paul lists specific practices to be "taken off" (sexual immorality, moral corruption, lust, evil desire, greed, and dishonesty). The nature to be "put on" includes compassion, kindness, humility, gentleness, patience, forgiveness, and love. Paul sums up in verse 17 CEB: *Whatever you do, whether in speech or action do it all in the name of the Lord Jesus and give thanks to God the Father through him.*

1 THESSALONIANS 1 – 5
FAITHFULNESS

Paul's first letter to the church at Thessalonica begins with words of thanksgiving and praise for the young fellowship. He rejoices in their faithfulness, even facing trials, and their good works of love. This theme is presented early, as in 1 Thessalonians 1:2-3 CEB we read: *We always thank God for all of you when we mention you constantly in our prayers. This is because we remember your work that comes from faith, your effort that comes from love, and your perseverance that comes from hope in our Lord Jesus Christ in the presence of our God and Father.*

Later, Paul focuses on holy living while waiting for the return of Jesus. In 1 Thessalonians 4:11-12 CEB we read: *Aim to live quietly, mind your own business, and earn your own living, just as I told you. That way you'll behave appropriately toward outsiders, and you won't be in need.* Sounds like good advice for the 21st century as well!

Regarding the return of Jesus, Paul writes in 1 Thessalonians 5:1-2: *We don't need to write to you about the timing and dates, brothers and sisters. You know very well that the day of the Lord is going to come like a thief in the night. So then let's not sleep like the others, but let's stay awake and stay sober.* Paul is giving his interpretation of Jesus' warnings and parables about being faithful and ready for his return, whenever it may occur (Matthew 24 and 25).

2 THESSALONIANS 1 – 3
MORE FOCUS ON FAITHFULNESS

This, the last of Paul's epistles to churches included in the New Testament, is similar in theme and style to his first letter to the church at Thessalonica. In fact, the beginning sounds very familiar, as we find in 2 Thessalonians 1:3-4: *We ought always to thank God for you, and rightly so because your faith is growing more and more, and the love every one of you has for each other is increasing. Therefore, among God's churches we boast about your perseverance and faith in all the persecutions and trials you are enduring.*

In chapter 2, Paul answers questions from the church about the return of Jesus. Note that many in the early church believed that Jesus' promised return was imminent. As a result, much of the apostles' writing, including that of Paul and Peter, focuses on holy living in preparation for Christ's return. Here, the young fellowship at Thessalonica is seeking reassurance that Christ has not already returned. Paul informs them that Jesus will return to destroy a man or person of "lawlessness". Some believe this person to be the same antichrist referenced in John's first letter (Day Ten).

Chapter 3 is reminiscent of Paul's rules for living found in 1 Thessalonians as well. He focuses here specifically on living a disciplined life. In 2 Thessalonians 3:10 CEB we read: *Even when we were with you, we gave you this command: "If anyone doesn't want to work, they shouldn't eat."*

Paul's last letter to the churches ends as they each begin, with his familiar subject-line greeting: *The grace of our Lord Jesus Christ be with you all* (2 Thessalonians 3:18).

1 TIMOTHY 1 – 6
PREPARATION FOR SERVICE

Have you ever had a mentor? Or maybe you have mentored someone else? A mentor encourages, teaches, and supports the mentee through a life experience or perhaps a new job. Paul's pastoral letters (1 and 2

Do God's Work

Jesus as Mediator

False Teachers

The Good Fight

Avoid Controversies

Onesimus

Timothy and Titus) are examples of what we might call mentoring.

Paul encourages Timothy and Titus in their new roles as pastors of churches. He also teaches them how to deal with problems that he is pretty sure will come up. And he includes some doctrine as well, to be sure that they have the foundation of spiritual knowledge to support their efforts. See the *ScriptureScope* below for an example.

A GODLY FOCUS

In 1 Timothy 1:3-4 we read: *As I urged you when I went into Macedonia, stay there in Ephesus so that you may command certain men not to teach false doctrines any longer nor to devote themselves to myths and endless genealogies. These promote controversies rather than God's work—which is by faith.*

Controversies...in the church? *(smile)* Yes, in Paul's day, in ours, and in every age in between. I find it both disturbing and encouraging to hear Paul warn Timothy about the same issues we deal with today: Disturbing because we haven't made much progress and encouraging because those of us who proclaim the gospel as Paul taught it need to know that God's message will prevail.

I am reminded of a brother in Christ that Keith and I met on a recent cruise. He and his wife were faithful to attend every Bible study. One day early in the cruise they invited us to join them afterwards to continue the day's discussion over lunch.

We soon learned that what he wanted to discuss was not the joy of God's word or even his personal salvation story. Instead, he wanted to argue semantics and what has come to be known as 'the historical Jesus'. In other words, exactly what did Jesus say, do, eat, drink and how much of the Bible can we actually believe? We might call this the 21st century version of "myths and endless genealogies." *(smile)*

We excused ourselves after explaining that, as missionaries of God's Word on that cruise ship, we did not want to be overheard in a public place arguing about it. Often, it is just this kind of discussion that puts off those who are thinking they might want to know more about Christianity.

The problem is not that people like our friend are offering wrong opinions. The problem is that they are asking the wrong questions.

The issue is not genealogies (Paul's day) or semantics and historical accuracy (our day). What the church should focus on, as Paul told Timothy, is the salvation Jesus brought to the world–to both Jew and Gentile, slave and free, and, yes, even to those who stir the pot.

So, rather than argue over semantics and the historical Jesus, let us spend our energy on knowing and living out the salvation he brings and rejoice in the gift of grace we have been given. Or, as the founder of Methodism John Wesley put it: *Though we can't think alike, may we not love alike? May we not be of one heart, though we are not of one opinion? Without all doubt, we may.*

Paul continues by instructing Timothy to pray for everyone because *"this is right and it pleases God."* In 1 Timothy 2:5-6 we read: *For there is one God and mediator between God and men, the man Christ Jesus, who gave himself as a ransom for all men—the testimony given in its proper time.* Remember Job 9:32-34? Job asks for such a mediator, a man to argue his case before God. We noted at the time that Job needed Jesus. Paul says: Here he is!

In the remainder of chapter 2 and chapter 3, Paul gives Timothy instructions on how to deal with various groups of people within the early church, including deacons, widows, elders, and slaves. In chapters 4 and 5 the focus shifts to leadership and pastoral direction for Timothy. Chapter 6 concludes with warnings about false teachers who *"see godliness as a way to make money."* In 1 Timothy 6:10 CEB we read Paul's conclusion to the discussion: *The love of money is the root of all kinds of evil. Some have wandered away from the faith and have impaled themselves with a lot of pain because they made money their goal.*

Paul concludes his first letter to Timothy with these words in 6:21: *Timothy, protect what has been given to you in trust. Avoid godless and pointless discussions and the contradictory claims of so-called "knowledge." When some people adopted this false knowledge, they missed the goal of faith.*

2 TIMOTHY 1 – 3
A LIFETIME OF SERVICE

Paul's first letter to Timothy was designed to prepare him to serve a sometimes-faithless congregation, riddled with controversy. His second letter seems to be designed to prepare him for a lifetime of service. He reminds him of the trials to come and encourages Timothy through his own, that is Paul's, example.

Paul first tells Timothy of his trials, including his current imprisonment. As you can see from the Paul's Ministry table, at least some historians believe that this letter and perhaps all the pastoral letters were written while Paul was under house arrest in Rome. He reassures Timothy of his faith in Jesus in 2 Timothy 1:12 CEB: *This is also why I'm suffering the way I do, but I'm not ashamed. I know the one in whom I've placed my trust. I'm convinced that God is powerful enough to protect what he has placed in my trust until that day.*

Chapter 2 and the beginning of chapter 3 are reminiscent of Paul's first letter to Timothy, as he warns against false teachers and *"foolish and stupid arguments."* Then, he reissues his charge to Timothy to serve the Lord. In chapter 4 Paul asks Timothy to come see him, saying that only Luke is with him (presumably in Rome). Indeed, some scholars have labeled 2 Timothy as "Paul's last will and testament", based in large part on 2 Timothy 4:6-7: *For I am already being poured out like a drink offering, and the time has come for my departure. I have fought the good fight, I have finished the race, I have kept the faith.*

Paul's letter concludes with greetings to his friends and partners in ministry, Priscilla and Aquilla.

TITUS 1 – 3
DOING WHAT IS GOOD

Paul's letter to another young minister, Titus, has many of the same themes found in 1 Timothy. Paul cautions him against divisions in the church and counsels him on what he should teach to different groups, specifically the older men, the older women, the younger women, and the young men. (Sounds a lot like Sunday School to me!)

Additionally, he directs Titus to appoint elders and overseers (bishops) in every town. This seems to indicate the growth of the church community, if a hierarchy of leadership is needed. In Titus 1:6-9 he gives Titus specific criteria upon which these appointments should be made.

Similar to 1 Timothy, we read in Titus 3:9: *But avoid foolish controversies and genealogies and arguments and quarrels about the law, because these are unprofitable and useless.* A final theme is "doing what is good." Paul reminds Titus that: *Our people must learn to devote themselves to doing what is good in order that they may provide for daily necessities and not live unproductive lives* (Titus 3:14).

PHILEMON
RECONCILIATION

The last of Paul's letters in the New Testament is his brief epistle to the slave-owner Philemon. Paul informs him that he is sending Philemon's slave, Onesimus, back to him. Paul calls Onesimus his "son" and asks Philemon to take him back, not as a slave but as a "brother in the Lord."

The brief letter to Philemon reminds us of the many stories of reconciliation we have read throughout our study. We remember when Esau forgave Jacob and Joseph forgave his brothers in Genesis. Later, after God's judgment on Israel and Judah, the exiled remnant returned to Jerusalem to rebuild Yahweh's temple. Finally, God reconciled the world to himself through the death and resurrection of his Son, Jesus Christ.

We might wonder why this little letter made it into the Bible, but when we consider that its story is also God's story, it makes perfect sense.

We have one more day of study ahead of us. Paul's letters comprise a significant portion of the NT wisdom literature, but what about the other apostles? Are there any writings from "the rock", Peter? How about James, the half-brother of Jesus who became the leader of the Jerusalem church? And then there's John, the "disciple whom Jesus loved". Surely they have something to say as well. Indeed, they do. We will explore their letters in Day Ten.

REFLECTING FORWARD

Use these questions to guide your discussion of Day Nine and prepare for our final day of study.

1. In the introduction to this chapter, I called Paul the first Christian theologian. We also talked about his focus on helping people understand who Jesus was, why he came, and what his crucifixion and resurrection mean. How do Paul's letters help you understand the gospels better? Do you have a favorite letter that is particularly meaningful to you?

2. We discussed at the end of Day Eight how Paul's "baggage" as an enemy of Jesus might impact his teaching and preaching. As we studied Paul's letters, did you get a sense of that? Paul talks about a 'thorn" that brings him pain. Could that be spiritual, rather than physical? Do you have "baggage" that brings you pain? How do you deal with your regrets and guilt?

3. Paul often focused on divisions within the fellowship of believers. To address these, he directed believers to focus on faith, love, goodness, kindness, and compassion. John Wesley directed his followers to think on those things we agree about rather than those we disagree about. We live in a time when there is much disagreement. How do you stay focused on living as Jesus would live in a world where even the church is divided?

4. Paul writes often about becoming a "new creation" in Christ. Can you think of any language Jesus used that says the same thing in another way? (Consider John 3.) What does being a "new creation" mean to you? What about your life has changed—or, what would you hope would change if you became a Christ-follower?

5. In Ephesians 2:8-9, Paul talks about grace, something we have seen throughout the scriptures, all the way back to Genesis (see page 32). Salvation comes only through the grace of God, which is extended to everyone who believes in Jesus, his resurrection, and the saving grace he offers. One of the most famous hymns is all about grace, amazing grace. It seems that all people—Christians and non-Christians—would like to believe in grace. How has your life changed because of grace? What opportunities have you had to extend grace to others? When have you failed to give grace to others? How did God grow your faith through those experiences?

6. As we approach the last books of the Bible, take a few minutes to think about and discuss the first nine days of this study. What have you learned? What seems to be in limbo? What do you still need to know to make this great story of the Bible complete?

DAY TEN

HEBREWS, JAMES, 1 AND 2 PETER

1, 2, AND 3 JOHN, JUDE, REVELATION

EPILOGUE

After our study of the letters of Paul, we now look forward to the rest of the New Testament—a combination of letters written by a variety of authors and a remarkable prophetic vision known as Revelation. The first letter we will study today, Hebrews, serves as a bridge within the wisdom literature.

Hebrews connects the thirteen letters most often attributed to Paul and the seven letters commonly attributed to others who knew Jesus. These others include the apostles Peter and John and Jesus' half-brothers James and Jude. As we cross this bridge, we leave Paul's literary style, imagery, and terminology related to Christ behind. On the other side, we find other early attempts at defining Christian theology and arriving at a common understanding and language. With the gospels, these twenty-one letters create the foundation upon which the liturgy, hymns, and sacraments of the Christian church have been built.

HEBREWS 1 – 13
JESUS, THE HIGH PRIEST

Jesus Above Moses

Covenant Comparison

Jesus as Mediator

Faith

Cloud of Witnesses

The book of Hebrews often comes across as less a letter and more an eloquent sermon on proclaiming Christ as the Messiah. Paul's letters addressed both Jews and Gentiles, but his readership was predominantly Gentiles in many of the churches to which he wrote. The writer of Hebrews is focused on a Jewish audience to convince them that Jesus is the Messiah. In this way, it might be seen as a companion piece to Matthew's gospel.

The author of Hebrews is not known, although most scholars agree that it was not Paul. The style is different, and the familiar greeting is missing. One possible author is Apollos, who Paul refers to as a fellow worker for the Lord.

In chapters 1 through 4 the writer establishes Jesus as God's messenger, greater than the angels and greater than Moses. Connection: Remember that Moses is the savior in the Hebrew salvation story, the deliverance from Egypt (Day Two). By placing Jesus above Moses, the writer emphasizes Jesus' divine nature as the Son of God. Chapter 4 includes encouragement to the readers not to miss the Sabbath-rest that Jesus brings which is available to them all.

In chapter 5, the writer introduces a deeper teaching, specifically a comparison of Jesus with the high priest of Yahweh's temple. He will elaborate on this later, but in this chapter he tells his readers that they need to mature in their faith to understand what he is about to teach them. See the *ScriptureScope* below.

THE DIVINE DIFFERENCE

In Hebrews 5:12-14 CEB we read: *Although you should have been teachers by now, you need someone to teach you an introduction to the basics about God's message. You have come to the place where you need milk instead of solid food. Everyone who lives on milk is not used to the word or righteousness, because they are babies. But solid food is for the mature, whose senses are trained by practice to distinguish between good and evil.*

The author of Hebrews is trying to explain that those receiving this letter need to mature in the faith. Rather than having to be taught basic truths of the faith again and again, they should be teaching others. Instead, they are still babies in the faith, living on milk rather than solid food. Because of this they have not learned how to live out their faith in righteousness and holiness.

And what is the benefit of being mature in the faith? Nothing less than being able to tell right from wrong, good from evil, the temporal from the eternal, the worldly from the Godly. But this ability does not come just from a solid meal here and there, but from 'practice'.

I can't speak for anyone else, but I can tell a significant difference–a divine difference–when I am reading God's Word regularly. The difference is in my ability to resist temptations and distractions of the world and focus on holiness and godliness. The more solid scriptural food I get, the less the world appeals. God is changing me from the inside out through his Word. Hallelujah!

In chapters 6 through 10 the author elaborates upon the analogy of Jesus as the great high priest. He compares Christianity, the new covenant with Jesus as high priest, to Judaism, the old covenant with Aaron as high priest. In Judaism the high priest made repeated guilt and sin offerings to obtain forgiveness for the people. In the new covenant, Jesus is the ultimate and final blood offering to cancel sin. (Remember John the Baptist's profession of Jesus as the Lamb of God?)

In Judaism the high priest enters the holy of holies to mediate for the people. Jesus is the mediator for all in the ultimate Holy of Holies, at the right hand of God in the heavenly tabernacle. (Remember in Day Seven when the curtain into the temple holy of holies tore apart from top to bottom when Jesus died on the cross? No longer would a high priest be needed to mediate for the people inside the holy of holies.)

In Hebrews 10:15-18, the writer quotes Jeremiah 31: *The Holy Spirit also testifies to us about this. First he says: "This is the covenant I will make with them after that time, says the Lord. I will put my laws in their hearts, and I will write them on their minds." Then he adds: "Their sins and lawless acts I will remember no more." And where these have been forgiven, there is no longer any sacrifice for sin.*

Chapter 11 begins with a description of faith: *Now faith is being sure of what we hope for and certain of what we do not see* (Hebrews 11:1). The rest of the chapter gives examples of Jewish ancestors with great faith, including many of the same people we focused on in our study of the Old Testament: Abel, Noah, Abraham, Isaac, Jacob, Joseph, Moses, Rahab, Gideon, Samson, David, Samuel and the prophets.

Hebrews 12:1-2 then concludes: *Therefore, since we are surrounded by such a great cloud of witnesses, let us throw off everything that hinders and the sin that so easily entangles, and let us run with perseverance the race marked out for us. Let us fix our eyes on Jesus, the author and perfecter of our faith, who for the joy set before him endured the cross, scorning its shame, and sat down at the right hand of the throne of God.*

The book ends with exhortations and encouragement. In Hebrews 13:2 we read: *Do not forget to entertain strangers for by so doing some people have entertained angels without knowing it.* And later, in Hebrews 13:8: *Jesus Christ is the same yesterday and today and forever.*

JAMES 1 – 5
FAITH IN ACTION

Most Biblical scholars now believe that the book of James was not written by James, one of the Twelve, but by James, the half-brother of Jesus. This James was

> *Handbook for Living*
>
> *Pure Joy in Trials*
>
> *Faith Must Have Works*
>
> *Power of the Tongue*
>
> *Power of Prayer*

also the leader of the church in Jerusalem, ultimately the bishop of Jerusalem. James' letter focuses on the importance of good works as a response to salvation received through grace. Note that it is not to be interpreted as direction to do good works to *earn* salvation. Jesus made it clear that salvation comes only through belief in him and acceptance of his gift of grace.

Remember Paul's letter to the Ephesians 2:8-9: *For it is by grace you have been saved, through faith—and this not from yourselves, it is the gift of God—not by works, so that no one can boast.* Some have suggested that James contradicts Paul by saying that, indeed, doing good works is required for salvation. In fact, because of the concern that James might be understood this way, his letter almost did not make the final cut when the Bible was being put together. Now that it's here, we will see that James' "handbook for Christian living" does not contradict Paul's teaching, but rather complements it.

James begins his letter with a greeting, similar to Paul. In this case, he describes himself simply as a slave of God and of Jesus Christ. He addresses his letter to the twelve tribes scattered throughout the nations, outside of Israel. This would indicate a desire for the letter to be passed among the churches for reading and teaching, which was the common practice.

After the greeting, James begins with encouragement to believers when they are faced with trials. We read in James 1:2-4: *Consider it pure joy whenever you face trials of many kinds, because you know that the testing of your faith develops perseverance. Perseverance must finish its work so that you may be mature and complete, not lacking anything.* Again, as in Hebrews, we see a desire for believers to mature in their faith.

James quickly turns to the importance of our actions as a response to our faith. In James 2:14-16 CEB we read: *My brothers and sisters, what good is it if people say they have faith but do nothing to show it? Claiming to have faith can't save anyone, can it? Imagine a brother or sister who is naked and never has enough food to eat. What if one of you said, "Go in peace! Stay warm! Have a nice meal!"? What good is it if you don't actually give them what their body needs?* Later, James makes it absolutely clear in James 2:26: *As the lifeless body is dead, so faith without actions is dead.*

In chapter 3 James focuses exclusively on the damage done by the tongue. See the *ScriptureScope* below for my favorite of his metaphors.

STAYING ON COURSE

In James 3:4-5a we read: *Consider ships: they are so large that strong winds are needed to drive them. But pilots direct their ships wherever they want with a little rudder. In the same way, even though the tongue is a small part of the body, it boasts wildly.*

So, now you know why this passage is a favorite. Not only does this image of a ship appeal to the cruiser in me, it also perfectly describes my tongue at times—boasting and out of control. And, it brings to mind what Keith and I learned from a friend who is also a cruise director.

Over dinner one night, our friend John posed the question: "So, how often do you think this ship is off course?" I thought for a minute and then said tentatively, "Never?" (No, this wasn't *Jeopardy*—I just answered with a question because I didn't have a clue.) John smiled and said: "Always."

Always? Seriously? That didn't make me feel too good on our transatlantic voyage. I needed an explanation. "Yes," John said. "Actually, it's always off course—not by a lot, but to some degree—and the captain is always working to get it back on course."

What a great description of the Christian life! We are always off course a bit—we are all sinners and fall short of the glory of God, as Paul put it. And God is working—through his word, through his messengers—to get us back on course. In fact, this is precisely what James is trying to help us with as well.

James concludes in chapters 4 and 5 with directions on prayer. In James 4:2b-3 we read: *You do not have, because you do not ask God. When you ask, you do not receive, because you ask with wrong motives that you may spend what you get on your pleasures.*

In chapter 5 James encourages his readers to be patient and wait for the Lord, whose return is near. (Connection: We will see a similar expectation in other letters in today's readings.) In James 5:16 CEB, he sums up his direction on prayer: *For this reason, confess your sins to each other and pray for each other so that you may be healed. The prayer of the righteous person is powerful in what it can achieve.*

1 PETER
GET READY

Holy Living

The End is Near

False Teaching

God's Timing

I mentioned earlier that each summer Keith and I spend a week with our grandchildren, typically on a little trip. We call this annual event Camp Clover, named after the street we lived on for several years. We spend time seeing new things, having fun, and studying the Bible.

When our third grandson, Henry, was nine years old, we took a short road trip to San Antonio. That year, I decided to teach them the entire Bible—similar to what you are reading here—but at a much higher level. We had four nights, so I presented it as a football game (we live in Texas, remember). The first two quarters were the Old Testament, the last two were the New Testament. And, the period we are living in now was "Overtime".

As we talked about Overtime, I said something about Jesus coming back to earth. Even though Henry has attended Sunday School and Vacation Bible School his entire life, apparently Jesus' second coming was not something that had registered with him previously. Suddenly he looked at me with an anxious look and cried out, "Nana! Jesus is coming back?" I nodded and then with the faith and honesty of a child, he announced, "We better get ready!" Indeed—and that's exactly what Peter is telling his readers in his first letter.

Peter begins, like James, with a greeting to *"God's chosen strangers in the world"*, scattered throughout the Roman Empire. He identifies himself only as Peter, an apostle of Jesus Christ. The remainder of the book focuses on righteous living with the return of Christ and the final judgment imminent.

Peter encourages the believers in their persecution and trials, saying that they may be suffering these things for "a little while". Nevertheless, they should remember that they should not give in to the evil desires they had before they became Christ-followers. In 1 Peter 1:15-16 he quotes Leviticus: *But just as he who called you is holy, so be holy in all you do; for it is written: "Be holy because I am holy."* Later, Peter offers another reason for living "good lives." See below.

CHANGE THE WORLD

In 1 Peter 2:12 we read: *Live such good lives among the pagans that, though they accuse you of doing wrong, they may see your good deeds and glorify God on the day he visits us.*

Are we living among pagans in the 21st century? Probably not in the sense that Peter knew it, but idol-worship is all around us. All you have to do is look at the internet or listen to the evening news. So, do the 21st century pagans see our good deeds? Do we distinguish ourselves in that way, as the first century Roman historian Tacitus noted about the first century Christians?

And do today's pagans still accuse us of doing wrong, as they did in the first century? Back then, Christians were condemned for failing to worship the gods of Rome, for putting their faith in a God you couldn't even see, for being unsociable by Rome's standards, and for foolishly believing in a deified man named Jesus who was nothing more than a religious teacher.

Today, it's much the same.

The world of celebrity, power, and self-indulgence often sees Christians as fools for believing in a God with a Son named Jesus who was crucified and rose from the dead. They call us boring and backward for choosing fellowship with believers over the hot spots around town. And, they see us as downright weird for turning away from the excesses of the world.

But, when disaster strikes, when the homeless need a place to sleep, when the hungry need a Thanksgiving meal, and when children have basic needs that must be met.... Christians are often among the first to reach out and the last to go home. As individuals and as the universal church—Catholic and Protestant—these events give us a very visible platform to "live good lives among the pagans."

But Peter is saying: Do that all the time. Christ is the answer to the world's problems. Christians *are* Christ in the world until he returns. Live out a life of holiness—not "holier-than-thou-ness", but true holy lives of love, humility, and selflessness. Do this and you will change the world.

In chapters 3 and 4 Peter continues to expand this idea of living as strangers in the world, reflecting back to his greeting. In 1 Peter 4:7-8 he writes: *The end of all things is near. Therefore be clear minded and self-controlled so that you can pray. Above all, love each other deeply because love covers over a multitude of sins.*

2 PETER 1 – 3
GOD'S TIMING

Peter's second letter contrasts with his first letter as he seems to shift his focus from the imminent return of Jesus to the dangers posed by false teachers. He also accepts that Jesus may not return in his lifetime and tries to help his readers understand that as well.

In 2 Peter 1:13-16 CEB he explains: *I think it's right that I keep stirring up your memory as long as I'm alive. After all, our Lord Jesus Christ has shown me that I am about to depart from this life. I'm eager for you always to remember these things after my death. We didn't repeat crafty myths when we told you about the powerful coming of our Lord Jesus Christ. Quite the contrary, we witnessed his majesty with our own eyes.*

Chapter 2 focuses on the destruction caused by false teachers. As with Paul, this is a theme that continues through these apostolic letters. We will also see this in the letter attributed to Jude.

Later he reflects on God's timing in 2 Peter 3:8-9: *But do not forget this one thing, dear friends: With the Lord a day is like a thousand years, and a thousand years are like a day. The Lord is not slow in keeping his promise, as some understand slowness. He is patient with you, not wanting anyone to perish, but everyone to come to repentance.* Remember the end of Ecclesiastes, when the teacher directs his students to "remember your creator in your prime" (Day Four). We reflected on C. S. Lewis' assertion that the reason Jesus does not return is because God is giving us plenty of time to 'come over to his side.' It seems he may have gotten that from Peter!

1 JOHN 1 – 5
WALKING IN LIGHT AND LOVE

> *God is Light*
>
> *The Antichrist*
>
> *God is Love*
>
> *Love is Obedience*
>
> *Practice What is Good*
>
> *Unrestrained Immorality*

This might be a good time to review John's gospel (Day Eight), as it will remind you of John's focus on Jesus' teachings about love. Knowing that, it should come as no surprise that love is also the focus of this first letter of the apostle John (not John the Baptist, but one of the Twelve--the John who Jesus asked to take care of his mother Mary).

The letter begins without a greeting, and John never identifies himself. The first words, however, reflect the Gospel of John without doubt. In 1 John 1:1 we read: *That which was from the beginning, which we have heard, which we have seen with our eyes, which we have looked at and our hands have touched—this we proclaim concerning the Word of life.* Compare to the first verse of John's gospel: *In the beginning was the Word, and the Word was with God, and the Word was God.*

John continues by comparing God to light. In 1 John 1:5-6 we read: *This is the message we have heard from him and declare to you: God is light; in him there is no darkness at all. If we claim to have fellowship with him yet walk in the darkness, we lie and do not live by the truth.* Then, later in verses 8 and 9: *If we claim to be without sin, we deceive ourselves and the truth is not in us. If we confess our sins, he is faithful and just and will forgive us our sins and purify us from all unrighteousness.*

In chapter 2 John warns his readers against "the antichrist". (Connection to Paul's second letter to the Thessalonians in Day Nine.)

As with Peter's first letter, John seems to believe that Jesus' return is imminent, as we read in 1 John 2:18, 22: *Dear children, this is the last hour; and as you have heard that the antichrist is coming, even now many antichrists have come. This is how we know it is the last hour.... Who is the liar? It is the man who denies that Jesus is the Christ. Such a man is the antichrist—he denies the Father and the Son.* With this definition of the "antichrist", John seems to indicate that it could be anyone who does not believe in Jesus Christ as the Son of God.

In chapters 3 through 5, John teaches that to walk as children in the light means to love God and love one another. In 1 John 4:8, 10 we read: *Whoever does not love does not know God, because God is love. This is love: not that we loved God, but that he loved us and sent his Son as an atoning sacrifice for our sins.* Later, in verse 19 we read: *We love God because he first loved us.*

John sums up his message in 1 John 5:11-12*: And this is the testimony: God has given us eternal life, and this life is in his Son. He who has the Son has life; he who does not have the Son of God does not have life.*

2 AND 3 JOHN
ELDER WISDOM

John's second and third letters contrast somewhat with the first. Unlike 1 John, both are very brief and are written to specific issues in the local church. John identifies himself in the greetings as "the elder", indicating his position to provide guidance. The second letter is addressed to *"the chosen lady (or gentlewoman) and her children"*, which most scholars take to mean a local congregation and its members. The use of the cryptic language probably suggests John's concern for persecution of that local church should the letter fall into the wrong hands.

In 2 John, the themes of love and warnings about the antichrist continue. In 2 John 4:7 we read: *And this is love: that we walk in obedience to his commands. As you have heard from the beginning, his command is that you walk in love. Many deceivers, who do not acknowledge Jesus Christ as coming in the flesh, have gone out into the world. Any such person is the deceiver and the antichrist.*

John's third letter is addressed specifically to a church leader, Gaius, who appears to be the pastor in a local congregation. The apostle commends Gaius on his faithfulness and promises him that he will come soon to visit. He seems to be concerned about two members (or leaders) of the church. One is Diotrephes, who is a negative force in the church, *"making unjust and wicked accusations against us"* and refusing to *"welcome the brothers and sisters"*. By contrast, John commends Demetrius who *"everyone speaks highly of."*

John sums up his concerns in verse 11 CEB: *Dear friend, don't imitate what is bad but what is good. Whoever practices what is good belongs to God. Whoever practices what is bad has not seen God.*

JUDE
AN INTERVENTION

The short book of Jude has much to say to us today. It is similar to 2 Peter in language and style, leading some scholars to believe that one borrowed from the other. The focus of the letter is on false teaching.

Jude introduces himself in the greeting as *"a servant [or slave] of Jesus Christ and brother of James."* Some scholars believe that, like James, he was a half-brother of Jesus. Others suggest that the language and style is too refined for a Jew who grew up in Nazareth. There are also differences in opinion as to when the letter was written. It is addressed to a general audience of *"those who are called, loved by God the Father and kept safe by Jesus Christ"* (verse 1 CEB).

Jude begins by stating his purpose. In verses 3 and 4 we see that his letter is intended to be what we might call an "intervention". He wants to call attention to an issue of concern and intervene before things go too far. We read: *Dear friends, I wanted very much to write to you concerning the salvation we share. Instead, I must write to urge you to fight for the faith delivered once and for all to God's holy people. Godless people have slipped in among you. They turn the grace of our God into unrestrained immorality and deny our only master and Lord, Jesus Christ. Judgment was passed against them a long time ago.*

Notice what Jude says about the grace of God—that these people have turned it into "unrestrained immorality." In the early church, groups emerged that saw God's grace—forgiveness of sins, just for the asking—as a "free pass" to do whatever they pleased. They could always ask for forgiveness and everything would be OK. This is what Jude wants to put a stop to.

Jude offers an "intervention" strategy of love and grace for believers in verses 20-23: *But you, dear friends: build each other up on the foundation of your most holy faith, pray in the Holy Spirit, keep each other in the love of God, wait for the mercy of our Lord Jesus Christ, who will give you eternal life. Have mercy on those who doubt. Save some by snatching them from the fire.*

The letter ends with a beautiful blessing in verses 24 and 25.

REVELATION 1 – 22
GOD WINS!

Messages to Churches

Lukewarm Laodicea

Scrolls, Seals, Trumpets

Behind the Curtain

Armageddon

Apocalyptic Literature

New Creation

In some older Bibles (such as the red-letter King James version I received from my grandparents when I was six years old) the book we know as Revelation was titled The Revelation of St. John the Divine. It was generally believed to be the record of a vision that came to the old apostle John when he was exiled on the island of Patmos at the end of his life. Contemporary Bible scholars now disagree (surprise!) on whether the apostle John was the one who actually received the vision or whether it was another John entirely (if someone named "John" at all).

It doesn't really matter, because the real author of Revelation is Jesus, as the first two verses make clear: *The revelation of Jesus Christ which God gave him to show his servants what must soon take place. He made it known by sending his angel to his servant John, who testifies to everything he saw—that is, the word of God and the testimony of Jesus Christ.* Thus, John simply reported—and apparently wrote down—what he saw.

In the first chapter we meet the risen Jesus coming on the clouds, who announces in Revelation 1:8: *"I am the Alpha and the Omega,"* says the Lord God, *"who is, and who was, and who is to come, the Almighty."* We are taken back through time to Genesis, as God is the Alpha (the beginning) and, now in Revelation, the Omega (the end). He is the great I AM.

The rest of chapter 1 provides a vivid description of Jesus as "one like a son of man", as Daniel described him in his vision (Day Five). Jesus is preparing to send messages to seven churches in Asia.

In chapters 2 and 3, Jesus proclaims a message to each of the seven churches. Each message is part praise, part rebuke, and part encouragement. I am reminded when I read these of parent-teacher conferences in school. As a principal I always tried to prepare beginning teachers for these sometimes-daunting experiences. I directed them to say something positive at first, even if it was difficult to come up with: "Johnny is always here!" Then, gently share your concerns: "But, he never seems to have his homework done." And, finally, offer encouragement: "I'm sure we can help him if we work together." I have to admit that I did not know the scriptures in those days as I do now. If I had, I might have known that Jesus invented that strategy a long time before I did!

See the *ScriptureScope* below for my favorite of his seven messages.

No Middle Ground

In Revelation 3:15-16 CEB we read: *I know your works. You are neither cold nor hot. I wish that you were either cold or hot. So because you are lukewarm, and neither hot nor cold, I'm about to spit you out of my mouth.*

Now, here is something to think about. Jesus is speaking to the church in Laodicea, in the region near Colossae. Paul mentioned Laodicea in his letter to the Colossians (Day Nine) and now it is one of the seven churches of Asia to whom Jesus speaks directly. In truth, each of the seven messages has meaning for the church today--but this one in particular caught my attention.

See, I've been lukewarm through most of my Christian life. I was baptized young and went to church my entire life, but I was never 'on fire' for Jesus–never a slave to righteousness and holiness, never addicted to reading his Word, never committed to living a life of witness to others–until around the year 2000.

So, I'm pretty familiar with lukewarm, and, honestly, it's a place that is easy for Christ-followers in this generation to be comfortable. Indeed, even some fellow believers condemn those who are 'hot' as fanatical and foolish. Better to be cool about your faith–a Christian who manages to walk the line between the world and the church.

In this passage, Jesus challenges the Laodiceans to get off that lukewarm fence, to make a choice–hot or cold.

If there is one thing I pray that you get from this study it is to start burning for Jesus in your life as a Christ-follower. All in. Or, as John Wesley preached, don't be an "almost Christian", but an "altogether Christian." According to Jesus, there is no middle ground.

In chapter 4, John sees God on his throne. Remember the visions of God that came to Isaiah, Ezekiel, and Daniel? This is John's vision. In Revelation 5:11-12 we read: *Then I looked and heard the voice of many angels, numbering thousands upon thousands, and ten thousand times ten thousand. They encircled the throne and the living creatures and the elders. In a loud voice they sang: "Worthy is the Lamb, who was slain, to receive power and wealth and wisdom and strength and honor and glory and praise!"*

Chapters 5 through 11 could be subtitled: *Seven Scrolls, Seals, and Trumpets.* These chapters are filled with symbols and images, an ancient code that would have meant a great deal to the early Christians suffering tremendous persecution under Rome. The breaking of each seal, the reading of the scroll, and the sounding of the trumpet reveal another step toward the destiny of humanity. When the seventh trumpet sounds, the end of the world and the final judgment have come. We read in Revelation 11:15b words used by G. F. Handel in the magnificent "Hallelujah" from the oratorio *Messiah*: *The kingdom of the world has become the kingdom of our Lord and of his Christ and he will reign for ever and ever.*

Chapters 16 through 20 tell the meta-narrative of the Bible from a different perspective. As Daniel's vision allowed him to see "behind the curtain" that separates the physical and spiritual worlds, this description takes us there as well. We see what we have been reading about from "the other side." The scene takes us from the creation of the world to Israel to Jesus to the church. The chapters conclude with the final war, the defeat of Babylon and the beast, and the final judgment. In Revelation 16:16 we read a description of the final battle: *Then they gathered the kings together to the place that in Hebrew is called Armageddon.*

These chapters are "apocalyptic" in nature, meaning they describe the apocalypse, or final destruction of the world. This was a common literary style between 200 BC and AD 150. Most of the world was in a crisis—Roman domination—and apocalyptic writings gave hope for resolution and a new age of peace.

Apocalyptic books and media are also common in our world today. The books and movies of the 21st century are often symbolic and mean something particularly to those of us living in this time. In the same way, the symbols and imagery in Revelation would have meant something to the early Christians. They would have understood Babylon to be Rome with Caesar as Lord. God's defeat of Babylon will usher in a kingdom of peace where Jesus is Lord.

While the specifics of the apocalypse and final judgment have been debated for centuries and continue to be today, there is one ending to the story: God wins. This amazing story that we have put together piece by piece is complete. The beast (whatever or whoever that turns out to be) is slain. Babylon (however that appears) is destroyed. Satan is gone; death is defeated. The Almighty One, the Ancient of Days, the great I Am, the triune God of Father, Son, and Holy Spirit rules forever!

But, that's not the whole story. There's more. See the final *ScriptureScope* below.

FINAL DESTINATION

In Revelation 21:1 we read: *Then I saw a new heaven and a new earth, for the first heaven and the first earth had passed away, and there was no longer any sea. I saw the Holy City, the new Jerusalem, coming down out of heaven from God, prepared as a bride beautifully dressed for her husband.*

After the apocalypse and the final judgment, what then? The last two chapters of Revelation show us the new creation. Note that the writer describes "a new heaven *and* a new earth"—not a new heaven *instead of* a new earth. Note also that the Holy City is coming *down* out of heaven to us; we are not going *up* to heaven to be in the Holy City.

Hmmm…When we read it like that, this verse seems to contradict all the hymns of "going to heaven" we've sung over the years. This almost seems like heaven is coming to us and that we might spend eternity not floating on clouds strumming harps but—seriously?—right here on earth.

But, not this earth. We will be on the "new earth", where the Holy City is and, yes, where God lives here among us. This is confirmed a few verses later when John writes: *God's dwelling is here with humankind. He will dwell with them, and they will be his peoples. God himself will be with them as their God* (21:3 CEB).

So, what does this passage mean to you? If our final destination is not "up" in heaven but "here" on the new earth, where do we go when we die? The "new earth" won't be available until after the apocalypse. And what about the thief that Jesus promised *"today you will be with me in paradise"* (Luke 23:43)?

Could there be two versions of what we call "heaven"—a temporary "heaven" and a final destination, the "new creation"?

Several years ago, we were connecting in the Miami airport with my 85-year old mother. Our plane out of Miami to Barcelona was delayed repeatedly until finally we were given vouchers to spend the night at a local hotel. The flight would go out in the morning, and we were to have cleared security (again) and be back at the gate by 5:30 am.

Since it was already 1:00 am at that point, Keith and I decided that going to a hotel and then coming back in a few hours was not realistic for us or Mom. So, I said a quick prayer and looked around for another option. Right behind us was a long escalator leading up, up, up....to the Admiral's Club, the American Airlines VIP holding pen.

We weren't VIPs, but all the VIP wranglers were gone at that hour, so we made ourselves comfortable there. It wasn't our final destination—we still hoped to make it to Barcelona and did about 18 hours late. But it was definitely the best place available. We were safe, and we were surrounded by loved ones.

I think of the "temporary heaven" being a lot like the Admiral's Club. It's not the final destination, but it's a significant improvement over where we have been and the best place to be in the meantime!

Revelation closes with Jesus' reassurance of his return. In Revelation 22:12 CEB Jesus says: *"Look! I'm coming soon. My reward is with me, to repay all people as their actions deserve."* The book closes with these words: *The one who bears witness to these things says, "Yes, I'm coming soon." Amen. Come, Lord Jesus! The grace of the Lord Jesus be with all.*

Epilogue

We have come full circle in God's amazing story. We studied 66 books, written over centuries and covering a period of more than four millennia. We connected characters, events, places, and teachings. We learned that the books of the Bible are not unrelated stories, but rather the pieces of one meta-narrative, a sweeping epic. The saga of the Bible is the story of people—like you and me—who have responded to God's call throughout history. The story is amazing because God is amazing.

We began our study focusing on three themes: creation, covenant, and salvation. We followed these themes through Israel's story in the Old Testament, the coming of Jesus in the New Testament, and all the wisdom and prophetic writings in both. In Revelation, we encountered a verse which connects all three themes, Revelation 11:15b: *The kingdom of the world has become the kingdom of our Lord and of his Christ, and he will reign forever and ever.*

Breaking that down, we see the connections:

The kingdom of the world: The world God created back in Genesis into which sin came to bring death and destruction. The world God first saved through Noah and later through Abraham and Moses. The world that seduced the Israelites away from God and brought on their judgment and exile. The world into which Jesus came. The world which dominates our lives today. The world in which we are strangers seeking to live as Christ would live.

Has become the kingdom of our Lord and of his Christ: The old covenant based on law has become the new covenant based on grace. The old world of sin and death has become the new world of eternal life.

Salvation dependent on high priests and sin offerings has become salvation based on faith in Jesus Christ as Lord and Savior. The kingdom of God is here and now in our hearts. The kingdom of God will ultimately change the world as every knee bows and every tongue confess Jesus as Lord. God wins!

And he will reign: Because of Jesus, God is with us in the new covenant, reigning as the Holy Spirit in our hearts. God is with us, just as he was with Adam and Eve in the garden before sin. God is with us just as he was with the Israelites in the temple. God will be with us in the perfect new creation. Our three-Person God is reigning over all of his creation as the Alpha and the Omega, the beginning and the end.

Forever and ever: The salvation Jesus brings will never end. The new covenant is forever. The new creation will be the eternal presence of God in our lives. The power of life and love has broken the power of hate and death. On the cross, Jesus conquered death once and forever for those who believe.

When we began ten days ago, I quoted John Newton's words from *Amazing Grace*:

> The Lord has promised good to me
> His Word my hope secures
> He will my shield and portion be
> As long as life endures.

His Word has become my shield and portion, my hope. I no longer see reading the Bible as part duty and part study or simply looking for inspiration. I see it as pure joy! I hope that this study will encourage you to read God's Word in this way—with joyful hearts and open minds.

Ask God to help you understand his Word and he will—I am living testament to that.

John Wesley called himself a "man of one book." It doesn't take much research to discover that Wesley was a student of many books. So, what did he mean? I believe he meant that the root of all his study and of all of his reading, was one book—this book, God's Word, the Bible. Other books may entertain. Other books may inform. But only one book holds all the questions and all the answers.

Let us be people of one book.

Amen? Amen!

FINAL DISCUSSION

1. Hebrews is one of my favorite books in the New Testament. I need to be reminded that I'm not a baby in the faith anymore—I need "solid food". Where are you in your faith journey? Are you "feeding" on the right food so that you will keep growing?

2. Peter summed up the Christian life by reminding us to be different than the pagans—to live counter-culturally in a good way, in God's way. How do you live in a way different from the world, and yet in the world? How does God help you to do this?

3. In Revelation we talked about how easy it is to be a lukewarm believer. Have you been lukewarm in your faith? How would your life be different if you were "all in" and on fire for Jesus?

4. Reflecting on the entire 10 days of our study, what are the highlights for you? What has God taught you through this study? How has God transformed you? What will you do differently? How have you grown in your faith and become a "new creation"?

5. What's next for you in your faith journey?

.

STUDY TOOLS

BIBLE CHRONOLOGY

KINGS AND PROPHETS

CHRIST'S LIFE AND MINISTRY

PAUL'S MINISTRY

BIBLE CHRONOLOGY*

OLD TESTAMENT [Creation—425 BC]

OT Note: The dates listed are scholarly suggestions of a timeline for the events recorded in the books, not the dates the books were written. The indented books without dates are books of wisdom or prophecy referencing the events recorded in the history books. Some were written during the timeframe; others were recorded much later.

Genesis [Creation—1800 BC]

Exodus/Lev/Num/Deut [1525—1406 BC]

Joshua [1406—1390 BC]

Judges/Ruth [1390—1100 BC]

1 Samuel/1 Chronicles [1100 BC—

      Psalms of David for Deliverance

2 Samuel/1 Chronicles

      Psalms of David and the Sons of Korah

1 Kings/2 Chronicles –930 BC]

      Psalms of Solomon

      Proverbs/Song of Songs/Ecclesiastes

2 Kings/2 Chronicles [930—535 BC]

      Obadiah/Joel/Jonah/Hosea/Amos
      Isaiah/Micah

      Nahum

      Zephaniah

      Jeremiah/Habakkuk/Ezekiel
      Lamentations

      Job/Psalms of the Exile

      Daniel

Ezra [535 B.C—

      Haggai/Zechariah

      Psalms of the Restoration

Esther

Nehemiah –425 BC]

      Malachi

NT Note: The dates provided for the Gospels and Acts are scholarly suggestions of the dates the events recorded happened, not the dates the books were written. The dates on all other books are suggested dates for the writing of the books.

Matthew/Mark/Luke/John [5 BC—AD 30]

Acts 1-15 [AD 30—

     Galatians [AD 50]

Acts 16-18:22

     1 and 2 Thessalonians [AD 51]

Acts 18:23-20:1

     1 and 2 Corinthians [AD 55-57]

     Romans [AD 56-58]

     James [AD 50-60]

Acts 20:2-28:31 --63]

     Colossians [AD 61-63]

     Philemon [AD 61-63]

     Ephesians [AD 61-63]

     Philippians [AD 61-63]

1 and 2 Peter [pre-AD 64]

1 Timothy [AD 63-64]

Titus [AD 63-65]

2 Timothy [AD 64-67]

Hebrews [AD 65-70]

Jude [AD 60-80]

1, 2, and 3 John [AD 90-95]

Revelation [AD 95-96]

*Adapted from *The Daily Bible*, compilation and commentary by F. LaGard Smith, published by Harvest House Publishers, 1984, www.harvesthousepublishers.com

KINGS AND PROPHETS**
(1100BC – 425BC)

KING OF ISRAEL	PROPHETS
Saul	Samuel
Ish-Bosheth	None named
David	Gad, Nathan
Solomon	Ahijah, Iddo

JUDAH	PROPHET(S)	ISRAEL	PROPHET(S)

(Reign in Years [m = months; d = days])   *Good character
Italicized names reference prophetic books of the OT

JUDAH	PROPHET(S)	ISRAEL	PROPHET(S)
Rehoboam(17)	Shemaiah, Iddo	Jeroboam I (22)	Ahijah
Abijah(3)	Iddo	Nadab(2)	None named
Asa(41)*	Azariah, Hanani	Baasha(24)	Jehu
		Elah(2)	None named
		Zimri(7d)	None named
		Tibni(?)	None named
Jehoshaphat(25)*	Jehu, Jahaziel Eliezer	Omri(12)	None named
Jehoram(8)	Elijah, Elisha	Ahab(22)	Elijah, Micaiah
Ahaziah(1)	Elijah, Elisha	Ahaziah(2)	None named
Athaliah(Q6)	None named	Joram(12)	None named
Joash(40)*	Zechariah, *Joel*	Jehu(28)	Elisha
		Jehoahaz(17)	Elisha
Amaziah(29)*	None named	Jehoash(16)	Elisha
		Jeroboam II(41)	*Hosea,Amos, Jonah*
		Zechariah(6m)	None named
		Shallum(1m)	None named

Azariah/Uzziah(52)*	*Isaiah*	Menahem(10)	None named
		Pekahiah(2)	None named
Jotham(16)*	*Isaiah, Micah*	Pekah(20)	Oded
Ahaz(16)	*Isaiah, Micah*	Hoshea (9)	None named
Hezekiah(29)*	*Isaiah, Micah, Nahum*		
Manasseh(55)	None named		
Amon(2)	None named		
Josiah(31)*	Huldah, *Zephaniah, Jeremiah*		
Jehoahaz(3m)	*Jeremiah*		
Jehoiakim(11)	*Jeremiah*, Uriah, *Daniel*		
Jehoiachin (3m)	*Jeremiah, Habakkuk, Ezekiel*		
Zedekiah (11)	*Jeremiah, Habakkuk, Ezekiel, Obadiah*		

KINGS AND PROPHETS OF THE EXILE AND RESTORATION

PROPHET	KING
Daniel	Nebuchadnezzar of Babylon
	Belshazzar
	Darius the Mede
	Cyrus of Persia
Haggai	Darius of Persia
Zechariah	Darius of Persia
Malachi	Artaxerxes II of Persia

TIMELINE OF THE WRITING PROPHETS—8th c. BC to mid 5th c. BC

722 BC—Samaria Falls
609 BC—First Deportation from Judah
587 BC—Jerusalem Falls
538 BC—First Remnant Returns
516 BC—Temple is completed
425 BC—City wall is completed, prophets fall silent

CHRIST'S LIFE AND MINISTRY**

EVENT	REFERENCE
Birth of Christ	Luke 2:1-7
Jesus circumcised and named 8 days after birth	Luke 2:21
Jesus presented in the temple 40 days after birth	Luke 2:22
Simeon and Anna see Jesus	Luke 2:25, 36
The Magi visit Jesus	Matt. 2:13-15
Herod has all male children age 2 and under killed	Matt. 2:16-18
Herod the Great dies; Joseph and Mary return from Egypt and settle with Jesus in Nazareth	Matt. 2:19-23
Jesus, age 12, at the temple during Passover	Luke 2:41-52
John the Baptist begins ministry as Jesus' forerunner	Luke 3:1-3
John baptizes Jesus	Mark 1:9-11
Jesus is tempted 40 days in the wilderness	Mark 1:12-13
Jesus calls first disciples	John 1:35-51
Wedding at Cana and Jesus' public ministry begins	John 2:1-12
Jesus' 1st Passover; merchants driven from temple	John 2:13-25
Jesus teaches Nicodemus	John 3:1-21
Jesus returns to Galilee by way of Samaria; woman at well	John 4:4-26
Jesus reads from Isaiah's scroll in Nazareth; rejected	Luke 4:16-30
Jesus teaches throughout Galilee with Capernaum as base	Matt. 4:12-17
Jesus at "the feast of the Jews" (2nd Passover?)	John 5:1
Sermon on the Mount	Matt. 5-7; Luke 6
Jesus' feet washed by sinful woman at Pharisee's home	Luke 7:36-50
Jesus calms the storm on the Sea of Galilee	Luke 8:23-27
Jesus sends "Legion" into pigs in Gerasenes	Mark 5:1-20

Jesus rejected again in Nazareth	Mark 6:1-6
Jesus sends out apostles to teach and heal in his Name	Matt. 9:35-11:1
John the Baptist killed	Matt. 14:1-12
Jesus feeds 5000 (2nd year of ministry)	Matt. 14; Mark 6; Luke 9; John 6
Jesus walks on water (Peter tries)	Matt: 23-33
Jesus extends ministry to Tyre, Sidon, and Caesarea Philippi	Matt. 15:21-16:13
Jesus is transfigured	Luke 9:28-36
Jesus at the Feast of Tabernacles (Sept.)	John 7:2, 10
Jesus prevents stoning of woman caught in adultery	John 7:53-8:11
Healing of man born blind	John 9
Jesus returns to Galilee for final 2 months	Luke 9:51-56
Jesus visits home of Mary and Martha in Bethany	Luke 10:38-42
Jesus at the Feast of Dedication (Dec.)	John 10:22-39
Jesus takes ministry east of Jordan River, to Perea	John 10:40-42
Jesus hears of Lazarus' death and returns to Bethany	John 11:1-53
Jesus goes to Ephraim with disciples (January – March)	John 11:54
Jesus travels to Jerusalem for Passover	Luke 19:28
Jesus arrives in Bethany 6 days before the Passover; has dinner with Simon the Leper, Lazarus, Mary, and Martha; Mary anoints Jesus with nard, angers Judas Iscariot	John 12:1-11; Mark 14:1-9 Matt. 26:6-13
Triumphal entry into Jerusalem; cleansing of temple	Matt. 21:1-22
Jesus returns to Jerusalem the next day	Mark 11:27
Jesus has final meal with disciples in Upper Room; is betrayed by Judas Iscariot; arrested in Garden of Gethsemane	Luke 22:7-53
Jesus is tried before the Sanhedrin at daybreak	Luke 22:66-71

Jesus goes to Pilate, to Herod, and back to Pilate	Luke 23:6-12
Jesus is crucified at 9:00 am	Mark 15:25
Darkness for 3 hours (Noon – 3:00 pm)	Mark 15:33
Jesus dies at 3:00 pm	Luke 24:44-46
Earthquake; temple curtain is torn from top to bottom	Matt. 27:51
Saints are resurrected	Matt. 27:52
Joseph of Arimathea and Nicodemus ask Pilate for body	John 19:38
Jesus is buried toward evening	Matt. 27:57-61
The tomb is sealed and a guard posted	Matt. 27:62-66
Jesus is raised from the dead at dawn on 3rd day	Matt. 28:1-2
Jesus appears to Mary Magdalene	John 20:11-18
Jesus appears to other women	Matt. 28:9-10
Jesus appears to Peter	Luke 24:33-35
Jesus appears to 2 disciples on the road to Emmaus	Luke 24:13-32
Jesus appears to 10 disciples Sunday evening	John 20:19-23
Jesus appears to 11 disciples one week later	John 20:26-28
Jesus appears to 7 disciples in Galilee; Peter called to lead	John 21:1-25
Jesus appears to the apostles and more than 500 disciples in Galilee	1 Cor. 15:6
Jesus appears to James, his brother	1 Cor. 15:7
Jesus ascends 40 days after his resurrection	Acts 1:3-9
Pentecost occurs 50 days after Jesus' resurrection	Acts 2:1-13

** Adapted from *Baker's Handbook of Bible Lists* by Andrew E. Hill, published by Baker Books, a division of Baker Publishing Group, Grand Rapids, MI, 2006.

PAUL'S MINISTRY**

EVENT	DATE AD
Saul persecutes the church; observes Stephen's stoning	33-35
Conversion of Saul on road to Damascus	35
1st Jerusalem visit, welcomed by Barnabas	38
Saul/Barnabas take famine gift from Antioch (Syria) to Jerusalem	46
1st missionary journey from Antioch with Barnabas and John Mark to Cyprus, Pamphylia (Turkey), and Antioch of Pisidia	46-48
Paul attends Jerusalem Council; takes message to Gentiles	49
Galatians written	50
2nd missionary journey, with Silas to Philippi, Athens, Corinth	49-52
Paul in Corinth with Priscilla and Aquila	50-52
1 and 2 Thessalonians written	51
3rd missionary journey, through Galatia and Phrygia to Ephesus	53-57
Paul in Ephesus	53-55
1 Corinthians written	55
Paul in Macedonia and Achaia	55-57
2 Corinthians written	56
Romans written; Paul arrested in Jerusalem	57
Imprisonment at Caesarea	57-59
Journey to Rome	59-60
Imprisonment at Rome	60-62/63
Colossians, Philemon, Ephesians, Philippians written	61-62/63
Paul released and in Macedonia or Spain (?)	63?
2nd imprisonment at Rome	63-64?
1 Timothy, Titus, 2 Timothy written	63-66/67

NOTES

Made in the USA
Coppell, TX
16 July 2020

31109339R00154